New Technologies and Renaissance Studies III

NEW TECHNOLOGIES IN MEDIEVAL AND
RENAISSANCE STUDIES 9

SERIES EDITORS William R. Bowen and Raymond G. Siemens

New Technologies and Renaissance Studies III

Edited by
Matthew Evan Davis and Colin Wilder

Iter Press
NEW YORK | TORONTO

2022

978-1-64959-016-9 (paper)
978-1-64959-017-6 (pdf)
978-1-64959-037-4 (epub)

Library of Congress Cataloging-in-Publication Data

Names: Davis, Matthew Evan, editor. | Wilder, Colin, editor. | Renaissance Society of America. | Sixteenth Century Society and Conference.
Title: New technologies and Renaissance studies III / edited by Matthew Evan Davis and Colin Wilder.
Description: New York : Iter Press, 2022. | Series: New technologies in medieval and Renaissance studies ; 9 | "Taken from papers given at the Iter-sponsored sessions at the annual meeting of the Renaissance Society of America and at the Sixteenth Century Society and Conference from the years 2011 to 2018"--CIP galley. | Includes bibliographical references. | Summary: "The essays in this volume explore problems with digital approaches to analogue objects of study; employ digital methods to study networks of production, dissemination, and collection, and reflect on the limitations of those methods; and speak to an often-noted truth of digital projects: Unlike traditional scholarship, digital scholarship is often the result of collective networks of not only disciplinary scholars but also of library professionals and other technical and professional staff as well as students"-- Provided by publisher.
Identifiers: LCCN 2020058522 (print) | LCCN 2020058523 (ebook) | ISBN 9781649590169 (paper) | ISBN 9781649590176 (pdf) | ISBN 9781649590374 (epub)
Subjects: LCSH: Renaissance--Study and teaching (Higher)--Congresses. | Archival materials--Digitization--Congresses. | Manuscripts, Renaissance--Data processing--Congresses. | Text processing (Computer science)--Congresses. | Electronic publications--Congresses. | Humanities--Technological innovations--Congresses. | Educational technology--Congresses. | Educational innovations--Congresses.
Classification: LCC CB361 .N493 2022 (print) | LCC CB361 (ebook) | DDC 940.2/1--dc23
LC record available at https://lccn.loc.gov/2020058522
LC ebook record available at https://lccn.loc.gov/2020058523

Cover Illustration

A composited image showing the stages of a 3D model of the statue of Charles I at Trafalgar Square in London, beginning with the dotmap at the bottom and graduating to the complete model at the top. Compositing courtesy of Matthew Evan Davis.

Contents

Collaboration

Introduction

Matthew Evan Davis

Colin Wilder

Durham University

University of South Carolina

The digital has become the sea in which we all swim. From the databases used to facilitate searching for and in texts to the social media platforms increasingly used alongside conferences as points of scholarly communication and information dissemination, the tools and methodologies of the digital age inform our thinking, our discussion, and the drawing of our conclusions. The concepts and terminology of the digital are the means through which our understanding of the world and the objects of our study are mediated. They are metaphors we use in the classroom, in our politics and media, and in our thinking about what it means to be human. We have all become digital scholars.

In this brave new world, the novelty of digital tools as a cause for discussion in and of itself has worn off. It is now common practice for scholars from the newest graduate student to the most august professor to be able to handle the transcription of manuscripts and printed works into XML-based markup schemes like that imposed by the Text Encoding Initiative; to plot points on a map using Geographic Information Systems software such as ArcGIS; to use statistical computing tools such as R to parse texts algorithmically; and to display the results of all of these tools in complex visualizations using tools like Gephi, or Javascript libraries like d3.js. Scholars in the humanities no longer have to justify the use of digital tools any more than we might have to justify our use of the library for research. Our toolkit overflows with options.

Perhaps nowhere in the humanities is this truer than among scholars of the medieval and early modern eras. We have long been digital pioneers, often from expediency. We work with geographically-disparate and unique items that are available to us only in small windows. The promise of the digital—that it would put us on equal footing with colleagues who enjoy a rich backlog of print materials and historical artifacts from more recent, accessible eras—has proven alluring. We have responded to this call ever since Roberto Busa, Josephine Miles, and their team of women put together the *Index Thomasticus*, completing the first volume while most universities were still using PDP-10 mainframes and timesharing protocols.

ISBN 978-1-64959-016-9 (paper) ISBN 978-1-64959-017-6 (pdf) ISBN 978-1-64959-037-4 (epub)

New Technologies in Medieval and Renaissance Studies 9 (2022) 1–5

With new opportunities come new challenges. To meet them, we have developed new methods; in so doing, we have gained insights not only into the role of the technological tool but into the ways that the objects of our study were produced, consumed, and disseminated during the medieval and early modern periods. New complexities have emerged, too, and we approach these in the way that Busa and Miles's team adopted during that first digital humanities project: collaboratively.

Taken from papers given at the Iter-sponsored sessions at the annual meeting of the Renaissance Society of America and at the Sixteenth Century Society and Conference from the years 2011 to 2018, the essays in this volume represent work that falls into three broad, if uneven, sections reflective of the history of our relationship with the digital—and of alliances between our disciplines.

The first section, "Challenges and Opportunities," includes essays that speak to the promising but potentially fraught relationship that the digital can have with our decidedly analogue objects of study. Travis Mullen employs both TEI text encoding and a database to consider the epistolary collection *The King's Cabinet Opened*, not as a single, distinct text but as a combination of abstract meaning and concrete interface. He suggests that separating the text and the traditional print interface, and instead making readers approach the text through digital mediation, provides needed insights into the book as both a construct and, in its original nature, as an already-mediated public printing of private correspondence by Charles I.

Peter Boot examines Renaissance emblems as an example of textual reuse to make a larger point about the ways in which digital tools sometimes fall short of our expectations. Rather than assume that a digital tool will answer the questions we ask of it, Boot posits that digital tools provide information that must then be analyzed by the scholar rather than simply accepted at face value. He goes on to suggest that the use of these tools results in information overload; he offers possible ways of mitigating that overload, and suggests a need for a tool laid over the top of existing infrastructure to handle that mitigation.

Claudia Resch's essay concludes the section by showing how there are still limitations to our ability to use algorithmic methodologies in the study of early modern texts. Resch availed herself of the Austrian Baroque Corpus (ABaC:us) in her study of the texts of Abraham a Sancta Clara, a seventeenth-century Discalced Augustinian. The tool allowed her to identify particular rhetorical patterns and measure certain aspects of a Sancta Clara's style, but fell short of being able to definitively provide the answers she sought.

The second section, "Methods and Insights," explores not just the scholarly methods used to examine material objects, but also the ways that digital methods can help navigate the networks of production, dissemination, and collection that have largely shaped our understanding of those objects. Thus, it is a section not just about the problems and promise of the digital, but about how digital tools provide new discoveries and concrete ways to approach medieval and early modern works.

Leading this section is Toby Burrows, whose essay is primarily interested in the manuscript collections of Sir Thomas Phillipps and Sir Alfred Chester Beatty, two manuscript collectors of the nineteenth and twentieth centuries, respectively. Their work was intertwined, with several of Phillipps's manuscripts ending up in Beatty's collection; consequently, analysis of their histories can be difficult. Burrows examines how the software *nodegoat* helps him to record these histories and to tease out the resultant connections between them. More important, however, is Burrows's insight into how the tool facilitates his ability to place the Phillips-Beatty manuscripts into a larger context.

Similarly, Colin Wilder's distant reading methodology attempts to determine the exact contents of the four early modern German libraries—the Marburg Collective High Court, the law faculty of Marburg University Library, the Hanau Leihbibliothek, and the Frankfurt Stadtbibliothek—from their title catalogs. Through a discussion that is as much about the methods and tools of distant reading as it is about the contents of the four libraries, Wilder determines that books dealing with feudal law are largely absent, books about canon law are very present despite common narratives of German legal history, and (what Wilder calls "Germanistic") titles with distinctly German associations are largely absent as well.

Moving from the study of libraries to a handful of texts by a single author, Alessandro Zammataro shows how a combination of ultraviolet spectrographic imaging and commodity image management tools, such as Adobe Photoshop, can be used as an aid to the process of recovering transcriptional errors and resolving textual cruces in Petrarch's work. His careful examination of multiple witnesses of the poet's work first shows how ultraviolet imaging recovers letter forms and illuminations lost via oil damage to the parchment. Then, he uses Photoshop's tool suite to show how both those spectrographic images and more conventional pictures of illuminations can be manipulated in order to resolve outstanding questions in Petrarchan studies.

The last essay in the section, by Marie-Alice Belle and Marie-France Guénette, explores the utility of translation network analysis by focusing on the printed translation as a material object. This object, in keeping with Latourian notions of Actor-Network Theory, is seen as an assemblage of both human and non-human actors involved in its production, dissemination, and reception. That assemblage, in turn, is reconstructed by the authors from the *Renaissance Cultural Crossroads Online Catalogue of Translations in Britain 1473–1640* (RCC), and the *Cultural Crosscurrents Catalogue of Printed Translations in Stuart and Commonwealth Britain, 1641–1660* (CCC), supplemented by reference to the *English Short Title Catalogue* and *Early English Books Online*. Applying this focused approach in reconstructing translation networks to two specific case studies—those of the St. Omer press and the seventeenth-century bookseller Humprey Moseley—Belle and Guénette examine the potential of network analysis to interrogate questions raised by the market for printed translations in a Great Britain split by culture, ideology, and religion.

The final section, "Collaboration," speaks to an often-noted truth of digital projects: that unlike our more traditional scholarship they are the result of collective networks of not only scholars with their deep subject specialties but also of library professionals and other technical and professional staff, as well as our students, who often serve as a source for insights into the objects of our study through time spent in the classroom.

Jessica Otis begins the section by examining how the Six Degrees of Francis Bacon project's use of Named-Entity Recognition (NER) allows a more nuanced understanding of the deeply collaborative *Oxford Dictionary of National Biography* (ODNB). In several instances, individuals who lack their own biographical entries are named frequently in the biographies of others. The Six Degrees project found these connections and, by foregrounding less-known individuals, was able to find new links with the Continent as well as connective tissue between a number of people of historical significance. Furthermore, these individuals were often women, suggesting points of connection and contact that have been otherwise obscured in the past. Finally, Otis examines points where NER algorithms need further refinement as well as the ways in which the *ODNB*'s structure has contributed to the obscuration found by the Six Degree's team.

In perhaps the purest example of collaboration in the third section, Andie Silva examines the use of digital editing tools as a pedagogical method, discussing the creation of a unique version of Shakespeare's works under the auspices of a course subtitled "Shakespeare in the Digital Age." Using the Scalar public editing platform, Silva's course created an edition of Shakespeare that draws heavily from pop-culture analogies, intending to present the finished result as public-facing scholarship. Silva goes on to reflect that the use of Scalar forced the students to engage with the text actively, questioning the assumptions of the canon and "remixing" canonic texts. These questions extended to the criticism used in their class edition as well, with the students challenging the assumptions of race, gender, class, and ethnicity assumed by academic critics and contemporary cultural representations.

Using collaboration as a tool to foster understanding is also at the center of Tanja Jones's essay. She examines women as artists, patrons, and subjects in the art of the early modern courts of Europe, noting where our understanding has improved involving these figures and where we still need dedicated work to expand our understanding. She then suggests that digitally-based methods of collaboration, such as the Early Modern Women in the Courts project, can help to address the points where work is still needed.

Even under these three broad categories, the essays differ greatly in their approaches to the use of digital tools and methodologies; yet they all take to heart the idea that if digital scholarship has become the new normal then it must *be* normal, treated as any other theoretical or methodological approach. They use digital tools not only to answer digital questions but often as a new approach to traditional research questions. In this way they speak, ultimately, to the truism this introduction began with: that we are all, in some way, digital scholars.

Challenges and Opportunities

The King's Cabinet Splintered: *The King's Cabinet Opened* and Digital Mediation

Travis Mullen

Center for Digital Humanities, University of South Carolina

In June of 1645, the Parliamentarian New Model Army seized a packet of King Charles I's private correspondence at the battle of Naseby. They carefully selected, arranged, and decoded portions of the letters that had been encrypted and had them printed as *The King's Cabinet Opened*.[1] This seizure and publication were a crucial propagandistic victory that did irreparable damage to Charles's public image. Through their purposeful curation of Charles I's letters, the Parliamentarians partially constructed and partially revealed him as a duplicitous ruler who cared more for the queen, Henrietta Maria, than for the English people. *The King's Cabinet Opened* invited the English public to engage with the king's private affairs through print, implicitly undermining his claim to absolutism. This essay considers a digital remediation of that book. The text of the digital edition, and that cited within, is based on the transcription available through the *Early English Books Online* (*EEBO*) project website. I corrected the transcribed text using the images available through *EEBO* and against a physical copy located at the Folger Shakespeare Library.[2] Each of the letters, the preface, and annotations have been individually encoded in extensible markup language (XML) using the guidelines set forth by the Text Encoding Initiative (TEI). Additionally, the documents have been inserted into a database with a custom interface where readers

---

[1] The printer for this edition is unknown, but it was "printed for" Robert Bostock by authorization of Parliament.

[2] *The King's Cabinet opened* (see Works Cited). For the Folger's copy, see call number C2358.2. All citations are taken from the Text Creation Partnership edition; hereafter, *KCO*. According to the *ESTC*, there were only two editions of the book produced—the second is listed as a rare close copy—but there are five states of the first edition. Copies correspond to more than one state; this essay's text corresponds to states two and four in which some numerals are missing in quire E and in which the cypher codes appear throughout. The descriptions of the states provided by the *ESTC* allow for a few conclusions about their differences that are important when considering whether they impact my argument: all states, except for state three, include numbered letters and all states include cypher codes to various extents (state five has fewer instances of this).

ISBN 978-1-64959-016-9 (paper) ISBN 978-1-64959-017-6 (pdf) ISBN 978-1-64959-037-4 (epub)

New Technologies in Medieval and Renaissance Studies 9 (2022) 9–32

can interact with them in new ways. *The King's Cabinet Opened Online* project seeks to maintain and enrich the diverse print features of this important historical text through the addition of semantic markup and the creation of an electronic edition. Digital remediation represents a change in interface that invites a critical reconsideration of the book while raising larger questions about epistolarity and textuality: how can thinking through interface shed new light on digital remediation, and what can digital remediation tell us about the physical objects from which they come?

By focusing on the impact of mediation on epistles, we can rethink the relationship between a book's content and form, seeing it, instead, as a relationship between interface and database. An important key term in this analysis is interface: the formal—material or virtual—frame or window and its features that act as the go-between for the reader, the text, and the codes that are reinscribed on the hard disc of the host server. Alan Liu argues that through the interface, text becomes "semiotically transcendental" as its meaning is disconnected from its presentation (Liu 2004, 59). For Alexander Galloway, it is "a gateway that opens up and allows passage to some place beyond" (Galloway 2012, 30). That place beyond is, in many cases, the database: the semi-structured information behind an interface that readers cannot otherwise access.[3] In the case of *The King's Cabinet Opened*, as well as in other epistolary collections such as James Howell's 1645 *Epistolae Ho-Elianae*, editors present their books as single windows—as interfaces—into an otherwise inaccessible archive of discourse. An edition, I argue, can be seen as a single selection among many possibilities contained within a database and, by thinking this way, a printed book can be reframed as an interface that displays the results of that selection. Such, at least, is the analogy that informs and motivates this essay. Examining *The King's Cabinet Opened* helps show that the protocols that govern databases are similar to those that govern epistolarity, especially in print. Consequently, the database can be a useful metaphor for understanding the book, epistolarity, and the digital humanities. Digital remediation, then, can be seen to transform printed books through a change in interface that sheds new light on their original printedness.

---

[3] Such is the case whether that interface is through specific coded queries or a graphical interface. The database, as it exists in a technical sense, is a semi-structured set of records that cannot be directly touched or examined, except through interface as it exists in sequences of numbers stored virtually in "memory." In "Database, Interface, and Archival Fever," (2007) Jerome McGann argues that in order for a database to function, it needs a user interface; the reader cannot experience the text directly from the database, but must have a gateway into the database.

1. Seventeenth-century epistolarity in manuscript and print

The seventeenth-century letter was a highly social document in which ideas of public and private were fluid and contingent. According to Gary Schneider, letters were "*the* material medium, *tout court*, of early modern sociocultural exchange and ... a critical means of pragmatic communication" (Schneider 2005, 13). As such, the letter typically ranged outside the purview of the recipient and into what Schneider calls an epistolary community. Letters were "sociotexts: collective social forms designed, understood, and expected to circulate within designated epistolary circles" (Scheider 2005, 22). Letters were intended to circulate within tightly controlled groups of people and as such were subject to manipulation and modification during circulation. The social nature of the letter made conceptions of public and private difficult to pin down: "letters, as bearers of information and intelligence, mediated intercourse in the public realm of administrative and state business; yet letters, as bearers of interiority and intimate expression, were also considered highly private documents" (Schneider 2005, 27). Letters were also highly suspect modes of communication; they were seen as potential sites of deception and subversion. The generic fluidity and sociality of the letter led to an overlapping of epistolary communities and, thereby, to possible publication. No matter how private the letter's content, however, "its transmission was always mediated by a third party" (Schneider 2005, 71). The letter, then, was always in circulation beyond the traditional conception of dyadic privacy—that of sender to receiver, point to point—and subject to possible interference. Letters were "crucial material bearers of social connection, instruments by which social ties were initiated, negotiated and consolidated" (Schneider 2005, 27). Letters functioned to create and maintain links—social ties—between people by functioning as material carriers of presence. Schneider argues that "even letters that said 'nothing'—that is, imparted little or no explicit news or information—nevertheless communicated alliance, fidelity, and homage; they bore weighty sociocultural significance, and were even perceived as testimonies, as material evidence of social connectedness" (Schneider 2005, 27).

The seventeenth-century letter was a place of social negotiation. A letter can be read as a physical connection between and declaration of relationship to those people involved in its communication circuit. As such, much of letter-writing consisted in adhering to practices designed to ensure that these epistolary relationships and communication continued; that is, the epistolary community was concerned primarily with ensuring its continuation and maintenance through the creation of more and more entries. James Daybell and Andrew Gordon argue that "much correspondence incorporated a phatic component—in a climate of uncertain delivery, confirming receipt of previous letters, advising of letters to be received, and detailing the networks of transmission through which a letter ought to pass, were important features" (Daybell and Gordon 2016, 3). In part, this is a recognition of the already dubious nature of relying on a third party for the delivery of letters, but it also indicates the iterative and cumulative nature of epistolarity—always looking backward and ever looking forward. Schneider explains that many letter writing conventions "reflect the sociotextual function of letters, and demonstrate a concern with connection and continuity" and that "epistolary language concerned with initiating and assuring epistolary continuity [was] perhaps the 'master theme' of epistolary communication" (Schneider 2005, 15, 55).

Letters were individual parts of a self-propagating network that was enabled by third-party carriers and maintained by complex social practices designed to ensure its continuation and maintain its relationships. They were relational entities and entities of relation. Carriers functioned as linking tables through which the relation was enacted. We can see this as a set of database tables in which there is a person table that houses senders and recipients, a letters table that houses the contents and metadata of the letters (date, location, etc.) and a reference to the person table, then the carrier table that links them all together with a column for each sender, recipient, and letter through which the contents can be accessed. In this way, epistolary communication is relational—it connects or links entities, in this case people, together. Letters were methods of maintaining and initiating connections. Like entries in a relational database, letters chosen for print represented a selection from a larger, hidden field of possibility. Seventeenth-century letter collections like James Howell's 1645 *Epistolae Ho-Elianae* seemed to recognize the social and selective qualities of a print collection. *Epistolae Ho-Elianae* describes letters glowingly as "those golden links that do enchain / whole nations" (Howell 1907, xxxiv). [4] More telling, "To the Reader" explains that "Letters may more than history enclose / the choicest learning both in verse and prose" (xxxiv). This line reflects the process of preparing a volume of familiar letters for print—the choicest letters for the choicest learning: "the highest points of state and policy, / the most severe parts of philosophy." In his letter to the king, Howell begins, "these letters, addressed (most of them) to your best degrees of subjects, do, as so many lines drawn from the circumference to the centre, all meet in your Majesty" (xxxvii). Here Howell tells the reader a number of things: that these letters might be understood to

---

[4] All quotations refer to the 1907 edition of James Howell's *Epistolae Ho-Elianae*.

create a network of people he is associated with, that that network connects to the king, and that the correspondence included will be one-sided; that is, the letters will all be going out from Howell and not in. Howell has selected those letters that "may all prove letters of credit" (xxxvi). It would seem that Howell recognizes that with letters, each mediation "refram[es] the meaning and function of the correspondence in question" (Daybell and Gordon 2016, 9). Howell has provided his reader with a window, an interface, into a selection of his correspondence and, thereby, put the letters to work and changed their meanings.

Epistles in print became important political tools for the instantiation of and appeal to a new public. Many letter collections were printed in pamphlets because the pamphlet was a popular genre that "enabled pamphleteers to compass news, history and opinion into a few sheets and to bring into focus diverse heterogeneous materials and voices" (Raymond 2003, 214). The flexibility of the pamphlet as genre allowed editors to collect diverse materials—letters, orders, prefaces, and annotations—in a single document and to experiment with their formal presentation. The new communication methods enabled by the flexibility of the pamphlet and the medium of print afforded editors the ability to invoke the first instances of appeals to public opinion (Zaret 2000, 174–75). The letter pamphlet was a widely popular genre that "permitted a slippage between the intended, often familiar, reader and a broadly constituted reading public" (Barnes 2013, 106–07). The slippage between the familiar recipient and the intended audience was often exploited: many of the letters in print were forgeries, entirely fictitious works, or the letters of important people long since dead (Raymond 2003, 215).[5] By publishing *The King's Cabinet Opened*, the Parliamentarians instead provided a window—which they went to great lengths to substantiate—into the life of their contemporary ruler.

---

[5] Schneider also notes that "it was not until 1645, with the combined sociocultural energy of James Howell's *Epistolae Ho-Elianae* and King Charles I's correspondence published as *The King's Cabinet Opened*, that personal vernacular letter collections by native letter writers were regularly published in England. Before this date, the sporadic collections in the vernacular published were essentially collections of moral-didactic letters, those 'Christian epistles' written and published for polemical, exhortatory, and consolatory purposes; after 1645 collections of personal letters and letters of state by Englishmen were published with increasing frequency" (Schneider 2005, 49).

2. *The seventeenth-century letter in print:* The King's Cabinet Opened

The printing of Charles's private letters exemplifies the publicizing power of print as a political act (Schneider 2005, 49). Parliament came together for the first time to authorize the printing of *The King's Cabinet Opened* (Barnes 2013, 107); whereas a single house previously authorized materials, this document was "Published by Special Order of the Parliament" as a whole (*KCO*, A3). The majority of the letters are from the king to Henrietta Maria, and the editorial apparatus places emphasis on this fact. Michael McKeon argues that in publishing the king's private letters, "the realm of the private takes on the semiotic authority of the public realm, and what it entails is the 'identity' of the king in the sense, not of name and lineage . . . but, more intimately of mind and motive" (McKeon 2005, 483). The editors emphasized this fact by choosing a title that suggested that by seizing the letters, Fairfax had seized the king himself.

Given the dubious nature and popularity of letters and pamphlets in print, they were accompanied by suspicion. Consequently, Parliament went to great lengths to assert the authenticity of the letters in their pamphlet. They started with the subtitle "Secret Letters & Papers, Written with the Kings own Hand," and included an authenticity statement after each letter—usually "this is a true copy, examined by" and the name of an authenticator like Miles Corbett (*KCO*, Title, 3; Barnes 2013, 117) The print version could never replicate the king's hand, however, so these authenticity statements are a means to address the limitations of the medium.[6] Here *The King's Cabinet Opened* provides insight into its own creation, to the limitations imposed by print, and to the challenges inherent in asserting the authenticity of something that has been transformed into a new form. Parliament also emphasizes the authenticity of the documents in the preface and challenges the king to come forward if the printed letters are forgeries, saying, "we dare appeale to his own conscience now, knowing that he cannot disavow either his own hand writing, or the matters themselves here written" (*KCO* A3v).[7] The emphasis on authenticity suggests the importance that Parliament placed on the reader's judgment of

---

[6] It is also important to note that these letters were written in cipher, so the printed letter is more akin to a translation than to the king's hand. Thus, it is also a means to efface the editors' hand in its construction.

[7] This is interesting in several ways: first, the assertion that the letters were written in the king's hand is unverifiable, since the text referenced by the preface and read by the reader was rendered in print using type and not a reproduction of the handwriting; second, the appeal to the king's conscience here is interesting since the text—and especially the editorial apparatus—call the quality of his conscience into question.

and response to the document and the importance of the reader's acceptance of the letters' text as Charles's own words. This assertion enabled typographical manipulation of the text that changed its meaning, but not its content. To assert the king's hand, Parliament printed particularly damning text in italics (see Figure 1). As Joseph Loewenstein writes, "in the rhetoric of the English page, the italic is the master-trope. To print in italics is to fracture the English body type, and to assert a human claim on the written"; that italics are used "to make the weariness of impression give way to inscription, to designate the truly *authentic*" (Loewenstein 2002, 76). By transitioning to italic type, then, the Parliamentarians broke the printed into the written and came as close as they could—mechanically—to replicating the king's hand; by choosing to italicize controversial parts of the letters' contents, the Parliamentarians establish a human link to the king's supposedly subversive behavior. The remaining content of the letters is subordinated as printed material that simply surrounds the hand-written. This allows the Parliamentarian ideological manipulation to function by taking Charles's statements out of context—even the context of the letter that they're included in. The italics in Figure 1 attempt to leverage and supersede the medium directly into a representation of the king's hand. The electronic edition takes this a step further by differentiating common print practice—that of italicizing nouns—from trans-media efforts at enforcing authenticity and authorship.[8]

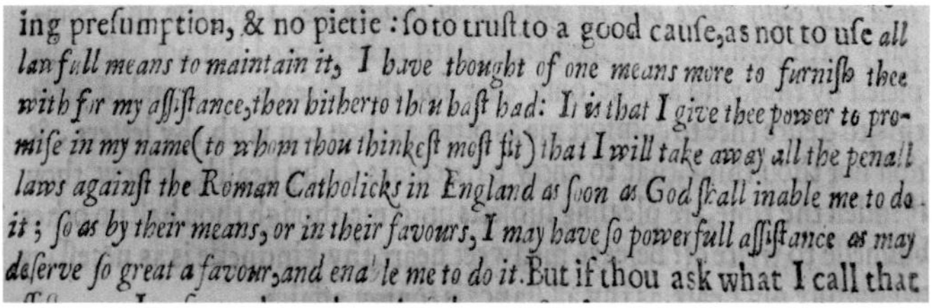
ing presumption, & no pietie : so to trust to a good cause, as not to use *all lawfull means to maintain it, I have thought of one means more to furnish thee with for my assistance, then hitherto thou hast had: It is that I give thee power to promise in my name (to whom thou thinkest most fit) that I will take away all the penall laws against the* Roman Catholicks *in* England *as soon as* God *shall inable me to do it; so as by their means, or in their favours, I may have so powerfull assistance as may deserve so great a favour, and enable me to do it.* But if thou ask what I call that

Figure 1. An example of the use of italicized text to emphasize a particularly damning section by representing it on the page as being in the king's own hand.

The ideological force of *The King's Cabinet Opened* rests in its editorial apparatus and in what Jerome McGann calls the book's "bibliographic codes" (McGann 1991, 12).[9] *The King's Cabinet Opened* is an excellent example of a text in

[8] I did not encounter any nouns that were supposed to be emphasized within the book. Rather, in emphasized text, nouns were printed in roman type rather than italics.

[9] McGann indicates that the meaning of a text is a function of the "most material . . . levels of the text: in the case of scripted texts, the physical form of books and manuscripts (paper, ink, typefaces, layouts) or their prices, advertising mechanisms, and

which the bibliographic codes powerfully inflect the meaning of the text but obfuscate the original manuscript meaning and characteristics. The printed version of the text takes advantage of scribal epistolary traditions to suggest the authenticity of the letters, including the use of typographical layout and font shifts. Parliament's use of the genre of the familiar letter convinced the public readership that they "were in such familiar proximity with his majesty that they could judge him as they would an equal" (Barnes 2013, 106; see also Raymond 2003, 217). The printed book represents the Parliamentarian's recognition and exploitation of the generic quality of both the familiar letter and the pamphlet to reproduce the printed equivalent of private letters which, ideologically at least, brought the reader into the king's company and the king into the reader's political and social circle.

Parliament's typographical emphasis on Charles's prioritization of love over friendship lost him a number of his advisors because the letters show that Henrietta Maria is Charles's "friend, confidant, advisor and wife and, as such, usurps the proper role of men [and that] she is at the centre of the personal rule" (Barnes 2013, 121–22). Charles violated an important convention of masculinity and betrayed his role as man and king. Charles's transmission of power to Henrietta Maria—beyond transgressing this masculine line and aligning himself with Catholicism—violated his absolutist kingship. The divestiture of power is itself a divestiture of absolutism. In a letter dated 5 March 1645, Charles writes to Henrietta Maria, "*I give thee power to promise in my name (to whom thou think most fit) that I will take away all penal laws against the Roman Catholicks in England*" (*KCO*, 7).[10] Here, Charles gives the power of his royal name and person over to Henrietta Maria, his "Dear heart." McKeon argues that in the letters "amatory intimacies have usurped the place of public judgment, a perversion intimated by the (conventionally) amatory language the editors use to announce that usurpation" (McKeon 2005, 485). The editors highlight Henrietta Maria's usurpation of the king's concern for and power over the state in the preface by mirroring his language in their description of his compromised position. Charles's letters were controversial because they were at once public and private: they were at the same time administrative and "bearers of interiority and intimate expression" (Schneider 2005, 68). Here the issue becomes one of medium: the letter is acting in two capacities,

---

distribution values." McGann also asserts that meaning is a function of all these matters, "whether we are aware of such matters when we make our meanings" or not (1991, 12).

[10] Parliament's emphasis. This is also an example of Parliament's emphasis of particularly damning sections of Charles's letters.

that of state and that of intimacy. Read in isolation and without Parliament's manipulation, this apparent conflict becomes nothing more than an acceptable fluctuation in an already fluid medium, the letter.

A letter anthology unhinges the letters from the context that originally gave them meaning. Parliament selectively arranged the letters to emphasize a narrative of the king's seduction by the queen and his betrayal of the people. The letters are arranged a-chronologically, with roman numerals that imply the given sequence is somehow correct (Daybell and Gordon 2016, 9; Schneider 2005, 255).[11] In a letter dated 12 July 1626, for example, the king complains of the "unkindesses and distastes [that] have fallen betweene [his] wife and [himself]" and concludes that he must "make her goe to Tiburn in devotion, to pray"; in the following letter, dated 1 January 1644, he requests that she write to him more often for, *"the distractions of London were never so greate, or likely to bring good effect as now lastly that assistance was never more needful, never so likely as now to doe good to him who is eternally thine,"* which is followed by a letter to his son Harry, dated 24 April 1645, in which he asserts that *"her health in the first place be cared for, then my affaires"* (*KCO*, 34–36).[12] The sequencing of the letters creates a narrative of transition from dissatisfaction at the level of desiring Henrietta Maria's exile, to her being a pleasant and necessary diversion, to her becoming the most important part of his life. Parliament's manipulation also makes evident the importance of a letter's material and social existence by imparting new meaning to their contents by separating them from their original material instantiation and sociocontextual situation.

In the next section, I explore the impact of digital mediation on *The King's Cabinet Opened.* The collection, already heavily mediated by the editorial decisions of the Parliamentarians, provides an excellent starting place for thinking through digital mediation generally and makes the impact of printedness more apparent in epistolary collections. By thinking about digital mediation, we come to understand the printed letter collection as an interface to a database, a selection against an otherwise inaccessible set of entries and relations.

---

[11] Schneider argues that "the recontextualization of [letters'] epistolary contents in the medium of print imparted a novel cultural meaning to the letters. In all of these cases, the exigencies of political maneuvering required the reframing, reorganization, and reevaluation of letters when transferred to print" (2005, 255).

[12] Parliament's emphasis.

3. *The digital* King's Cabinet Opened

I have argued that epistolarity in early modern England was an activity concerned with the development and maintenance of social relationships, and I also suggested that letters could be understood as entries selected from a private "reality" that, like a database, is accessible only through some interface. I now turn to *The King's Cabinet Opened* in its electronic form. The text of the digital edition is based on the Text Creation Partnership's transcribed edition which was itself derived from a microfilm scan, made for *Early English Books Online*, of an original copy located in the Huntington Library. After revising the text against *EEBO*'s page images and a physical copy in the Folger Shakespeare library, itself a copy from the Huntington, I encoded the text in XML using the Text Encoding Initiative's guidelines. After encoding, the text was transformed into HTML and inserted into an electronic semi-structured database for retrieval by the user via web interface.[13] Like the printed text, *The King's Cabinet Opened Online* has at its heart questions of *interface*. In the case of the print edition of *The King's Cabinet Opened*, the Parliamentarians were presented with a collection of letters to which we have no access. Given the relational nature of letters generally, and the unknown number and contents of the letters in Parliament's seizure, we can conceive of this collection as a database that we only have access to through an interface. We will consider the book as presenting one query against that database—a single view into its whole relational content—with the printed book as its interface. The implications of this framework for thinking through digital mediation include, among others, the flattening out of apparent differences between print and digital, allowing us to perceive the similar materiality of each. Digitally, the database can be queried in multiple ways through its interface. This sheds new light on the original editorial work—typography and chronology, for example—while opening up the text in new ways by adding new information, highlighting editorial decisions, enabling recombinability, and presenting the letters individually. Like the encrypted letters in their pre-print form, the text has become code, has been re-encoded, transformed again into a coded language that can obfuscate or clarify its meaning depending on what users bring to their experience. The digital edition reimagines the text by presenting it in a malleable format to a new public and inviting them to formulate and interpret the text and, especially, the work that Parliament and I have done to it through print and digitization.

---

[13] In converting the text of *The King's Cabinet Opened* I attempted to maintain all of the linguistic and bibliographic codes that were present.

Typography has special significance for this document. In the printed edition of *The King's Cabinet Opened*, both nouns—persons and places—and emphasized text are italicized. In the electronic edition there is now semantic differentiation between nouns—which are tagged with <i> or italic tags—and the emphasized text—which are tagged with <em> or emphasis tags—thus, there is a bibliographic emphasis on the text that the Parliamentarians meant to emphasize. This new differentiation enhances and complicates the Parliamentary message through the elaboration of new bibliographic codes.

In the code of Figure 2, we can see the initial <p> tag that delineates a section of text within the overall <div type='letter'> that contains a section of text the Parliamentarians printed in italics.[14] This text is enclosed in <emph> or emphasis tags that semantically mark its emphasis—the text is not italicized until it is translated into HTML and marked with <em> tags—that is, it denotes the emphasis in the text in a way that is not presentational, but hierarchical.[15] The text enclosed in the <emph> tag is hierarchically differentiated from the rest of the text in the paragraph. Also present here are <persName> and <rs> tags. These tags are used to identify people within the text, <persName> being a person's name and <rs> being a reference string for the person. Each person has been assigned a key by which they are linked to an identity entry in the personography. These tags separate the nouns—which are also italicized—from the text that is designated as receiving emphasis. When translated into HTML, these tags are made into hyperlinks, wrapped in <i> or italics tags, to the personography page. The difference in <em> and <i> tags maintains the semantic differentiation between the types of text in the HTML presentation. (See Figure 3.) The nouns, being hyperlinks, are now both visually and semantically distinct from the text that the Parliamentarians chose to highlight through emphasis.

---

[14] A <div> is a division in the hierarchy of the semi-structured document. In the case of each of the letters, the divisions are of the type "letter" within the <body> of the whole document.

[15] The choice of <emph> and subsequently <em> tags is a choice made among many options including highlight tags. The choice of emphasis was made to reflect and make apparent the initial choices made by the text's editors.

```
<p>
<emph> Now I must make a complaint to thee of my <persName key="CCD122">Sonne
     Charles</persName>, which troubles me the more, that thou maist suspect I seeke
by equiocating to hide the breach of my word, which I hate above all things,
especially to thee: It is this he hath sent to desire me, That <persName
     key="JGZR021">Sir John Greenfield</persName> may be sworne Gentleman of his
Bedchamber, but already so publikely ingaged in it, that the refusall would be a
great disgrace both to my <rs type="person" key="CCD122">Sonne</rs> and the young
     <rs type="person" key="ZGZR021">Gentleman</rs>, to whom it is not fit to give a
just distaste, especially now, considering his Fathers merits, his owne
hopefulnesse, besides the great power that Family has in the West: </emph> 'Yet I
have refused the admiting of him untill I shall heare from thee. Wherfore I desire
thee first to chide my <rs type="person" key="CCD122">Sonne</rs> for ingaging
```

Figure 2. The XML representation of a paragraph of a letter that includes emphasized text.

Now I must make a complaint to thee of my Sonne Charles, which troubles me the more, that thou maist suspect I seeke by equiocating to hide the breach of my word, which I hate above all things, especially to thee: It is this he hath sent to desire me, That Sir John Greenfield may be sworne Gentleman of his Bedchamber, but already so publikely ingaged in it, that the refusall would be a great disgrace both to my Sonne and the young Gentleman, to whom it is not fit to give a just distaste, especially now, considering his Fathers merits, his owne hopefulnesse, besides the great power that Family has in the West: 'Yet I have refused the admiting of him untill I shall heare from thee. Wherfore I desire thee first to chide my Sonne for ingaging himselfe without one of our consents; then, not to refuse thy owne consent; and lastly, to beleeve*

Figure 3. The rendered and styled HTML version of the XML from Figure 2.

The user can choose to view the letters in their original printed sequence with the preface and annotations, or sort them by date or by sender-receiver, or view all the letters that reference an individual, and so on. The letters have been re-individuated as separate pieces and returned to individual pieces of a conversation, now accessible through the screen. Previously, the annotations and the letters were only spuriously connected—they existed in the same physical document but not the same physical page. Now the user can view the relevant annotations and the letters on the same screen through the interface. This provides users with the opportunity to better understand and relate the commentary of the annotations to their intended letter—if they so choose. Separating the text from its editorial apparatus also reveals the holes that the apparatus created in space, time, and content. It reveals the very standard and conventional character of Charles's epistles. Because of the digital interface, users also have more apparently variant paths through *The King's Cabinet Opened* and therefore can construct their own image of King Charles I and of Parliament. In this way, I think, the electronic edition of *The King's Cabinet Opened* represents the incarnation of Parliament's professed, ideal invocation of the public.

Scholars of digital mediation tend to emphasize the new functionality offered by markup features, especially hyperlinks. While the digital interface allows for explicit connections between texts through hyperlinks, these connections already exist in print form. These connections come in the form of allusions, textual notes by scholars, references, addresses, co-authorship, the social circumstances in which the book was produced, and so on. The preface to *The King's Cabinet Opened*, for example, states that the authors will not "smother this light under a Bushell" (*KCO*, 1) which is a clear biblical allusion that invokes another text—that links from this text to that text (Ben-Porat 1976, 107–08).[16] *The King's Cabinet Opened* attempts to leverage the print interface to make ideological and social connections; the digital edition makes these connections explicit and invites reorganization.

Explicit connections in the digital *King's Cabinet Opened* extend beyond relationships that are merely textual. They enable analysis that allows us to see Charles's lived social network, admittedly one that is at least partially constructed by the editors of the volume, with weight given to the individual's proportional involvement in that network rather than that assigned to them by historians. They reveal the collaborative and social nature of epistolarity in a tangible way—people such as couriers are made present, are given weight in their communication circuits. Digital remediation, then, reinforces those arguments being made—very recently—by scholars of epistolarity (Daybell and Gordon 2016).[17]

As you can see in Figures 4 and 5, analysis of this collection reveals a very different social network for Charles than that compiled by historians.[18] In this

---

[16] Ziva Ben-Porat argues in her article "The Poetics of Literary Allusion" that allusion is the "simultaneous activation of two texts," which "results in the formation of intertextual patterns whose nature cannot be predetermined" (107–08). The allusion, then, reinvigorates the text alluded to in the invocation, resulting in a dialogic interaction between the two texts which creates new meaning for the reader who activates the link by recognizing the allusion.

[17] Daybell and Gordon's collection *Cultures of Correspondence* challenges the standard dyadic model of correspondence and asserts that correspondence always involved at least a third party. They argue that bearers were crucial in "conveying the material letter and in supplementing it with information not confided to the text" and that "an awareness of the collaborative nature of epistolary practices, the multiagent possibilities of letter writing—in addition to 'letter writers' . . . and recipients, which could involve secretaries, amanuenses, bearers, clerks, and archivists—erodes notions of letters as private and complicates our understanding of early modern subjectivities" (4). The digital edition of *The King's Cabinet Opened* allows for analysis that makes this more apparent.

[18] This comparison uses the social network graph generated for King Charles I on *Six Degrees of Francis Bacon* (Accessed 4/15/2015, http://www.sixdegreesoffrancisbacon. com/?ids=10011670&min_confidence=60&type=network). This network is compiled by "scholars and students from all over the world" (Accessed 4/15/2015, http://www. sixdegreesoffrancisbacon.com/about).

selection of Charles's correspondence network, controversial figures—like Henrietta Maria—and subversive ones—like carriers—loom large. The graph makes apparent those connections—and their magnitudes—that the Parliamentarians tried to highlight with their editorial apparatus and type shifts. Here, then, the digital allows us to examine a manifestation of Parliament's intention and concern: Henrietta Maria, spies, and "evil advisors" played a large role in Charles's personal rule. In this way, network analysis allows us to visualize and quantify the effectiveness of the editorial work done by the Parliamentarians. While the network is not an explicitly historical representation, it is a representation of the relationships constructed by this text.

The King's Cabinet Opened is a valuable case study in the similarity of the print and digital interface. The print document can be viewed as a snapshot of the interface to a database, as the result of a single query to a database. Here, the seized letters, the packet in its entirety, function as the database—the set of records stored and organized in a central location from which the user chooses—and the printed pamphlet as the interface to that database. The printed book might be seen as the result of a query that could be—roughly—structured: SELECT letters FROM packet WHERE Charles = [Deceptive AND (Duplicitous OR Loving)] SORT BY severity. The appended preface and annotations function as the user guide for interpreting the result of the query—the frame around the data pour (Liu 2004, 59).

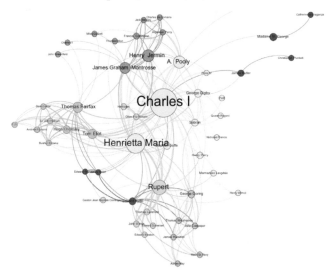

Figure 4. King Charles's social network as generated using the letters of *The King's Cabinet Opened.*

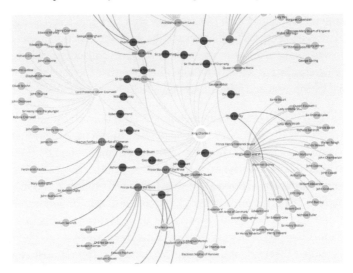

Figure 5. King Charles's social network from *Six Degrees of Francis Bacon* as generated in April of 2015.

This metaphorical representation of both text and web interface places the text in an architecture and understanding called Model-View-Controller. The model representing the data set and its structure—the original letters for Parliament, the available letters for the users of the digital edition. The model from which Parliament selected is a truly unknown domain, but that of *The King's Cabinet Opened Online* is filled with and structured by the selections that Parliament made against their model. The new electronic model is derived from the original model—a representation of the original data set. *The King's Cabinet Opened Online* represents a change in interface for *The King's Cabinet Opened*, for a data set that I have attempted to replicate entirely. The change in interface represents a change in the reader's possible experience and interaction with the text, not a change in the text itself. In this way, the print and digital editions are the same; they reframe and restructure data selected and extracted from a finite collection in order to present specific relationships by manipulating the interface to those selections.

The view represents the selection performed on the data set, the letters that are printed in the pamphlet and that populate the database of *KCO Online,* plus the appended editorial apparatus. In the case of the codex, print can be seen as the interface and each individual book as a view. Parliament's selections, which were guided by their political motives, were made by their controller—those motives that structured the selection performed on the model and transmitted to the view. In the electronic edition, the letters—those selected by Parliament—combined with the database structure make up the model. My code, and the user requests facilitated and limited by it, function as the controller (the instructions that the server utilizes to select collections of letters from the overall collection of letters). Finally, the page that the user sees—which is structured by my own editorial and design choices—represents the view.

The digital and print versions of *The King's Cabinet Opened*, then, mirror each other in form and functionality. The display on the website is an instance of the text—and a query performed against the database—just as the printed pamphlet is an instance of the text. Each is rife with interpretive possibilities and mutability that are arrived at through editorial guidance and user/reader interaction. The difference lies in the user's ability to re-generate the text in a way that has not yet been printed—in their ability to re-instantiate the text. The electronic edition is, therefore, only dynamic in its re-generability which is enabled through, and only through, its new interface. It represents a rapid shift in presented text akin to the bibliographic states that books can appear in.[19] Digitally, the web interface and user perform the functions of compositor and printer in a more immediate and less permanent way.

The user can come to the text, and recombine and reconstitute its content, but, as is the case with print, cannot escape from the interface through which they are viewing the text. For example, the user is forced to notice the new distinction between nouns—which are hyperlinked, italicized, and colored—and emphasized text. This change influences the experience and interpretation of the text; it invites, hints at, and draws the user to new information and, in some cases, it invites them to leave the text itself. The new formal elements distract from the content, in a sense reduce the importance of the king's words to the experience of the text and highlight new—and old—editorial decisions. The new elements function as possible interruptions to the text and its continuity, as possible junctures in the narrative of the user's experience with the text.

The user is given the opportunity to reconfigure the document and thus to consider the text itself in new ways—though with or without Parliament's specific guidance—while still within the confines of specific editorial decisions. The new interface has not eradicated the print interface but extended it. The formal structures that are inherent in the print interface have been enhanced, not replaced: the letters remain as letters; they are still presented within a frame (now called the viewport); the allusions and references to people remain but are more evident.

---

[19] Or, if we take this idea further, a commonplace book.

4. Digital mediation and the book as interface

Scholars are increasingly recognizing the fruitfulness of investigating the connection between print and digital media. In the case of *The King's Cabinet Opened*, both print and digital can, I think, show that the print and digital books represent changes in, and not to, interface and allow us to consider the interface as the primary site of mediation for text. That books exist in multiple states—and can be changed by each reading or reader—lends itself to an understanding of the book as an instantiation of a view to an interfaced database. Like epistolary collections, then, each instantiation of a print book can be seen as a selection against an unknown set of possibilities, like *The King's Cabinet Opened*. As such, this section departs from the text of *The King's Cabinet Opened* itself. Instead, it builds on the previous sections to explore the usefulness of thinking through books—digital or print—as mediated by interface. While the analogy of thinking of a book as a query against a database may be striking or strange, I think that reframing the book in this way can allow us to examine the effect and sites of change involved in digital remediation in new ways by acknowledging the similarities between print and digital.

Johanna Drucker argues for an understanding of interface that is "what we read and how we read combined through engagement, [that] is a provocation to cognitive experience, but [that] is also an enunciative apparatus" (Drucker 2014, 147). For Drucker, the interface contains both text and instructions for reading that are in part constituted by and constitutive of the reader. In going forward, there is a need to rethink the interface, for, "so long as we think of interface as an environment for doing things, performing tasks, work, structuring behaviors, we remain linked to the idea that 'reading' the digital environment is restricted to an analysis of its capacity to support the doing of tasks" (Drucker 2014, 144). A reconsideration of the interface, then, requires a reconsideration of the target of analysis and the function of the interface as a whole. Drucker's argument is about the continued development of interface, but I think that it is useful for considering interface as a whole. The interface is a window to a selection of text with instructions for how to interpret that text; it is a site of mediation that impacts the reception and understanding of text. As we have already seen, *The King's Cabinet Opened* and its editorial apparatus does just this. To limit our understanding of this complex structure to its capacity to support the completion of tasks is to miss the effect that the frame through which we view a book has on any particular instance of a text or its constitutive impact on our reception of that text.

John Milton wrote in *Areopagitica* that "books are not absolutely dead things, but do contain a potency of life in them to be as active as that soul was whose progeny they are" (Milton 2007, 930). Books have, and have had, a life beyond their final printed form; they exist in conversation with other texts, within a system of circulation and use, are bound or rebound with other texts, added to, revised, are the product of complex social interactions that do not cease upon its completion, and exist in multiple printed states. Each state, issue, or edition can be seen as representing an—at least slightly—different query on the database of the material from which the text was generated—the work that the text is an attempt at embodying. G. T. Tanselle, in his book *A Rationale of Textual Criticism*, argues that the text on a page does not constitute the work and therefore "any alterations one makes in the manuscript do not automatically alter the work" (Tansalle 1989, 27). The work, then, of the text consists not in its manifestation on the page, just as it does not consist of its manifestation on the screen. The database and Tanselle's work are similar in that they both lie behind and structure what is presented to the reader. The print text, like a web page, can be seen to represent an instance of an organization of pieces. *The King's Cabinet Opened* is a highly organized instance of its constituent pieces; the ability to manipulate this organization makes its constructedness more apparent. Its printed form represents a selection against an unknown set of data with a tightly controlled and constructed interface. The printed page can act as an interface that mediates between the reader and the work that impacts, creates, or guides their understanding of this particular instantiation of records retrieved from the database. States, issues, and editions can represent various instantiations of views to interfaces, whose text is the result of different queries to the same database, that guide our reading of that data set and its underlying source.

As Drucker explains, the graphic features of books all serve particular structural purposes:

> They work as presentation (what's inscribed and present), representation (content of a text and/or image), navigation (wayfinding across the spaces of the book), orientation (sense of where one is in the whole), reference (into the sources and conversations on which a work is drawn), and social networking (the dialogues of commentary, footnotes, endnotes, and marginalia). (Drucker 2014, 162)

Here, the discussion of the physical features of the printed book also represents the architecture of the book's interface. We can see that the book features many of the characteristics that we attribute to the digital interface and can come to the conclusion that the transition from print to digital is a change *in* interface, not a change *to* interface for text.

If we see the print to digital remediation in this way, we can consider the interface as the primary zone of mediation for text, both printed and electronic. Interface functions as the go-between for text and reader-user, but not without having an effect on the experience of the text. Alexander Galloway explains in *The Interface Effect* that representation through interface is "a map, a reduction or indexical and symbolic topology" (Galloway 2012, vii). It is common to look at the transition from print to digital as a liberation from the formal restrictions of print, as a method that allows for freedom in the user's experience of the text. While I think that this is to some extent true, it is important to recognize that there are inherent limitations in interfaced media—the user is limited to our structured map, our indexical topology that guides, as Parliament did, the user's experience and understanding of the text, albeit in new ways. The new interface compounds editorial decision upon editorial decision, resulting in a text that is doubly restricted and constructed but that is freshly and contradictorily mutable in its openness to recombinability. The result is not a new text or even a new edition, but a new *experience* of the text and of reading. The same can be said of a printed collection of letters: its new medium creates new meaning through new experience—through a new social and material context.

The underlying database represents an inaccessible highly-structured and indexed set of data from which to select. This means, as Lev Manovich and others have noted, that the world of *The King's Cabinet Opened* is represented as a list (Manovich 2002, 255; Folsom 2007a, 1573). The user thus experiences *The King's Cabinet Opened* through an interface that displays the letters in what Alan Liu calls a "data pour" (Liu 2004, 59). These are places on a page where the author or editor surrenders the act of writing to that of parameterization, designated zones where unknown content pours into the manifest work from databases or XML sources. The letters selected from the list now appear in locations on the screen that are designated for the display of information that is unknown—the user determines which letter or letters to see at any given time. For Liu, this is the characteristic of encoded text—the content of the work is separated from the "material instantiation or formal presentation" (Liu 2004, 58). For us, this is characteristic of printed epistolarity and especially *The King's Cabinet Opened*. The letters are separated from the editorial apparatus in two ways: they can be viewed without the preface or annotations, or they can be viewed without Parliament's careful sequencing. Therefore, the meaning of *The King's Cabinet Opened* is now more explicitly mutable at any given moment while maintaining a singular static organization in the database on the hard drive.

The database, through its interface, enables new narratives while challenging the original or official one. Manovich, despite his description of database and narrative as natural enemies, links them in a way saying "the 'user' of a narrative is traversing a database, following links between its records as established by the database creator" (Manovich 2002, 227). Therefore, narrative in itself is composed of a database. The narrative of an interfaced database, then, is composed of what Ed Folsom calls fractal pieces (Folsom 2007a, 1574). In *The King's Cabinet Opened*, each letter, the preface, the annotations, the added personography and social network maps can each be seen to generate fractal pieces of the whole narrative of a single experience with the electronic edition of *The King's Cabinet Opened*, or with other digital texts. In the print edition, this narrative is composed of links that the Parliamentarians tried to create through material and editorial manipulation; these links are made more explicit by the digital manifestation of the text.

The exploration of, and interaction with, each of these fractals leads to what Folsom explains is a rhizomatic experience of the text that is characterized by "an intertwined web of roots" (Folsom 2007a, 1573). The letters themselves—whether the static collection that is represented as a reproduction of the print book or the individual or user-sequenced—now have identities all their own that lead to other fractals; each letter contains a list of persons which links to the personography which links to the *Oxford Dictionary of National Biography*. Users can generate their own and multiplicative narratives constructed from these fractals; can construct their own sequencing of the letters; can choose to see the annotations or preface, in addition to the narrative of their experience with the site and of their path of information access.

The database, then, rather than being the enemy of narrative, enables the creation of narratives through interface. Katherine Hayles indicates that database also relies on narrative "because database can construct relational juxtapositions but is helpless to interpret or explain them it needs narrative to make its results meaningful" (Hayles 2007, 1603–08). *The King's Cabinet Opened*'s new database allows the user to create new connections and then interpret them—to construct a new narrative and therefore a new image of Charles's private and political life.

Since the interface allows for a mutable experience of the text, the letters can be seen as distinct from the Parliamentary editorial apparatus. The letters viewed without the editorial apparatus appended to them mean very little individually but can enable the user to come to a new understanding of a particular piece of English history and of the printedness of Parliament's edition. Viewing the letters individually also makes the incomplete nature of any printed letter collection more apparent through their conspicuous isolation. Though the primary editorial apparatus—preface and annotations—is disconnected, the typographical conventions remain and are enhanced and therefore can communicate a different message. The social networks and links in the letters can lead to a new understanding of seemingly minor characters in the English Revolution. As Diana Barnes indicates, for the printed edition, "in a peculiarly intellectual fashion readers were invited to participate by reading and judging the king's epistolary rhetoric" (Barnes 2013, 134).

Now, the digital edition draws out the Parliamentarians' rhetorical choices while encouraging readers to explore alternate or even external possibilities. The semi-structured nature of an interactive document allows for new connections to be made—or severed—by the user in the specific instance of reading. The king's cabinet is no longer simply opened—revealing a structured, selected content—but has been splintered and left for the user to reassemble.

WORKS CITED

Akkerman, Nadine. 2016. "Enigmatic Cultures of Cryptology." In *Cultures of Correspondence in Early Modern Britain*, edited by James Daybell and Andrew Gordon, 69–84. Philadelphia: University of Pennsylvania Press.

Barnes, Diana G. 2013. *Epistolary Community in Print, 1580-1664*. Surrey, UK: Ashgate.

Ben-Porat, Ziva. 1976. "The Poetics of Literary Allusion." *PTL: A Journal for Descriptive Poetics and Theory* 1: 105–28.

Daybell, James, and Andrew Gordon, eds. 2016. *Cultures of Correspondence in Early Modern Britain.* Philadelphia: University of Pennsylvania Press.

Drucker, Johanna. 2014. "Interface and Interpretation." In *Graphesis: Visual Forms of Knowledge Production*, by Johanna Drucker, 138–79. Cambridge, MA: Harvard University Press.

England and Wales. Sovereign (1625–1649: Charles I). *The King's Cabinet Opened: or, certain packets of secret letters & papers, written with the Kings own hand, and taken in his cabinet at Nasby-Field, June 14. Early English Books Online*: Text Creation Partnership. University of Oxford Text Archive. Accessed 20 October 2014. http://downloads.it.ox.ac.uk/ota-public/tcp/Texts-TEI/free/A31/A31932.xml.

Folsom, Ed. 2007a. "Database as Genre: The Epic Transformation Of Archives." *PMLA: Publications of the Modern Language Association of America* 122.5: 1571–79.

———. 2007b. "Reply." PMLA: Publications of the Modern Language Association of America 122.5: 1608–12.

Galloway, Alexander R. 2012. *The Interface Effect.* Cambridge: Polity.

Habermas, Jürgen. 1989. *The Structural Transformation of the Public Sphere: An Inquiry into a Category of Bourgeois Society.* Cambridge, MA: MIT Press.

Hayles, N. Katherine. 2007. "Narrative and Database: Natural Symbionts." *PMLA: Publications of the Modern Language Association of America* 122.5: 1603–08.

Howell, James. 1907. *Epistolae Ho-Elianae: the familiar Letters of James Howell,* edited by Bruce Rogers and Agnes Repplier. Boston: Houghton, Mifflin and Co. Accessed 20 October 2014. https://archive.org/details/epistolhoelianf01reppgoog.

The King's Cabinet opened: or, certain packets of secret letters & papers, written with the Kings own hand, and taken in his cabinet at Nasby-Field, June 14. 1645. By victorious Sr. Thomas Fairfax; wherein many mysteries of state, tending to the justification of that cause, for which Sir Thomas Fairfax joyned battell that memorable day are clearly laid open; together, with some annotations thereupon. 14 July 1645. Early English Books Online: 2205:08. Web.

Liu, Alan. 2004. "Transcendental Data: Toward a Cultural History and Aesthetics of the New Encoded Discourse." *Critical Inquiry* 31.1: 49–84.

Lowenstein, David. 1999. "The King among Radicals." In *The Royal Image: Representations of Charles I,* edited by Thomas N. Corns, 96–121. New York: Cambridge University Press.

Loewenstein, Joseph. 2002. *The Author's Due: Printing and the Prehistory of Copyright.* Chicago: University of Chicago Press.

Manovich, Lev. 2002. *The Language of New Media.* Cambridge, MA: MIT Press.

McGann, Jerome. 1991. *The Textual Condition.* Princeton: Princeton University Press.

———. 2007. "Database, Interface, and Archival Fever." *PMLA: Publications of the Modern Language Association of America* 122.5 (October): 1588–92.

McKeon, Michael. 2005. *The Secret History of Domesticity: Public, Private, and the Division of Knowledge.* Baltimore: Johns Hopkins University Press.

Milton, John. (1644) 2007. *Areopagitica.* In *The Complete Poetry and Essential Prose of John Milton,* edited by William Kerrigan, John Rumrich, and Stephen M. Fallon, 927–66. New York: Random House. Citations refer to the Random House edition.

Raymond, Joad. 1999. "Popular Representations of Charles I." In *The Royal Image: Representations of Charles I,* edited by Thomas N. Corns, 47–73. New York: Cambridge University Press.

———. 2003. *Pamphlets and Pamphleteering in Early Modern Britain.* Cambridge: Cambridge University Press.

Schneider, Gary. 2005. *The Culture of Epistolarity: Vernacular Letters and Letter Writing in Early Modern England, 1500-1700.* Newark: University of Delaware Press.

Sharpe, Kevin. 1993. "The King's Writ: Royal Authors and Royal Authority in Early Modern England." In *Culture and Politics in Early Stuart England,* edited by Kevin Sharpe and Peter Lake, 117–38. Stanford: Stanford University Press.

Tanselle, G. Thomas. 1989. "The Nature of Texts." *A Rationale of Textual Criticism,* by G. Thomas Tanselle, 11–38. Philadelphia: University of Pennsylvania Press.

Zaret, David. 2000. *Origins of Democratic Culture: Printing, Petitions, and the Public Sphere in Early-Modern England.* Princeton: Princeton University Press.

Lost in Pools of Data: Text Reuse in the Emblem Genre and the Nature of Humanities Research Data

Peter Boot

Department of Literary Studies,
Huygens Institute for the History of the Netherlands

Introduction

This essay will be about a limitation of the tools that we develop in the digital humanities. Its central thesis is that the tools we design to answer our questions need to be embedded in an environment that helps us organize, evaluate, and annotate their outcomes. Tool outcomes provide not answers but data that need interpretation (Sculley and Pasanek 2008). Each outcome is the result of a number of choices. The interpretation of the tool's outcomes requires an awareness of the choices that were made in its application. And as the researcher usually applies his or her tools multiple times, each time with different choices for settings and input material, each time with (slightly or radically) different outcomes, the question for the researcher begins to move. What was a question about, say, the topics in a collection of medieval texts, turns into a question of keeping track of input and output of multiple tool runs, motivations for choosing certain settings, judgments about the usefulness of certain outputs, etc. The core intellectual problem that the tool was designed to solve gives way to a more general information overload problem that was out of scope in its development—or more probably not even considered as an issue.

This is not just a concern for the individual researcher trying to make sense of the data. It has a wider impact when considering the transparency of the research process and the need to avoid cherry-picking our results. It is relevant when we want to share our data with other researchers. And it becomes particularly urgent when we want to use our tools for distant reading applications.

These general questions will be discussed in the context of quotation and reference in the Renaissance genre of the emblem. The widely popular emblem (in its simple form, a motto, an engraving or woodcut, and an explanatory poem) reused sayings, concepts, and pictorial motifs from older literature (Bible, classical authors, wisdom literature), and in its turn its contents were

ISBN 978-1-64959-016-9 (paper) ISBN 978-1-64959-017-6 (pdf) ISBN 978-1-64959-037-4 (epub)

New Technologies in Medieval and Renaissance Studies 9 (2022) 33–62

reused in later writings and visual culture. The detection of text reuse (a younger text reusing shorter or longer pieces of an older text) looks like a simple problem that the computer should be able to handle. And indeed, there are many digital humanities projects that have developed more or less sophisticated tools for finding quotations, allusions, or overlap between texts more generally.

To begin, I will discuss our experiences in developing and using text reuse detection software in the context of the Nederlab digital library. Nederlab is an ambitious digital library project that brings together for research purposes the main Dutch collections of digitized texts. In a pilot project, designed to test the usability of the Nederlab collections, we developed software to locate text reuse in emblem texts or reuse of emblem texts in later literature. This turned out not to be an easy task, but what is most relevant in the context of this essay is that the work isn't done when the parallel texts, i.e., potential quotations, have been identified. The real work is then only beginning. What is a relevant parallel? When two texts use the same Bible quotation, this is text reuse, but the younger text is probably not quoting the older. How do we compare the output of multiple tool runs with different settings and slightly modified input files? If we have decided a certain parallel is irrelevant, how do we avoid the same parallel turning up again in subsequent runs?

In another experiment, I wrote a prototype for a management tool that provided support for the information management needs that intensive use of a text reuse tool brings with it. The text reuse detection tool compared two corpora (e.g., the books of the Vulgate Bible and a collection of emblem books) in search of text parallels. The management tool stored all input parameters, hashes of input files, and all output for each run of the text detection tool, and made it possible to explore and annotate the information by run, by corpus, or by individual file. Discussion of this management tool will show how such a tool can indeed provide some overview of the text reuse detection runs and their results, though some aspects remain elusive.

However, the question about this meta-level tool that I will discuss is what the need for such a tool shows us about the nature of humanities data and the fundamental characteristics of tool use and computation in the humanities. For many of the choices a researcher has to make, be they in text reuse detection, in authorship attribution, in topic modeling, or really anywhere, there are no *a priori* reasonable settings. Always when we compute, the details of how we compute affect the outcome. As there is usually no obviously correct way to compute, we are faced with a choice between multiple outcomes.

For our own overview we need a facility to compare and annotate multiple outcomes, but even without taking into account our own needs, we would have a scholarly obligation to store the outcomes of our tool runs and to give account of the choices that we made.

In conclusion, I will look at the question of what this means for the tools that we develop. Facilities like the management tool discussed here should help humanities researchers, in our case Renaissance scholars and medievalists, manage the information overload resulting from using powerful and complicated tools, and focus on the core investigation. They should help other researchers evaluate and replicate scholarship. But does this imply that all tools should be embedded into a virtual research environment for organizing and evaluating their output? Could such a facility be sharable? Maybe tools could provide hooks for extension with facilities for further analysis? It is in no way certain that general-purpose management tools are actually feasible; at the level of the individual application, they may be prohibitively expensive. At present, there does not seem to be an easy way out of this dilemma.

Tools for detecting text reuse

Scholars have always been interested in text reuse, be it in the form of allusion, quotation, or unacknowledged borrowing of text. Text reuse can indicate literary influence, and a recognized quotation can clarify an otherwise obscure passage. Especially in ages that didn't value originality as much as we do, borrowing text was also an accepted way of building literary or philosophical works. As text reuse seems a more or less objective, simple phenomenon that just requires patience to find, its detection seems an ideal task for the computer (at least in those cases where the text is quoted in its original language). A number of digital humanities projects have developed software to do so. Mark Olsen and colleagues worked on detecting borrowed text in the *Encyclopédie* (Olsen, Horton, and Roe 2011), similar work on medieval encyclopaedic texts was done at Monash University (Zahora, Nikulin, Mews, and Squire 2015). Kane and Tompa developed a text detection tool, for a collection of Latin quotations, to help find both the sources of the quotations and later reuse (Kane and Tompa 2011). The *Tesserae* project is specifically interested in finding allusions, rather than full quotations (Coffee et al. 2012). There is a long list of related work, some of it, like the work at Monash, inspired by plagiarism detection software.

Text reuse in the emblem

One of the genres where text reuse detection seems particularly appropriate is the emblem book. The emblem was created by Italian lawyer Andrea Alciato, who published his *Emblematum liber* in 1531.The emblem as he created it would develop over the next two centuries from a learned game for humanists to a vehicle for mass moralization, but the essential ingredients remained the same: image and text (motto and subscription) jointly providing a witty, edifying, or instructive message. The emblem, originally in Latin, spread all over Europe, and emblem books in the various vernaculars soon began to appear.

From the beginning, emblem book writers took pride in reusing older texts and images. The sources that were used included medieval bestiaries, classical coins and medals, ideas about Egyptian hieroglyphs, as well as classical history, mythology, and literature (Daly 1998; Moseley 1989). For explicitly Christian emblem books, the Bible also became an important source. Henkel and Schöne's *Emblemata* (1976) shows the extent to which emblem writers reused the same pictorial motifs. Bath (1994) stresses how much the emblem book owed to learned collections of proverbs and sayings, such as Erasmus's *Adagia,* and notes that emblem books in their turn also contributed to these commonplace books, such as Mirabellius's *Polyanthea*. The emblem's influence on later literature was discussed by Daly (1998). The pictorial motifs used in emblem books were often reused in paintings (De Jongh 2000), in churches (Cieslak 1995) and as "applied emblems" in, for example, interior decoration (Heckscher and Wirth 1959).

In this essay, I will look specifically at text reuse in or based on emblems from the Low Countries (Porteman 1977; Stronks 2008). The Low Countries produced their fair share of Neolatin emblem books, as well as multilingual books and books in Dutch. The two main topics for Dutch emblem books were love and religion, often combined. The love emblem, though not strictly a Dutch invention (Saunders 2007) was brought into blossom in the Netherlands in the early seventeenth century in a series of successful emblem books, such as Otto van Veen's *Amorum emblemata* (Van Veen 1607/8). Van Veen's book, featuring Cupid on every page, was simultaneously published in multiple editions, each containing texts in a different combination of languages. The love emblem shared the emblem's predilection for intertextuality (Bloemendal 2007), reusing, for example, the vocabulary of Petrarchism and quoting canonical classical authors. It was turned to religious use by Van Veen himself (Van Veen 1615) in his *Amoris Divini Emblemata* (Boot 2012). This book reused texts and motifs from the books about secular love in writing about religious love, but replaced the classical authors by the Bible and the church fathers. Jacob Cats wrote realistic emblems about love, but added a social and religious application (Cats 1618). A series of other books, such as Van Leuven's *Amoris divini et humani antipathia* (Van Leuven 1629), opposed secular and religious love (with a preference for the religious variety, of course). All these books, and others in the same genre, borrowed heavily from each other, with respect to emblem concept, texts and pictorial motifs. The most prominent later Dutch emblematist was Jan Luyken. After *Duytse Lier* (Dutch lyre), an emblematically embellished book of poems and songs about love (Luyken 1671) and an emblem book titled *Jesus en de ziel* (Jesus and the soul) (Luyken 1685), he published a series of religious emblem books with emblems based on everyday objects and activities, such as *Het leerzaam huisraad* (Instructive household objects) (Luyken 1711). In his later emblem books, each emblem is followed by one or two pages of Bible quotations. I used Luyken's books to test systematically the best approaches to detect as many quotations as possible. Another book that I will look at is Willem den Elger's *Zinne-beelden der liefde* (Emblems of love) (Den Elger 1703). Den Elger reuses images from the religious emblem books' tradition in a mostly secular setting. The reason his book is interesting is that he quotes many other poets and emblem writers, and it is therefore suitable material for evaluating techniques for text reuse detection.

In this essay, the focus is on how the introduction of digital tools often does not solve the problem that they were introduced to solve. They do contribute to a solution, of course, but they also move the problem to a new level of abstraction which may at a cognitive level be harder to manage than the original problem. Before moving to this (meta-)issue, let me summarize what we found with respect to text reuse in the (Dutch) emblem genre. We discovered hardly any intellectual debts that were previously unknown. The forms of text reuse that we encountered were primarily shared quotations. Emblem book authors do not usually quote longer text fragments from each other. What they quote are usually other quotations. (From each other, they quote mottoes, but these are so short they escape detection; they are often only two or three words long.) The classical authors and the Bible are the main sources for these quotations. The favorite classical author is Ovid, which is unsurprising given the Dutch emblem book's focus on love. Another form of text reuse occurs in those emblem books that mix the emblem and the song book genre, such as the *Nieuwen ieucht spieghel* (New mirror of youth) (Anonymous 1617). There we encounter many songs from earlier collections of songs, such as *Den nieuwen verbeterden lust-hof* (The new improved garden of delights) (Vlack 1607). We encountered hardly any reuse of emblem texts in later works, with the exception of explicitly anthological works such as *Een lees- en zangboekjen voor de jeugd* (A reading and song book for young people; 1853).

Detecting text reuse in Nederlab

Nederlab (http://www.nederlab.nl/) is a digital library targeted at research-ers. It brings together the most important collections of digital text from the Netherlands: the collections of newspapers, journals, and books digitized by the National Library, the collections from the *Digital Library of Dutch Literature* (*DBNL*), now also managed by the National Library, as well as linguistic corpo-ra and other texts; collections from other institutions will follow shortly. To test the usability of the Nederlab infrastructure, in 2015 we looked into the possibility of doing text reuse detection on the Nederlab text collections.[1] In our research we looked into the sources for emblem text as well as the reuse of emblem texts in later texts. We created four collections of text: emblem books available within Nederlab (39 titles), Dutch Bible translations (6 titles), poetry until 1750 (199 titles) and books for children and young people (466 titles). We started looking for textual parallels without specific hypotheses about the quantity or type of text reuse that we were going to detect or about the books that we were going to find it in.

A simple text reuse detection tool was developed, inspired by the Text Pair software developed for the *Encyclopédie* project (Olsen and Horton 2009). The logic of that program was rewritten from Perl into Ruby, because Ruby was a better fit for our infrastructure. The idea was that after the experiment, the resulting software could be implemented within the Nederlab environ-ment for wider use. It is fair to say that we underestimated the effort re-quired to replicate the Text Pair functionality, and what we could deliver in the limited amount of time available for the project was only a limited amount of functionality. The software compares a query text file against an indexed base corpus, looks for corresponding shingles (n-grams of words), and merges adjoining hits into larger parallels. Some options are available to fine-tune the creation of the n-grams: n itself is a parameter and could be set to 3, 4, 5, or any other value; words from a stopword list could be ignored; a minimum word length could be imposed; words could be cut off after a certain length; and some elementary rewrite rules could be applied

---

[1] This was an "in kind" contribution to Nederlab development financed by the Huy-gens Institute for the History of the Netherlands. The researcher on the project was the author of this essay; development work was done by Meindert Kroese.

to combat orthographical variation.[2] As output, the tool produced a CSV file with pointers to the parallel texts (based on filename and position in the XML hierarchy) and the parallel text fragments with some context. Table 1 shows a brief extract of such a CSV file. The file in the first column is the States' Bible; the files in the third column are various emblem books.[3]

File location 1	Parallel in file 1	File location 2	Parallel in file 2
_sta001stat01_01.TEI.2.(…).p.17100	Uytspansel in * het midden der Wateren; * ende dat make	brun001embl02_01.TEI.2.(…).p.1456	bevrijd waren, en door * het midden der wateren, * dwers door die dorre woestijne maakte * die twee groote Lichten: dat groote Licht tot heerschappye * des
_sta001stat01_01.TEI.2.(…).p.17191	maeckte * die twee groote Lichten: dat groote licht tot heerschappye * des	luyk001schr02_01.TEI.2.(…).p.978	daags
sta001stat01 01.TEI.2.(…).p.17191	kleyne * Licht tot heerschappye des nachts; * oock de Sterren.	luyk001schr02 01.TEI.2.(…).p.978	groote * Licht tot heerschappye des * daags,
_sta001stat01_01.TEI.2.(…).p.17191	kleyne * Licht tot heerschappye des nachts; * oock de Sterren.	luyk001schr02_01.TEI.2.(…).p.978	kleine * Licht tot heerschappye des nachts; * ook de Sterren.
_sta001stat01_01.TEI.2.(…).p.17203	te heerschen in * den dach, ende in de nacht, * ende om scheydinge	hard001godd02_01.TEI.2.(…).q.24463	verheventheyt Godts. Dat ick * den dach ende nacht in dese * mijne pelgrimagie

Table 1. Extract of CSV file giving potential parallels. The words delimited by asterisks are the parallel, the rest is context (here shortened). The references to the file locations are also shortened. The extract shows both true and false parallels.

Unfortunately, what transpired immediately is that there is no single best setting for the parameters: no setting, certainly, that is applicable for all research questions and all corpora, but even for a single corpus it is necessary to run this tool, or probably any tool, a number of times with different parameter settings. That necessity arises mostly because quotations are almost never literal, character-by-character, identical to the text they quote (Kolak and Schilit 2008). When the Bible says "Honor thy father and thy mother," the text may be quoted as "We were told to honor our fathers and our mothers," and these texts only share the words "honor" and "and." For historic texts, an additional complication is that spelling was much more variable than today.

The parameters serve to limit the impact of this (usually irrelevant) variation. Ignoring words from a stopword list, usually of frequently occurring

---

[2] We hardly used the rewrite facility. Creating a set of acceptable rewrite rules would have been a project in itself.

[3] The parallels all supposedly refer back to verses in the first chapter of Genesis. The first parallel, however ("het midden der wateren" [in the midst of the waters]), comes from a retelling of the story of Exodus in De Brune's *Emblemata of Zinne-werck* (De Brune 1636). The next three are true quotations, the last one is again a coincidental agreement in word usage.

function words, would in the example probably remove "and," "thy," and "our," reducing the relevant texts to "Honor father mother" and "honor fathers mothers." Ignoring words below a minimum word length can have a similar effect. Cutting off words beyond a certain length (say six) would make that "Honor father mother" and "honor father mother." Apart from the capital, the texts are now identical and would be selected by our algorithm—that is, if we look for trigrams. If we were looking for four-grams, we would find nothing, as in the present context there are only three words left. So even a literal quotation of "Honor thy father and thy mother" would be overlooked if we applied stopword filtering with four-grams. This illustrates that parameter settings can work both ways: they can remove irrelevant variation, increasing the possibility of finding a quotation, but they can also remove evidence for quotation, and thus decrease that possibility.

Another way in which a parameter setting can be a double-edged sword is by increasing the number of located parallel texts while at the same time increasing the number of false hits. When we cut off words after a certain length, or replace words by their lemmas, we lessen the amount of variation and therefore increase the number of hits, true or false. Technically, we may increase recall (the proportion of true parallels retrieved by our system) at the cost of diminishing precision (the proportion of true parallels among our hits). This is especially visible when switching for instance from four-grams to trigrams. By loosening the requirements, the number of hits increases spectacularly. In a run where we compared the Dutch States Bible, the authoritative 1637 Bible translation (Anonymous 1637), against the Nederlab emblem corpus, 6,866 potential parallels were found when looking for four-grams, but no fewer than 49,836 when looking for trigrams (other settings being equal: minimum word size three, word cut-off length six, simple spelling uniformization, and no stopword removal). But often these potential parallels are the results of very generic trigrams (in Dutch) such as "ende dat ghy" (and that you/thou) or "den houwelicken staet" (the married state). On the other hand, the trigrams run does locate a number of true parallels that the four-grams run does not, such as the words from Genesis that God "schiep den Mensche" (created man). Inconsistent spelling is by far the most important reason why trigrams retrieve parallels that cannot be located using four-grams: Luyken's *Schriftuurlyke geschiedenissen en gelykenissen* (Scriptural histories and parables) (Luyken 1712) actually contains the entire Bible verse (Gen 1:27), as well as a wider context, but the words before and after "schiep den Mensche" are spelled differently by Luyken. It is clear that with 49,836 potential parallels, it has become impossible to check them manually.[4]

---

[4] For some projects, this problem of low precision becomes so urgent that the main

I give a few more examples, all from the book of Genesis, illustrating how a single run, with one choice of parameters, is insufficient. Using five-grams and minimum word length three, we find the parallel "Licht tot heerschappye des nachts" (light to rule the night) between the States Bible and Luyken; the parallel disappears when we use four-grams and minimum word length four (other settings being equal). Conversely, the second setting detects "mensche alleen zy; ick sal hem eene hulpe" ([It is not good that the] man should be alone; I will make him a helper). Both combinations of settings also report false parallels that the other one does not locate (e.g., "des eenen tegen den anderen" [of the one for the other], again a very general formulation from II Macc. 14), and there are true parallels that neither locates, as when Luyken quotes Gen 1:14. Neither run is by itself sufficient, nor is their combination. Similar examples could be given for many other combinations of parameter settings.

Once we have found the textual parallels, the work of evaluation begins. Is the text parallel really an example of the younger text quoting the older? In some cases, clearly not: for example, the parallel text may occur in an editorial note from a later age. In other cases, the parallel text may be from the printing privilege. In many cases, what we find are shared quotations: both the emblem book and a later volume of poetry quoting an older text—for our corpus, mostly the Bible and classical authors. This is no doubt a significant form of text reuse and shows an important fact about the textual culture of the time, but it does not show that the author of the younger work quoted, or even knew, the older work.

If each run of the text reuse detection tool is bound to retrieve a number of true and a number of false parallels, where the true ones may or may not be relevant to the research question, and if it is necessary to run the tool multiple times with different parameter settings, this implies that the researcher will need to inspect a large number of CSV files. Many of the detected parallels will be identical, some will overlap, some will occur only once. The question of the researcher now changes from "is there meaningful text reuse in these text collections?" to "what parameter settings are suitable for this corpus?" (based on language, quality of transcription, spelling variation, quotation density, and size), or "how do I find the new parallels in this CSV file given the ones I have already inspected?" or "what parameter settings did I use for this run again?" The researcher needs to keep track of

---

task switches from locating (potential) parallels to filtering out unlikely parallels (Forstall, Coffee, Buck, Roache, and Jacobson 2015).

the encountered true and false parallels as well as the settings they resulted from and will need some form of automated support for that.

Managing the text reuse research data

This management problem was the starting point for a second experiment. Here I decided to use the Text Pair software *as is*. The goal was not to develop software that would become part of a maintainable infrastructure but to use a suitable tool for detecting textual parallels; to build onto that tool an experimental environment for displaying and annotating parallels, and thus to evaluate the multiple parameter settings that the tool could use. To what extent could such a tool overcome the information overload problem?

I identified five main requirements for this management tool:

1. Store data. It should store all the settings that were used in the index and query steps of the detection process and it should store the information about the retrieved parallels.

2. Display. Based on the stored information it should allow display of a detection run, the parameters that were used, and the parallels that were found. It should also be able to display together the parallels that were found between the same text pair in different runs, and to display retrieved parallels based on a query on the parameter settings (for instance display the textual parallels found between text a and text b when using stopword removal but no minimum word length). This requirement is the only one that is often, to some extent, implemented in text reuse detection tools.

3. Annotate. It should facilitate annotation at all levels of the reuse detection process—run, parameter setting, text collection, text, and parallel—and on combinations of those levels, such as the usefulness of a parameter setting for a certain pair of texts in run x. While for most annotations free-format text is probably sufficient, for the retrieved parallels it should be possible to state unambiguously whether they should be considered true or false positives. This requirement relates to the next ones, about summary statistics and auto-annotation.

4. Compute summary statistics. When the researcher has annotated the retrieved parallels for a certain detection run as true or false positives, the tool should be able to compute for that run the standard information retrieval quality measures: recall, precision, and F1. See below for further discussion of the applicability of these measures in this context.

5. Auto-annotate. One of the biggest issues for the researcher in evaluating multiple parameter settings is having to find new parallels in a run among the many parallels he or she has already inspected. The management tool should therefore be able to auto-annotate parallels as true or false based on annotations to parallels from earlier runs.

With respect to the summary statistics: they should deliver a first and rough estimate of the quality of a run using a certain set of parameters. It is important to understand that, as we have no ground truth for the true amount of quotation in our corpora, the quality of a run can only be judged in terms of the amount of quotation that it detects with respect to other runs of the tool. We define recall as the overlap between the parallels detected in a run and the true (approved) parallels from all runs on the same corpus pair. Formally, for a run r, the recall for that run is defined as:

$$R_r = \text{length}(APar \cap Par_r) / \text{length}(APar)$$

where APar is the set of approved parallels for the corpus pair and Parr is the set of parallels detected in run r. Similarly, the precision is defined as the approved parallels in a run as a fraction of all parallels retrieved in that run, technically:

$$P_r = \text{length}(APar \cap Par_r) / \text{length}((APar \cup RejPar) \cap Parr)$$

where RejPar is the set of rejected parallels between the two corpora. Both precision and recall vary between 0 and 1, and are ideally 1. $F1_r$ the overall quality measure, is the harmonic mean between P_r and R_r. For each of the three numbers, we also define a count-based variant, where we don't take into account the length of the parallels, but just their numbers.[5] The values of these statistics change, and approach their true values, as more detection runs are done (or more precisely, as the results of more runs are annotated as either relevant or not). It remains up to the researcher to choose a criterion for approving or rejecting parallels: Is textual agreement in itself sufficient to approve a parallel? Or should there be more than mere linguistic agreement and should the texts actually quote a same text, or should one text quote the other? The latter can never be decided based on local textual evidence alone, but requires as a minimum knowledge about the dates of origin of the texts as well as knowledge about the textual traditions in which they were written.

---

[5] Definitions inspired by Potthast, Stein, Barrón-Cedeño, and Rosso 2010.

I developed a tool that fulfilled most of these requirements.[6] The text::pair index and query script were modified to so as to save the input parameters and the output into a MongoDB database. An application was developed to browse the database, to annotate its contents, and to compute the summary statistics.[7]

The next figures show some runs where I compared the Den Elger book with a merged Nederlab collection, including other emblem books, books for younger people, poetry, and bibles. The spelling of all texts has been uniformized based on a series of regular expression.[8] Figure 1 shows an overview of runs. For each run, we see some information about the corpora that were compared to each other and the summary statistics, if they were computed. From here it is possible to view all parameter settings for the run, to view the retrieved parallels at file pair level, or (using the filter options) to view the information at file pair level for multiple runs, selecting by query corpus, index corpus, or both. Figure 2 shows a selection of results at the corpus pair level, sorted by query file (text b). We see that parallels were retrieved for the text with filename _aem001aem01_01.txt (*Een Aemstelredams amoureus lietboeck* [An Amsterdam book of love songs]) (Anonymous 1589) in runs 251 and 259. These parallels (1 in run 251, 3 in 259) were rejected (that's what the "n" in "3n" says). We also see the total length for these parallels. The "notes" option gives access to an annotation window, the "view" option to the retrieved hits and the "filter" options allows display of hits filtered by indexed (base) text, query text or both. Figure 3 shows the hits for De Brune's *Emblemata of Zinne-werck* (De Brune 1636) in run 255. The one in red has been rejected ("het krieken van den dag" is a current expression meaning "at the crack of dawn"), the two in green have been accepted. They are quotations from Ovid's *Remedia Amoris* and Horace's *Epistles*. The "y" (yes) and "n" (no) buttons are used to approve or reject the quotations. At the bottom of the screen we see a view of both texts with the hyperlinked quotations in red. Figure 4, finally, shows the hits in different runs between the same two texts, here sorted by their offset in the first text. It allows us to inspect which parallels are detected in which runs. We see one hit ("amor formae condimentum," as mangled by the spelling uniformization) that was only detected once, in run 259.

---

[6] It doesn't do auto-annotation (requirement no. 5) or retrieval by parameter setting (part of no. 2).

[7] Developed in Python, using MongoDB, the Bottle Web framework and the jQuery Datatables plugin.

[8] Uniformized, not modernized or regularized. The purpose was to map spelling variants to the same form, not to create a modern or correct spelling.

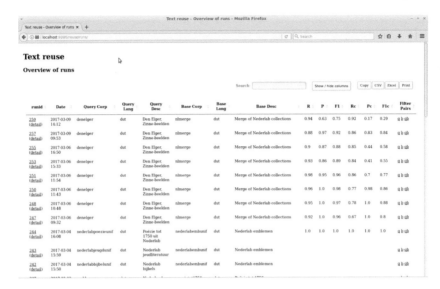

Figure 1. Overview of runs with summary statistics.

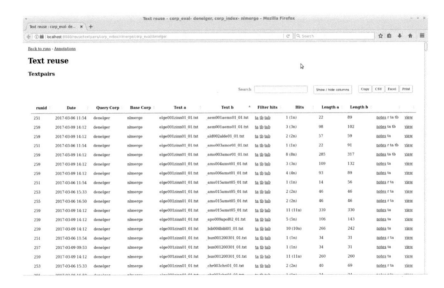

Figure 2. Results for different text pairs in multiple runs.

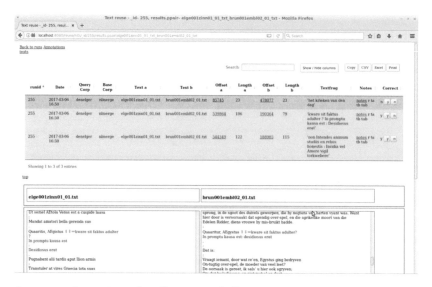

Figure 3. Hits, rejected and approved, for one text pair in one run.

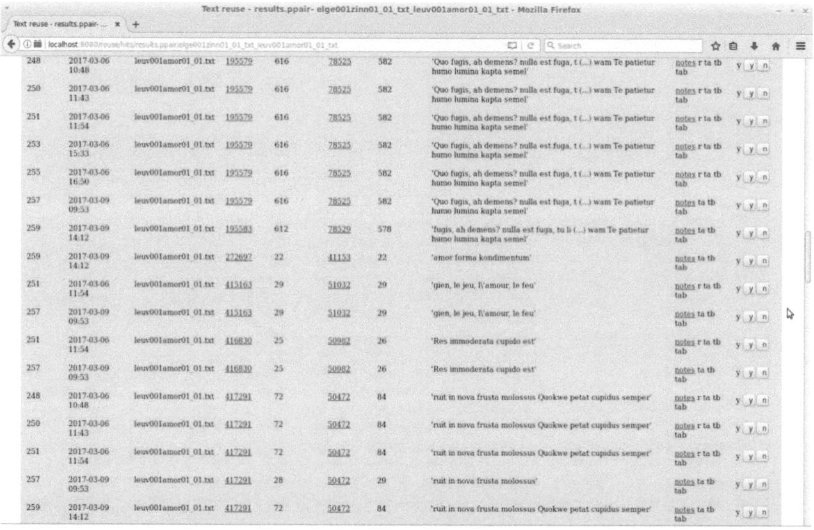

Figure 4. Hits for one text pair in multiple runs.

Armed with this tool, I did an experiment in text reuse detection for the Den
Elger book (1703). Table 2 shows the settings I used; the corresponding results are reported in Figure 1. Run 247 was the first run for this experiment.
The settings were just a first guess. The parameters are those that were
mentioned above, except for the minimum pair of shingles parameter which

gives the number of shingles that the texts should share before an overlap is considered a hit (a single shared n-gram is only considered a hit if the minimum pair parameter is set to 1). The other runs should be seen as attempts to find hits in other parts of the parameter space, without retrieving too many false positives. In run 248 I lowered the required minimum pair of shingles to three; in 250 I set the cut-off size to four. Both increase the number of hits. In run 251, I set the minimum shared pairs to two. This located a number of extra parallels, but also, for the first time, introduced a lot of noise. We see (in Figure 1) that the overlap-based precision is still at .95, but the count-based precision here drops to .70. The difference is caused by the true parallels being much longer than the spurious ones. In response, I increased the shingle size and experimented by no longer filtering out stopwords in run 253. This did not have the desired effect. The remaining runs attempted to locate very short parallel passages (minimum pair of shingles set to 1). In run 259, the last one, I set shingle size to three, increasing the minimum word size to four, hoping to find some three-word quotations. This had the desired effect (count-based recall is higher than in any other run), but only at the cost of producing a large number of false hits. The reported count-based precision of .17 is actually much higher than it should be, as the number of false positives was just too large to annotate all of them.

run	shingle size	min # pair	stopwords	min word size	cutoff size
247	3	4	yes	3	5
248	3	3	yes	3	5
250	3	3	yes	3	4
251	3	2	yes	3	4
253	4	2	no	3	4
255	5	1	no	3	4
257	4	1	yes	3	5
259	3	1	yes	4	5

Table 2. Settings that were used in the experiment on Zinne-beelden der liefde.

Did the management tool actually help me to stay on top of the research data? The answer is: to some extent. I used all the shown functionalities in order to understand the effect of the different settings. I often went back to the parameter display in order to check which were the parameters for a given run. I used the annotation facilities. The summary statistics quickly became an indispensable tool for judging the quality of parameter settings.

However, the tool also has limitations. On a practical level, the facilities for rejection/approval of hits should be much more powerful. It should for instance be possible to approve or reject all found parallels between two texts in a single action. The auto-annotation feature was sorely missed. It would also be helpful if it were possible to simultaneously display the parallels from multiple runs in the context of the texts.

A more serious limitation is that the tool compares parallels from multiple runs based on offset. It cannot, therefore, compare runs where the input files have undergone some transformation that changes the offsets in the files. For instance, I would have liked to compare the performance of the algorithms on texts with and without spelling uniformization. But as the uniformization changes offsets, it is impossible to look at overlap between parallels in runs with and without uniformization. The same problem would arise if we were to introduce lemmatization, or filtering of text by language or similar operations. There are several ways out of this, but none of them would be simple.

Furthermore, for the count-based statistics, however necessary they are to give due weight to shorter parallels, it is a fundamental flaw that runs that retrieve exactly the same parallel text score differently, if one run splits a retrieved fragment in a number of pieces and another one doesn't.[9] To some extent, decisions based on those statistics must also be flawed.

The last limitation that I want to mention is that the tool forces the annotator to make a binary decision: a parallel is either a true parallel or not.[10] That can be a difficult choice to make, for instance because an undoubted parallel may not be a quotation (either because we recognize the text as a quotation from a third writer or because we don't know whether the older text is the source for the younger text). When Otto Vaenius in his *Amoris Divini Emblemata* (1615) writes "Amor qui desinere potest, nunquam verus fuit" (Love that

---

[9] For those who are interested, suppose the following: Run1 result (length, offset): 10,5 15,5 20,5 40,10, all approved. Run2 result (length, offset): 10,15 50,10, both approved. Now, for run 1: FN = 1, TP = 4, Rc = 0.8; for run 2: FN = 1, TP = 2, Rc = 0.67 (FN: False negative; TP: True positive; Rc: count-based recall = TP / (TP + FN)). The length-based recall would in both cases be 15 / (15 + 10) = .6.

[10] Actually, the researcher can also refrain from annotating the parallel if the choice is too hard.

can end was never true), at one level he is quoting Jerome, at another level he is quoting his own quotation of Jerome in his earlier book *Amorum Emblemata* (1607–8). Another reason may be that a younger text quotes an older one but inserts a new text fragment within the quotation. Depending on parameter settings, text::pair may ignore the new words and consider the whole text a quotation. But the researcher evaluating the retrieved parallels might want to tag it as "partly correct." The researcher will have to lay down very clear guidelines on when to approve or reject a parallel, but even so, the resulting statistics tell only part of the story.

Summarizing, there is no doubt that a management tool such as this can be a useful extension to a text reuse detection tool. But it is also clear that the tool can suggest a measure of certainty that is not always correct. Especially if quotations are sometimes retrieved in multiple fragments, or the status of a quotation is not quite clear, uncertainties remain. This is unavoidable because of the nature of the research question (maybe most research questions in the humanities are in that respect similar). In the next section, I will look into the question of how this approach to tool usage is applicable to other technologies used in digital humanities research.

Complex tools and complex data in humanities research

In fact, the problems that we encounter in doing text reuse detection are not unique to this problem area or technology. There are many technologies that share similar properties. Verhaar, writing about algorithmic criticism, notes:

> Scholars who aim to compare texts can commonly choose from a broad range of statistical techniques, and it can often be taxing to select an appropriate method. The differences between two distinct classes of texts may be examined using supervised learning techniques, of which Student's t-test, logistic regression and Naive Bayes all form concrete examples. When scholars aim to subdivide a corpus into smaller clusters, they can make use of k-means clustering, calculations of Euclidean distances, PCA or nearest neighbor analyses. These different methods are all based on different algorithms, and they consequently produce different results. Such differences can be subtle in some cases, but also quite dramatic in other cases. Even when scholars have decided to make use of one particular technique, they frequently have the possibility to influence the results by varying some of their initial parameters. In the case of classification, the results of the analyses can often be

manipulated directly by varying the sizes of the training sets and the test sets. In this study, it was found, for example, that the nature of the network diagram displaying formal similarities between poems can change dramatically along with the variables which are considered. (Verhaar 2016, 207)

To give a number of examples: the popular stylometry tools developed by Eder, Kestemont, and Rybicki (2013) have multiple choices for the features to use in computation, choices for the number of most frequent features to include, multiple distance measures, multiple clustering algorithms, and multiple ways of visualization. In topic modeling, gensim (Řehůřek and Sojka 2010) offers more than fourteen parameters to influence the computation of LDA models. For text categorization algorithms, the same issue is discussed by Koster and Beney (2006).

Parameter settings are hardly ever discussed in the literature. However, bad parameter settings can destroy the efficacy of an algorithm, as shown for instance by Hoste, Hendrickx, Daelemans, and Van den Bosch (2002). It implies that in many cases there is a need for systematic exploration of the behavior of the algorithm in the parameter space. Riedl and Biemann (2012) systematically evaluate the performance of text segmentation algorithms given certain parameter settings, Kievit-Kylar and Allen (2013) do the same for a semantic model of philosophical texts.

The situation for topic modeling is different from the situation for text reuse detection, in that the computation is not deterministic: a second run with the same parameters can result in a different outcome. This makes it even harder to evaluate a single outcome. On the other hand, there exist several measures to automatically evaluate and compare topic models, such as semantic coherence and exclusivity (Roberts et al. 2014).

The situation of a large number of parameter settings resulting in different outcomes creates a number of challenges. The first challenge is the one that we have seen for the text reuse detection case: it is the cognitive burden for the researcher who has to weigh the advantages and disadvantages of many different parameter settings and combinations of settings all producing slightly different results. A related challenge is keeping the administration of all these runs in order: how to make sure that we remember which combination of settings was used to create which outcome or combination of outcomes. This is especially problematic in cases where no ground truth is available. Why should we trust a clustering of authors by their hundred most frequently used words rather than by two hundred or three hundred? To avoid the human tendency to look for confirmation of our expectations, Eder, Kestemont and Rybicki include in their script the facility to generate bootstrap consensus trees, based on multiple parameter settings. This is an example of an ensemble method (Zhou 2012), methods that combine in some way the output of multiple algorithms or algorithm executions in order to create a better result. Ensemble methods are popular solutions in machine learning applications and other fields. When we try to locate examples of text reuse using multiple runs with different settings, we are applying an informal ensemble technique.

Another situation where the multiplicity of parameter settings and the impossibility to select a single best setting could create problems is when we try to employ tools for computational analysis in the service of exploring a digital collection. Even though practical applications are still relatively rare, much research has been done into interfaces where a digital library can be browsed on the basis of computed characteristics. Chuang, Ramage, Manning, and Heer (2012) describe a topic model-driven tool for exploring a library of PhD theses. Kolak and Schilit (2008) describe the "Popular Passages" tool used to facilitate navigating Google Books on the basis of shared quotations. The Commonplace Cultures project (Morrissey 2016) built a large database of cases of test reuse in eighteenth-century English works. But if there is no single best setting for the parameters of the tool underlying this navigation, the user should be aware that the completeness and correctness (let alone the relevance) of the created links cannot be guaranteed.

How can tools prepare for this?

Given the fact that tools consume and produce data, and that, as we have seen, most problems seem to require multiple tool runs, many research problems easily end up in a small data deluge. I described above how I tried to handle this deluge for the case of text reuse detection. But the question arises: how can we deal with the issue in a more general way? It doesn't seem feasible to require every new tool to come with its own virtual research environment for organizing and evaluating its output. Would it be possible to develop wrappers around tools that store tool input and output? And perhaps a generic reporting and annotation facility around the input and output data, whose application in a certain tool domain should be largely parameter-driven?

It is interesting to note that the requirement of storing information about input, parameters, and output of tool runs is being widely discussed in other scholarly domains and mostly for other concerns than the ones discussed in this essay. Storing provenance information about scientific data is important for a number of reasons, including the need to assess data quality, to provide an audit trail, to provide replication recipes, and to facilitate recognition of individual contributions (Simmhan, Plale, and Gannon 2005). It is also essential for effectively sharing research data (Kowalczyk and Shankar 2011).

A number of tools are being developed to support storing provenance information for scholarly data. I mention two of them. YesWorkflow is a tool for storing and displaying what is called *prospective* provenance (McPhillips et al. 2015). Prospective provenance provides insight in the structure of a script and the steps that are taken to create a certain output file. YesWorkflow requires that the scripts that implement a scholarly workflow are provided with annotations that indicate program blocks, data flows, and connections between scripts. Software can display the information in graphical form, either in a process-oriented or a data-oriented view, and can answer queries about the provenance of an output dataset. In contrast to prospective provenance, *retrospective* provenance is based on capturing runtime information. An example of that approach is noWorkflow (Murta, Braganholo, Chirigati, Koop, and Freire 2014). noWorkflow captures information during the execution of a Python script. What it captures is information about the environment (operating system, environment variables, libraries that the script depends on) as well as information about the execution steps, including function calls (with input and output) and the content of all files accessed by the script.

In the humanities, application of tools like these up to now has been experimental. Senseney (2016) describes an experiment to annotate with Yes-Workflow some of the scripts for Ted Underwood's research (Underwood and Sellers 2015). Clark (2012) produces provenance information for XSLT transformations. Clark and Holloway (2012) describe a possible formalization of provenance information in two digital humanities virtual research environments. They stress that storing provenance data is really a traditional humanist virtue: "The humanities as a discipline has traditionally exhibited great care in documenting sources and establishing authentic chains of object transmission," however, "to date, little published research in e-humanities explicitly focuses on data provenance."

In situations where noWorkflow has been used for storing retrospective provenance data, it becomes possible to analyze multiple runs, to look at their differences, and to re-execute runs with or without changes (Pimentel, Freire, Braganholo, and Murta 2016). This opens the door to using tools for provenance detection not just to understand how the output of a single run was created, but also to understand why output from another run might be different. Bennett et al. (2016) speculate about how provenance data from multiple script runs could be input for machine learning and other data science approaches and thus point to improvements in the scripts.

However, a common complaint about noWorkflow and other systems for capturing retrospective provenance data is that the systems produce very large amounts of data that can easily overwhelm the researcher. In that respect, they may not be the best answer to a problem that is basically one of having to handle too much information. Also, capturing provenance data by itself does not help us in presenting the output of different runs in a way that makes it easy to compare their effectiveness, or in annotation of the results, or in the computation of summary statistics.

The management tool that I described above relied on additional coding added to the scripts that saved the input parameters and the script output into a database. A middle course between this semi-manual approach and capturing complete provenance information would be a management system that allows the researcher to set up runs in a database, by defining parameter settings, defining the files or collections of files to be processed, including metadata describing these files, attaching a script, and selecting the output from the script that should be saved into the database. It should then be possible to execute such a run from the database. The database would then no longer have the status of an afterthought but would be the controlling instance in script execution. A disadvantage might be that the script will have to be written in accordance with the expectations of the management system. This approach begins to resemble scientific workflow systems, such as Taverna or Kepler (Talia 2013); however, in the context of this essay we do not necessarily need their facilities for managing the details of workflow execution, calling web services, or sending jobs to high performance computing clusters.

The desired functionality for displaying and annotating the results and for computing derivative statistics would probably need to be specific to the relevant technology. In our case, lines in the CSV output files correspond to potential parallels. When doing topic modeling, for example, the outcome is a distribution of words over topics and of topics over documents. When doing stylometry, the output of a run might be a dendrogram or a principal components analysis. The different sorts of output are completely different, and it is hard to imagine a generic tool that knows how to display all of them satisfactorily. But it should be possible to work out an architecture where the general functionality of browsing runs with their input and their output is supplemented by plugins handling specific output and input types. The computation of quality measures such as precision and recall could also be handled in plugins.

It is worth noting that an environment like the one sketched here is very different from the popular Jupyter (IPython) notebook computing environment. When using notebooks, we work interactively. If a step in our computations fails, we change a few things, go back a few steps, run again, and this interactivity has many advantages. Most notably, unlike in the case of a failed script execution, all variables keep their values, and we can continue the computations more or less where the problem occurred. Similarly, after our computation is done, we can immediately continue the analysis based on the outcomes of the preceding steps. In a script execution environment, if we need a further analysis, we add the steps for the extra analysis to the script; we have to run the preceding steps again, and when after twenty minutes our added steps should be executed, they fail because of some small coding error. It is clear that a management system would certainly not be conducive to flexibility. On the other hand, finding out after a few weeks of intensive notebook use which notebook did which computation and which files it produced can be quite challenging. The two approaches probably lend themselves to different situations: the notebook approach to the situation where we are experimenting and still do not know which algorithms to select; the management approach once we have chosen the algorithms and want to explore systematically the best settings. However, for now, given the absence of such a management tool, this remains speculation.

Conclusion

Many questions in the humanities lend themselves to an approach based on or supported by software. Much work in the digital humanities goes into devising algorithms to answer these questions. But when we want to run those algorithms, we have to make choices: choices in the preparation of the input files, in the parameter settings, in the content of a stopword file, and in the visualization of the results. Often, we have no real reasons to prefer one choice over another, and so we try a few settings. But these settings result in different outcomes and often we have no other way of judging those outcomes than our own intuitions. Or, in the text reuse detection case that was discussed in this essay, each of the outcomes may contribute something to the complete answer, but we don't know in advance what they will contribute and how many tries we will need. Unlike topic modeling, text reuse detection is really simple; understanding the algorithms requires no training in mathematics or statistics. Yet it is only by trial and error that we find the settings that work; most runs find some true parallels and some false ones, and miss other true ones.

In this essay I have argued that in both situations we need software beyond the initial programs devised to tackle the original question. We need that additional software (I called it a management tool) in order to organize, compare, and evaluate the input and output of the initial algorithms. An ingredient in this additional software layer is the facility for unstructured and structured annotation as well as the computation of quality measures for the original results. This additional software may not require the intellectual brilliance of a fundamentally new algorithm; on the other hand, considerations of usability (clarity, flexibility, affordances, response time) become much more important. Maybe the two sorts of program should even be written by different developers.

There is much to be said for trying to develop a generic management system: a large part of the functionality for comparison and evaluation in different technologies should be similar. A generic structure with plugins for specific output types seems most promising. In the absence of such a tool, experimentation with technology-specific tools for managing (storing, viewing, comparing, evaluating, and annotating) the output of scholarly software can teach us what a more general tool should look like. For text reuse detection tools, certainly, it should be possible to define a common output format that would allow the creation of a shared tool for managing the tools' output. For text reuse detection in historic text genres, sensitive as it is to parameter settings, this would certainly help.

This sensitivity to parameter settings is not specific to software applications in early modern studies, but recurrent spelling variation and OCR issues of early modern texts do make the problem particularly urgent in our field. However, the issue also occurs in technologies that are not text-based. A good example is the recent study by Masías, Baldwin, Laengle, Vargas, and Crespo (2017) which uses social network analysis to assess the prominence of characters in Shakespeare's *Romeo and Juliet*. The network construction can be based on different aspects of the play, the centrality of characters can be based on different aspects of the network, and resulting computations are also dependent on a parameter setting. The outcomes are widely different, for instance in how they rate Juliet's importance. Giacometti et al.

(2017) note how results in multispectral imaging of an eighteenth-century manuscript depend on camera, light source, and algorithm. Here, like before, choices that may seem technicalities are in fact methodological choices that should be discussed and evaluated systematically. In order to come to grips with its growing amounts of research data, as well as to clarify provenance and facilitate replication, scholarly research should save and make accessible the complete tool runs on which its arguments are based.

WORKS CITED

Anonymous. 1589. *Een Aemstelredams amoureus lietboeck*. Amsterdam. Accessed 17 February 2020. https://www.dbnl.org/tekst/_aem001aems01_01/.

Anonymous. [1617]. *Nieuwen ieucht spieghel*. No place. Accessed 17 February 2020. http://emblems.let.uu.nl/nj1617.html.

Anonymous. 1637. *Biblia, dat is: De gantsche H. Schrifture* [. . .] [Dutch States' Bible]. Leyden. Accessed 17 February 2020. https://www.dbnl.org/tekst/_sta001stat01_01/.

Anonymous. 1853. *Een lees- en zangboekjen voor de jeugd*. Amsterdam. Accessed 17 February 2020. https://www.dbnl.org/tekst/_lee015lees01_01/.

Bath, Michael. 1994. *Speaking Pictures*. London: Longman.

Bennett, Kristin P., Johm S. Erickson, Hannah de Los Santos, Spencer Norris, Evan Patton, and John Sheehan, et al. 2016. "Data Analytics as Data: A Semantic Workflow Approach." 30th Conference on Neural Information Processing Systems. Accessed 23 August 2019. https://archive.tw.rpi.edu/media/latest/semanlaytics.pdf.

Bloemendal, Jan. 2007. "Love Emblems and a Web of Intertexuality." In *Learned Love*, edited by Els Stronks and Peter Boot, 1:111–18. The Hague: DANS.

Boot, Peter. 2012. "Similar or Dissimilar Loves? *Amoris Divini Emblemata* and Its Relation to *Amorum Emblemata*." In *Otto Vaenius and His Emblem Books*, edited by Simon McKeown, 157–73. Glasgow Emblem Studies 15. Glasgow: University of Glasgow.

Cats, Jacob. 1618. *Silenus Alcibiadis, sive Proteus.* Middelburg. Accessed 17 February 2020. https://www.dbnl.org/tekst/cats001sile01_01/.

Chuang, Jason, Daniel Ramage, Christopher Manning, and Jeffrey Heer. 2012. "Interpretation and Trust: Designing Model-Driven Visualizations for Text Analysis." SIGCHI Conference on Human Factors in Computing Systems, 443–52. Accessed 17 March 2017. https://www.researchgate.net/publication/254005264_Interpretation_and_trust_Designing_model-driven_visualizations_for_text_analysis.

Cieslak, Katarzyna. 1995. "Emblematic Programs in Seventeenth-Century Gdansk Churches in the Light of Contemporary Protestantism: An Essay and Documentation." *Emblematica* 9.1: 21–44.

Clark, Ashley M. 2012. "Meta-stylesheets: Exploring the Provenance of XSL Transformations." Presented at Balisage: The Markup Conference 2012, Montréal, Canada, 7 – 10 August 2012. In *Proceedings of Balisage: The Markup Conference 2012.* Balisage Series on Markup Technologies 8. Accessed 23 August 2019. https://doi.org/10.4242/BalisageVol8.Clark01.

Clark, Ashley M., and Steven W. Holloway. 2012. "'The Past Is Never Dead. It's Not Even Past': The Challenge of Data Provenance in the e-Humanities." Presented at Digital Humanities 2012. Accessed 23 August 2019. http://www.dh2012.uni-hamburg.de/conference/programme/abstracts/the-past-is-never-dead-its-not-even-past-the-challenge-of-data-provenance-in-the-e-humanities.1.html.

Coffee, Neil, Jean-Pierre Koenig, Shakthi Poornima, Christopher W. Forstall, Roelant Ossewaarde, and Sarah L. Jacobson. 2012. "The Tesserae Project: Intertextual Analysis of Latin Poetry." *Literary and Linguistic Computing* 28.2: 221–28.

Daly, Peter. M. 1998. *Literature in the Light of the Emblem: Structural Parallels between the Emblem and Literature in the Sixteenth and Seventeenth Centuries.* 2nd ed. Toronto: University of Toronto Press.

De Jongh, Eddy. 2000. *Questions of Meaning: Theme and Motif in Dutch Seventeenth-Century Painting.* Leiden: Primavera Press.

De Brune, Willem. 1636. *Emblemata of Zinne-werck.* Amsterdam. Accessed 17 February 2020. https://www.dbnl.org/tekst/brun001embl02_01/.

Den Elger, Willem. 1603. *Zinne-beelden der Liefde*. Leiden. Accessed 17 February 2020. http://emblems.let.uu.nl/el1703.html.

Eder, Maciej, Mike Kestemont, and Jan Rybicki. 2013. "Stylometry with R: A Suite of Tools." Presented at Digital Humanities 2013. Accessed 15 February 2017. http://dh2013.unl.edu/abstracts/ab-136.html.

Forstall, Christopher, Neil Coffee, Thomas Buck, Katherine Roache, and Sarah Jacobson. 2015. "Modeling the Scholars: Detecting Intertextuality through Enhanced Word-Level N-gram Matching." *Digital Scholarship in the Humanities* 30.4: 503–15.

Giacometti, Alejandro, Alberto Campagnolo, Lindsay MacDonald, Simon Mahony, Stuart Robson, and Tim Weyrich, et al. 2017. "The Value of Critical Destruction: Evaluating Multispectral Image Processing Methods for the Analysis of Primary Historical Texts." *Digital Scholarship in the Humanities* 32.1: 101–22.

Heckscher, William S., and Karl-August Wirth. 1959. "Emblem, Emblembuch." *Reallexikon zur Deutschen Kunstgeschichte* 5: 85–228.

Henkel, Arthur, and Albrecht Schöne. 1976. *Emblemata. Handbuch zur Sinnbildkunst des XVI. und XVII. Jahrhunderts*. Stuttgart: Metzler.

Hoste, Véronique, Isis Hendrickx, Walter Daelemans, and Antal van den Bosch. 2002. "Parameter Optimization for Machine-Learning of Word Sense Disambiguation." *Natural Language Engineering* 8.4: 311–25.

Kane, Andrew, and Frank W. Tompa. 2011. "Janus: The Intertextuality Search Engine for the Electronic *Manipulus florum* Project." *Literary and Linguistic Computing* 26.4: 407–15.

Kievit-Kylar, Brent, and Colin Allen. 2013. "Kant Be Understood? Probing the Parameters of Semantic Models of Philosophy." International Association for Computing and Philosophy Conference. Accessed 1 March 2017. http://www.iacap.org/proceedings_IACAP13/paper_36.pdf.

Kolak, Okan, and Bill N. Schilit. 2008. "Generating Links by Mining Quotations." *Proceedings of the Nineteenth ACM Conference on Hypertext and Hypermedia*, 117–26. Accessed 23 August 2019. https://sites.google.com/site/schilit/kolak_ht08.pdf.

Koster, Cornelis H., and Jean G. Beney. 2006. *On the Importance of Parameter Tuning in Text Categorization.* International Andrei Ershov Memorial Conference on Perspectives of System Informatics. Accessed 23 August 2019. https://link.springer.com/chapter/10.1007/978-3-540-708 81-0_24.

Kowalczyk, Stacey, and Kalpana Shankar. 2011. "Data Sharing in the Sciences." *Annual Review of Information Science and Technology* 45.1: 247–94.

Luyken, Jan. 1671. *Duytse Lier.* Amsterdam. Accessed 17 February 2020. http://emblems.let.uu.nl/lu1671.html.

Luyken, Jan. 1685. *Jesus en de ziel.* Amsterdam. Accessed 17 February 2020. http://emblems.let.uu.nl/lu1685.html.

Luyken, Jan. 1711. *Het leerzaam huisraad.* Amsterdam. Accessed 17 February 2020. https://www.dbnl.org/tekst/luyk001leer01_01/.

Luyken, Jan. 1712. *Schriftuurlyke geschiedenissen en gelykenissen.* Amsterdam. Accessed 17 February 2020. https://www.dbnl.org/tekst/luyk001schr02_01.

Masías, Víctor H., Paula Baldwin, Sigifredo Laengle, Augusto Vargas, and Fernando A. Crespo. 2017. "Exploring the Prominence of Romeo and Juliet's Characters Using Weighted Centrality Measures." *Digital Scholarship in the Humanities* 32.4: 837–58.

McPhillips, Timothy, Tianhong Song, Tyler Kolisnik, Steve Aulenbach, Khalid Belhajjame, and Kyle Bocinsky, et al. 2015. "YesWorkflow: A User-Oriented, Language-Independent Tool for Recovering Workflow Information from Scripts." *International Journal of Digital Curation* 10.1: 298–313. Accessed 19 August 2019. http://www.ijdc.net/article/view/10.1.298.

Morrissey, Robert. 2016. "Commonplace Cultures: Mining Shared Passages in the 18th Century using Sequence Alignment and Visual Analytics." *Humanities Commons.* Accessed 19 August 2019. http://dx.doi.org/10.17613/M66369.

Moseley, Charles. 1989. *A Century of Emblems: An Introductory Anthology.* Aldershot: Scolar Press.

Murta, Leonardo, Vanessa Braganholo, Fernando Chirigati, David Koop, and Juliana Freire. 2014. "noWorkflow: Capturing and Analyzing Provenance of Scripts." In *Provenance and Annotation of Data and Processes*, edited by Bertram Ludäscher and Beth Plale, 71–88. Berlin: Springer. Accessed 23 August 2019. https://link.springer.com/chapter/10.1007/978-3-319-16462-5_6.

Olsen, Mark, and Russell Horton. 2009. "PAIR: Pairwise Alignment for Intertextual Relations." Chicago. Computer software. Accessed 23 August 2019. https://code.google.com/archive/p/text-pair/.

Olsen, Mark, Russell Horton, and Glenn Roe. 2011. "Something Borrowed: Sequence Alignment and the Identification of Similar Passages in Large Text Collections." *Digital Studies/Le champ numérique* 2.1. Accessed 23 August 2019. http://doi.org/10.16995/dscn.258.

Pimentel, João F., Juliana Freire, Vanessa Braganholo, and Leonardo Murta. 2016. "Tracking and Analyzing the Evolution of Provenance from Scripts." In *Provenance and Annotation of Data and Processes*, edited by Marta Mattoso and Boris Glavic, 16–28. Berlin: Springer.

Porteman, Karel. 1977. *Inleiding tot de Nederlandse emblemataliteratuur.* Groningen: Wolters-Noordhoff.

Potthast, Martin, Benno Stein, Alberto Barrón-Cedeño, and Paolo Rosso. 2010. "An Evaluation Framework for Plagiarism Detection." *Proceedings of the 23rd International Conference on Computational Linguistics: Posters* 997–1005. Accessed 23 August 2019. https://www.aclweb.org/anthology/C10-2115.

Řehůřek, Radim, and Petr Sojka. 2010. "Software Framework for Topic Modelling with Large Corpora." *Proceedings of LREC 2010 Workshop: New Challenges for NLP Frameworks, Valletta, Malta.* Accessed 23 August 2019. http://www.lrec-conf.org/proceedings/lrec2010/workshops/W10.pdf.

Riedl, Martin, and Chris Biemann. 2012. "Sweeping through the Topic Space: Bad Luck? Roll Again!" *Proceedings of the Joint Workshop on Unsupervised and Semi-Supervised Learning in NLP*, 19–27. Accessed 23 August 2019. https://www.aclweb.org/anthology/W/W12/W12-0703.pdf.

Roberts, M. E., B. M. Stewart, and D Tingley. 2016. "Navigating the local modes of big data". *Computational Social Science*, edited by R. Michael Alvarez, 51–97. New York: Cambridge University Press.

Saunders, Alison. 2007. "Creator of the Earliest Collection of French Emblems, But Now Also Creator of the Earliest Collection of Love Emblems? Evidence from a Newly Discovered Emblem Book by Guillaume de la Perriere." In *Learned Love: Proceedings of the Emblem Project Utrecht Conference on Dutch Love Emblems and the Internet (November 2006)*, edited by Peter Boot and Els Stronk, 1: 13–32. The Hague: Edita.

Sculley, D., and Bradley M. Pasanek. 2008. "Meaning and Mining: The Impact of Implicit Assumptions in Data Mining for the Humanities." *Literary and Linguistic Computing* 23.4: 409–24.

Senseney, Megan. 2016. "Pace of Change: A Preliminary YesWorkflow Case Study." Center for Informatics Research in Science and Scholarship (CIRSS) Technical Report 201601-1. Illinois: University of Illinois at Urbana-Champaign.

Simmhan, Yogesh L., Beth Plale, and Dennis Gannon. 2005. "A Survey of Data Provenance in E-science." *ACM Sigmod Record* 34.3: 31–36.

Stronks, Els. 2008. "The Emblem in the Low Countries." In *Companion to Emblem Studies,* edited by P. M. Daly, 267–289. New York: AMS Press.

Talia, Domenico. 2013. "Workflow Systems for Science: Concepts and Tools." *ISRN Software Engineering* 2013, article ID 404525. Accessed 23 August 2019. https://www.hindawi.com/journals/isrn/2013/404525/.

Underwood, Ted, and Jordan. Sellers. 2015. "How Quickly Do Literary Standards Change?" *Figshare*. Journal Contribution. Accessed 10 March 2017. https://doi.org/10.6084/m9.figshare.1418394.v1.

Van Leuven, Ludovicus. 1619. *Amoris Divini et Humana Antipathia.* Antwerp. Accessed 17 February 2020. http://emblems.let.uu.nl/ad1629.html.

Van Veen, Otto. 1607–8. *Amorum Emblemata.* Antwerp. Accessed 17 February 2020. http://emblems.let.uu.nl/v1608.html.

Van Veen, Otto. 1615. *Amoris Divini Emblemata.* Antwerp. Accessed 17 February 2020. http://emblems.let.uu.nl/v1615.html.

Valck, Michiel. 1607. Den nieuwen verbeterden lust-hof [. . .]. Amsterdam. Accessed 17 February 2020. https://www.dbnl.org/tekst/vlac002nieu03_01/.

Verhaar, Peter. 2016. "Affordances and Limitations of Algorithmic Criticism." Unpublished PhD. Leiden: Leiden University. Accessed 19 August 2019. https://openaccess.leidenuniv.nl/bitstream/handle/1887/43241/PhD_PeterVerhaar.pdf.

Zahora, Tomas, Dmitr Nikulin, Constant J. Mews, and David. M. Squire. 2015. "Deconstructing Bricolage: Interactive Online Analysis of Compiled Texts with Factotum." *Digital Humanities Quarterly* 9.1. Accessed 23 August 2019. http://www.digitalhumanities.org/dhq/vol/9/1/000203/000203.html.

Zhou, Zhi-Hua. 2012. *Ensemble methods: foundations and algorithms.* New York: Chapman and Hall/CRC.

Digital Approaches to Analyzing and Understanding Baroque Literature

Claudia Resch

Austrian Centre for Digital Humanities and Cultural Heritage,
Austrian Academy of Sciences

Opportunities for researchers interested in the early modern period have never been better. Libraries are making their inventories and collections available to the public, and providing digital access to large amounts of primary source material. Researchers involved in a broad range of projects already benefit from the increasing numbers of digitized page images. However, while page-per-page scans of early modern prints are becoming more available, machine-readable versions of these sources remain scarce and full-text transcriptions exist for only a fraction of these. Given the typographical and structural complexity of early modern printed texts on the one hand, and the period-typical linguistic features and structures on the other, books from this time pose challenges with regards to digitization, normalization, and encoding. Although a few ongoing projects[1] deal with digital textual data, the technical means for processing these texts remain underdeveloped, which is thus impeding the ability of researchers to perform more dynamic queries and corpus-based analyses on the German language of the early modern period.

This essay describes key results and observations from the project Text-Technological Methods for the Analysis of Austrian Baroque Literature[2] made up of an interdisciplinary team of literary scholars and (computer) linguists working together to explore the potential of a predominantly digital approach to early modern texts. The project started from a linguistic and philological viewpoint, while also seeking to provide results that could be relevant to various other disciplines. Over the course of our work, the

---

[1] Examples of language resources from that time period are found in the *Bonner Frühneuhochdeutschkorpus*, the *GerManC Project*, the *Deutsches Textarchiv*, and the *Wolfenbüttel Digital Library*. See Works Cited.

[2] The project Text-Technological Methods for the Analysis of Austrian Baroque Literature was carried out with support from the Anniversary Fund of the Österreichische Nationalbank (OeNB 14738; principal investigator: Claudia Resch).

ISBN 978-1-64959-016-9 (paper) ISBN 978-1-64959-017-6 (pdf) ISBN 978-1-64959-037-4 (epub)

New Technologies in Medieval and Renaissance Studies 9 (2022) 63–86

team was faced with questions like how to transform the texts into machine-readable format, what needs to be done to apply automatic tools to annotate "non-standard" texts, and where potential benefits of enriching those texts with additional linguistic knowledge could lie. The outcomes of this work are presented herein, along with insights into all stages of the process that led to the creation of a digital corpus: transcription, structural and linguistic annotation, and digital representation in an integrated online environment. This essay will explore and exemplify methodological approaches to analyzing the enriched primary sources from the perspective of literary scholarship, while also reporting in general terms on the advantages and potentials, as well as the limitations of digital approaches to the sources in question.

1. Towards a digital collection of baroque literature

The object of investigation as well as the visible result or "by-product" of this endeavor is a research collection called Austrian Baroque Corpus (ABaC:us)[3] that contains thematically connected *memento mori* prints. It is now freely available through the Austrian Centre for Digital Humanities and Cultural Heritage (ACDH-CH) at the Austrian Academy of Sciences in Vienna. The web application (https://acdh.oeaw.ac.at/abacus/) can be seen as the institute's first prototype for the digital representation of historic sources of that period and provides additional documentation about the corpus and the texts included.

The contents of the ABaC:us collection are characterized by the prevalence of sacred literature and made up of mainly textual sources with a strong thematic focus on death and dying. Prime examples of these are the very popular and richly illustrated German emblem books (Boot 2009) with texts in prose and verse, which were a focal point of baroque culture. The collection in its current form can be described as a historical, thematic, or specialized corpus that foregrounds a specific topic and provides a wealth of data for a wide range of further inquiries.

The digital collection mainly includes texts written by or ascribed to the Discalced Augustinian Abraham a Sancta Clara (1644–1709) (Eybl 2008, 10–14; Eybl 1992), who, in the seventeenth century, was regarded as one of the best preachers in the German-speaking area. His considerable reputation within

---

[3] The present corpus was compiled between 2010 and 2015 at the former Institute for Corpus Linguistics and Text Technology (ICLTT) and at the Austrian Centre for Digital Humanities (ACDH) of the Austrian Academy of Sciences, which was recently renamed Austrian Centre for Digital Humanities and Cultural Heritage (ACDH-CH).

the Habsburg Empire arose from the force of his language, the grotesqueness of his humor, and the impartial severity of his lectures. In Vienna, people flocked to his sermons in large numbers and the emperor appointed him imperial court preacher in 1677. In the following years, Abraham a Sancta Clara also started to publish pieces of didactic literature using the same satirical-dramatic style, vivid representation, and entertaining devices as in his sermons. His style was a forceful combination of scholarship, parables, stories, and word play.

Figure 1. Historic and contemporary depictions of Abraham a Sancta Clara (1644–1709).

When Vienna was struck by the plague in 1678, Abraham was very concerned about the souls of those who were unexpectedly carried off by the "Black Death." As a monk and the spiritual director of a confraternity caring for the dead, he was often faced with death and dying, so that the topos of baroque transience and the idea of *memento mori* shaped and permeated five of his most popular texts: *Mercks Wienn* (1680), *Lösch Wienn* (1680), *Grosse Todten Bruderschaft* (1681), *Augustini Feuriges Hertz* (1691), and *Besonders meubliert- und gezierte Todten-Capelle* (1710), all written by or attributed to him.

Figure 2. Title pages of the books included in ABaC:us.

The authorship for some of his works still is (and will probably remain) in doubt, because as his popularity grew across German-speaking Europe, a number of reprinted editions of his works were reproduced several times—in whole or in part, including many spurious interpolations. Peter Šajda confirms this observation: "The fact that Pater Abraham's books sold well, led several publishers to the idea of combining parts of his already published works with texts of other authors, ascribing the literary hybrid to the Augustinian preacher" (Šajda 2009, 3). Because of his literary talent and peculiar style, Abraham a Sancta Clara had become so popular that publishers distributed books purposefully attributed to his well-known name, using his successful "brand" to sell texts which were, in effect, counterfeits.[4]

It is hardly surprising that the question of which texts were written by Abraham himself, and which derived from the clergyman's circle or imitators or publishers, has captivated Abraham scholars[5] for years. While this is a reasonable question, and a conclusive answer would be of considerable significance for the task of situating his works within a canon, a computational approach to the task of separating his work from those of others may prove less useful than expected in this particular case. The prospect of producing exact quantifications with the help of stylometric tools may seem promising, but the specifics of period-typical writing practices complicate the matter. Examples from the texts *Lösch Wienn* (written by Abraham) and *Todten-Capelle* (attributed to Abraham) show how difficult it is to trace distinctive styles, because imitators frequently reproduced short extracts from his texts and inserted them into a new context. This can be observed, for example, in a paragraph that appears in both texts with only some slight changes to the original wording: The form of address "ihr Wienner Kinder!" (you children of Vienna) was transformed into "ihr Welt-Kinder" (you children of the world) to adapt the phrase to the changed circumstances of the newer publication, which was printed not in Vienna but in Nuremberg. The other changes are insignificant, concerning merely spelling variations. Occasionally, however, such minor formal changes can have rather momentous semantic consequences, as in the case of the phrase "Hetzen vnd Fischen" (to hunt and to fish), which has turned into the less appropriate "Hertzen und Fischen" (to cuddle and to fish):

---

[4] Abraham a Sancta Clara is often compared to the German author Hans Jakob Christoffel von Grimmelshausen (1621–76), whose works were disseminated under similar circumstances.

[5] On the topic of authorship attribution, see Horber 1929, Wunderlich 2000, 194 and Eybl 2012, 104–21.

Figure 3. Comparison between a paragraph of *Lösch Wienn* and *Todten-Capelle*, carried out by the commonly-known software Juxta[6], an open-source tool for collating different text versions and precisely tracking where differences are to be found.

With reference to these apparent acts of plagiarism, it should be noted that it was quite common for imitators to take passages of Abraham's earlier works and use them to construct and compile something new, a working method that was not considered reprehensible at that time. As Abraham himself also made use of phrases and ideas deriving from other authors, it would not make sense to try to distinguish "authentic" texts from "false" ones in his particular case. In many well-known debates of digitally-supported authorship attribution (e.g., William Shakespeare), investigations start from the presupposition that each author has an individual writing style that can reliably be determined by some set of observable features. In fact, an author's language and authorial fingerprint—which form a complex package consisting of many traits—always depend on the genre, the intent of the work, and stylistic conventions, as well as the intended audience. It should be considered that someone's personal style of writing can of course change over time, which likewise presents a challenge to computer-based recognition. In order to successfully attribute a text to a specific author, authorship attribution software, like the stylo "R" package[7], needs a critical amount of texts to learn from. Not only do these samples have to be representative of the specific style for the author in question, the software also needs a pre-selected array of alternative candidates for the authorship and a sufficient amount of texts that can securely be ascribed to them. Unfortunately, in the case of Abraham we have neither further candidates nor a representative amount of comparable texts in digital form. Taking into consideration additional external information, we can only assume that some texts may derive from the preacher's field of influence, for example from other friars in his religious order, or his publishers and other imitators.

---

[6] See http://www.juxtasoftware.org/about/. Accessed 20 February 2020.

[7] See https://sites.google.com/site/computationalstylistics/stylo. Accessed 20 February 2020.

Despite the question of authorship and attribution being a not fully attainable goal (regardless of the use of computational methods), the project operated under the assumption that digital text analysis may provide valuable insights for research into early modern texts. Following a corpus-based approach, the project group created a digital collection of texts from Abraham a Sancta Clara's sphere—be they written or ascribed to him—and tested various software tools for potential applications in their analysis. We were particularly interested in the identification of recurring patterns and regularities that characterized Abraham's writing style, or could at least be considered as "Abrahamic features" on a lexical and syntactic level.

2. Building up ABaC:us from scratch

In building up the corpus from scratch, our aim was to gather attested, naturally-occurring textual data from the baroque era and actual authentic instances of language in use. The corpus consists of computer-readable full texts and includes neither fragments nor samples, but always the full length of the text in the earliest known version that could be identified ("editio princeps"/first edition where available). In contrast to other corpora that contain millions of words, this digital resource of 200,000 words is rather small. The limited size of the corpus is due to the characteristics of the language under investigation. A reliable corpus of historic word forms with the level of detail in editing and annotation that we were aiming for is not easily realized on a large scale. As our experiences show, the computer-generated annotations still require a lot of secondary manual editing. The specific challenges, as well as our suggested approach to solving these problems, will be elaborated below.

Even though computational text analysis usually relies on "big data," in this specific case working with a relatively small selection of texts has proved advantageous. As the computer-generated output requires considerable amounts of reviewing and editing, it is helpful for researchers to be familiar with the individual texts. The texts in ABaC:us were carefully selected and thoroughly documented. After being transcribed by the computer, they were then painstakingly collated by hand. In their final versions the transcriptions are therefore essentially flawless and provide an optimal basis for further inquiry. Although at the moment there is no prospect of the corpus becoming a vast digital collection, we embrace any opportunity to expand it in order to contribute to its overall usefulness.

As indicated above, the process of digitizing historical prints and converting them into an electronic form is an immense challenge and not as straight-forward as building a modern-day corpus. Since the books were valuable old prints, often housed in monastic libraries and not accessible to the public, we asked for high-resolution digital images, which were converted into machine-readable characters by an Optical Character Recognition software. As OCR technology is optimized for contemporary print and performs poorly with most baroque texts, carrying out OCR procedures was no easy task. Both the quality of paper and ink, as well as the properties of font, layout, and orthography in printed editions from this era, presented a challenge for the OCR software. The best results were achieved with Abbey Fine Reader 7, a tool that is capable of reading both roman and black letter fonts (Fraktur). Since then, the ACDH-CH has made considerable progress in applying a method for black letter text recognition offered by the Transkribus platform which combines OCR and HTR technology and is currently being used for the digitization of other early modern textual sources.

In the next step of the digitization process, the cleanly transcribed digital text was encoded in accordance with the Text Encoding Initiative (TEI)[8]. The TEI guidelines are an international, community-based open standard, which are regularly revised in order to meet the needs of scholarly editing, textual research, lexicography, and corpus linguistics. The markup applied is comprised of several layers of annotation—capturing, first, fundamental structural units (chapters, headings, paragraphs and verse lines); second, named entities (place and personal names); and third, basic linguistic information, which allows for more complex linguistic search queries that go beyond mere string matching.

2.1. Applying a basic linguistic annotation

As the "Abrahamic" texts are not always easy to understand for those who are not experts in the field, the value of this collection partly consists of the aforementioned basic linguistic annotation. It makes the corpus intelligible and useful to larger audiences and opens up a number of additional search functionalities. To ensure optimal usability, the raw corpus has not only been automatically enriched with labels indicating the word class of each item in a text (part-of-speech-tagging or POS tagging), but also with lemma information. The result of this is that each historic word-form has been labeled with a base form: all variant spellings of the word "Arzt" (physician) like "Artzten," "Artzt," "Aertzte," for instance, were mapped to a corresponding

---

[8] See http://www.tei-c.org/Guidelines/P5. Accessed 20 February 2020.

lemma "Arzt," i.e., the form of the word that would occur as the headword in a dictionary. Different forms of a verb were also attributed to one base form, so that a search for "helfen" (help) leads to all inflections of this verb and its different spellings, such as "helffen," "geholffen," "helfft," "hüllft," "hilfft," etc. By linking each word form in the text with its respective lemma, we enabled the computer to identify all occurrences of a word despite the existence of many competing spelling variants and inflected forms.

In the early modern period, before the establishment of orthographical standards, authors (or even printers) more or less freely used whichever spelling variant they preferred, with no particular regard for consistency even within a single text. As the tools and coding schemes[9] used in automatized tagging were originally developed for modern and not for pre- or non-standardized German, we had to cope with a great linguistic variety and at the same time a vast amount of mismatches caused by the TreeTagger[10] which could not cope with the different spelling variants and the very complex nature of baroque style.[11] Since this kind of annotation can only be useful if it is done well, we put significant effort into manually correcting all the mismatches caused by the automatic tagging. In order to obtain an optimally tagged corpus, the team ultimately checked more than 200,000 running words.

Although the corpus has been manually post-edited and we have undertaken a significant amount of highly labor-intensive manual editing[12] in order to

---

[9] To support a growing consensus in the community and to maintain the interoperability of ABaC:us we decided to use the tags of the Stuttgart-Tübingen-TagSet, see http://www.sfs.uni-tuebingen.de/resources/stts-1999.pdf (accessed 20 February 2020) which can be seen as a "de facto standard" for modern German language and was used by many corpus projects in the past. Most of the tags worked for the baroque language, while others have been adopted for particular historic forms of the language.

[10] See http://www.cis.uni-muenchen.de/~schmid/tools/TreeTagger/. Accessed 20 February 2020.

[11] Erhard Hinrichs and Thomas Zastrow have already noted that, compared to other texts, Abraham a Sancta Clara's style exhibits by far the highest average sentence length, which might also be a reason why the author's test data had "the highest number of tagging errors." See Hinrichs 2012, 11.

[12] Since the ABaC:us working group insisted on high-quality linguistic annotation and description throughout the project, most phases of the project would not have been feasible without external funding. Two research assistants have worked independently on the manual correction and a senior researcher supervised their decisions,

find the right attributions, it is nonetheless unlikely to achieve 100% accuracy. In some cases, the classifications were further complicated by ambiguity and the assignments had to be based on subjective interpretations and assessments which may be contested with regards to their "correctness."[13] Users of the data should keep in mind that annotating a historic corpus is a very complex interpretation task and can have far-reaching consequences. There is nothing we could call the "absolute truth" or a "gold standard" annotation against which the reliability of the present data can be measured at the moment. Nevertheless, the manual examination and correction was imperative for the quality of this data.

2.2. The quality of annotation matters

The result, a painstakingly annotated corpus with basic linguistic information, can be useful for the above-mentioned inquiries as well as in distinguishing homographs (i.e., words that have the same spelling, but different meanings). For example: "sein" could be a personal pronoun (his), or an infinitive verb form (to be). The additional word class information helps researchers to generalize their search (e.g., "Find all prepositions in the text"), and can also help to specify the results (e.g., "Find the word 'sein,' but only those word forms that are used as an infinitive"). Anything that has been marked up in the data in the form of these basic linguistic annotations can then be extracted and used in various ways.

Due to this linguistic annotation, the corpus provides a versatile basis for various inquiries. For the first time, researchers are able to explore lexical as well as linguistic structures and regularities in works attributed to Abraham a Sancta Clara in a corpus-based approach. The corpus-based investigation of the antiquated but still fascinating "Abrahamic" texts, made possible by linguistic annotation, opens up an unbiased view at the author who, in literary histories, is repeatedly portrayed as an eloquent, verbally gifted, and imaginative writer with a tendency to linguistic exaggeration and creative language usage.

---

not only but especially in cases of doubt.

[13] Geoffrey Leech explains that "'Correctness' is defined by what the annotation scheme allows or disallows." Leech emphasizes that the applied annotation scheme has to correspond with linguistic realities. At the same time, it is true that even the most detailed scheme has to deal with all (unpredictable) peculiarities and eventualities of language that crop up in a corpus, which often leads to compromises. See Leech 2004.

In order to demonstrate the diverse applications of the corpus and the utility of the linguistic annotation, we provide some examples for the kind of investigation made possible by using text-technological methods with a resource such enriched. The following paragraphs will present several of these methods, through which we explore how digital analysis can help to elucidate "Abrahamic" style and to identify typical textual features that constitute, at least in part, the specific manner of writing that was so often imitated by Abraham's contemporaries.

3. Memento mori: *coming to terms with death*

Considering that *memento mori* literature has the expressed purpose to remind people of the fragility and impermanence of mortal life, it is not surprising that the word "death" is more frequently used than any other noun in these texts. A visual representation of all the lexical items occurring in the corpus shows that the lemma "Tod" (death) is the most frequent noun in these texts, followed by "Gott" (god), "Mensch" (human being), "Herr" (Lord), and "Leben" (life).

Figure 4. Word cloud consisting of the most frequent nouns within the corpus (the more frequently a specific word appears in the textual data, the bigger and bolder it appears in the word cloud).

The most straightforward way to search through ABaC:us is by means of the concordance tool[14] that automatically constructs a list of keywords in context and automatically yields frequency lists. For example, a search for the frequent lemma "Tod" (death) returns all instances of this specific term and displays them in a list centered on the word in the middle of the page, and provides the context in which it occurs (usually up to fifteen words on each side of the search term). The screenshot (below) shows that the lemma "Tod"

---

[14] The following investigations were carried out using Sketch Engine (see "Software" in Works Cited).

occurs 642 times in total. Due to the lemma information, all spelling variants (Todt/Tod) and declined forms (Todts/Todes) are included in the list.

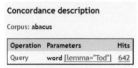

	seelig verschieden ; gleich aber nach dem **Todt** /NN/Tod	erscheint sie der H . Jungfrauen Ludgardi
von den Hebræischen Lotters=Knechten zum **Tod** /NN/Tod	geschleipfft worden . Weil du bist der
Sand=Hauffen ? Weist dann nicht / daß auch der **Todt** /NN/Tod	vnzeitige Aepffel schitle / vnd die Fleischhacker
sich aber schreibt Theophilactus bey dessen **Todt** /NN/Tod	etwas wunderliches ereignet ; nemblichen
gestatten / daß er solt eines vnglückseeligen **Todts** /NN/Tod	sterben / dann die Gutthaten / so man den
mit den Frey=Brieff / daß sie eines üblen **Todts** /NN/Tod	nicht können sterben : Anno 1600 . die
Geister ernstlich ermahnt / er solle sich zum **Tod** /NN/Tod	bereitten / alldieweil sein letztes Stündl
dann von Stund an auff das eyffrigst zum **Todt** /NN/Tod	bereitet / vnd müglichste Reu vnd Leyd
verricht ; stirbt den andern Tag deß gähen **Todts** /NN/Tod	. Wird dahero nicht bald jemand eines üblen
Wird dahero nicht bald jemand eines üblen **Todts** /NN/Tod	sterben / der gegen den Todten mitleydig
sc : Mercks Wienn / Das ist Deß wütenden **Todts** /NN/Tod	ein vmbständige Beschreibung Jn Der berühmten
Farben / führet den Pembsel / in Willens den **Todt** /NN/Tod	mit möglichsten Fleiß zuentwerffen ; er
vnersättlichen / den Menschen=Mörder den **Todt** /NN/Tod	so natürlich / daß der kunstreicheste Mahler
mich ein Todts=Bild nicht / Dan ich der **Todt** /NN/Tod	selbsten bin / Weil ich deß Todts = Ambt
ich der Todt selbsten bin / Weil ich deß **Todts** /NN/Tod	= Ambt verricht / Und raub deß Menschen
gleichwohl vnterfangen / den Wiennerischen **Todt** /NN/Tod	nach meiner Geringfügigkeit zuentwerffen
würden vnnd Gnaden disen meinen auffgeputzten **Todt** /NN/Tod	/ vnd wüntsche beynebenst ein langwieriges
Entwurff deß sterblichen Lebens / vnd daß der **Todt** /NN/Tod	ein Regel ohne Unterscheid allen vorschreibe
Lebens Athem ist schon ein Seuffzer zum **Todt** /NN/Tod	/ vnd der erste Augenblick deß menschlichen
erworbnes Leben schon worden ein Vigil deß **Todts** /NN/Tod	. Wann ein Weib von ihrer Leibs=Bürde loß

Figure 5. Excerpt from the query for the lemma "Tod" (death).

By evaluating such matches and the words surrounding them, we can begin to take into account the context in which a single word is placed. This method of displaying search results is referred to as "key word in context" (or KWIC) and reveals the varying contexts in which terms occur. This may be more insightful than just looking at words in isolation. Concordance analysis is an effective technique that allows researchers to carry out closer examinations. One expectation surrounding the genre which could be confirmed through our research is the fact that the term "Tod" constitutes a keyword and a thematic focus in the texts in question.

Given that "Tod" is the most frequently occurring lexical item, it seems worthwhile to examine its use on a deeper level by investigating typical language patterns surrounding the term. By looking at the words and phrases that occur to the left and right sides, we try to pick out similarities in language use. In these investigations, we have found out that the given term, "Tod," is frequently preceded by attribute adjectives that classify and characterize it. Based on this insight, it seemed reasonable to proceed with a combined query. The next figure shows the results of a search for all nominal phrases consisting of the noun "Tod" (death) and a preceding attributive adjective in the left position term (sorted in alphabetical order).

Figure 6. Excerpt from the query for the lemma "Tod" (death) and a preceding attributive adjective.

At first sight, the data above seems to contain a great variety of adjectives, notably the attributes "tobend" (raging), "türmisch" (infuriated), and "wütend" (furious), which are related to the destructive rapidity and the frenzy of death. Adjectives formed with the prefix "un-", such as "vnersättlich" (insatiable), "vnhöflich" (discourteous), and "unparteiisch" (impartial), characterize a personified Death of immense recklessness and give a vivid insight into the contemporary conception of death and its power to seize human lives—a power that renders all human beings equal regardless of their age, sex, or social status.

When running searches on a particular term (e.g., a noun such as "death") it is important to keep in mind that there might be determiners or pronouns for the term as well, which makes the process of analysis more complex. One particular stylistic feature of the specific genre under investigation is that authors like Abraham a Sancta Clara were extremely inventive in modifying and describing death and dying. To capture the wide range of death-related linguistic occurrences, the project group decided to categorize epithets for Death personified in single-word nouns, compound nouns, and nominal phrases (multiword units): for example, "Mader" (reaper) or "Jäger" (hunter); "Lebensfeind" (enemy of life) or "Menschenwürger" (strangler of human beings); "Herr von Beinhausen und Sichelberg" (Lord of Boneham and Sickle-berg) or "Reuter auf dem fahlen Pferd" (Rider on a pale horse). These phras-ings are reflective of the fact that the baroque era and its writers had a broad range of forms for encoding experiences with death and dying. Meanings were conveyed by a choice of vocabulary which nowadays has shifted out of fashion. These metaphorical paraphrases pose a particular challenge to search engines as they cannot be identified as types referring back to their respective target token unless they have been previously labeled. After an-notating these terms, however, we can also carry out semantically-oriented queries[15] which provide empirical, quantitative evidence of how the culture of death and dying was encoded, represented, and transmitted in lexical and linguistic patterns. Investigating these patterns may help to uncover the culturally specific "patterns of mind" of a given period, or the mental se-mantic structures related to particular concepts. Through the identification of frequently used words, phrases, and collocations, we can catch a glimpse of the significant phrases that circulated in the social world and informed the shared mental representation of culturally significant concepts like death and dying. Epithets making use of occupational titles or ranks such as "Herr Doktor Tod" (Doctor Death) or "General Haut und Bein" (General Skin and Bones) suggest that death has a human-like appearance, whereas "Jäger" (hunter) or "Mann auf langen Füßen" (man with long legs) express the swiftness of death. "Reuter auf dem fahlen Pferd" (Rider on a pale horse) invokes a biblical image, namely the Horsemen of the Apocalypse. By making a specific lexical choice over others, writers contributed to the construction of an imagery of death in some manner. However, we should note that com-munication about death and dying was not confined only to the verbal do-main. *Memento mori* messages were often embedded within images—a mental representation of death and dying could therefore emerge via interaction between verbal *and* visual texts.

Figure 7. Examples of a riding or cutting personified Death, using a scythe, a pair of scissors, or an arrow.

---

[15] As the annotation scheme had a more experimental character and has not been completed yet, this kind of enrichment is not accessible to the public at the moment.

The religious literature featured in ABaC:us represents the concept of death in its various forms of appearance. Although personifications of death were very popular at that time, the texts also allow other conceptual representations. To remind people, and to encourage them to be aware of their mortality, the term "death" often remains an abstract notion or exists as a metaphor. The uncertainty, or rather the openness of the entity (also shown in the amount of different attribute adjectives), is one of the parameters that made these picture-text combinations as successful and striking as they were.

4. Identifying rhetorical patterns

The part-of-speech tagging of ABaC:us can also be seen as a first stage of syntactic analysis. One of the main purposes of mapping word classes was the possibility to search the text collection for more complex stylistic patterns and recurrent phrases that can be found in various works of this particular period. With the help of searches based on part-of-speech tagging, certain stylistic phenomena can be shown to occur frequently in the examined texts. The first phenomenon that could be identified is a pair formula consisting of a foreign language element and an equivalent German lexeme, in which the latter provides a translation for the non-native element. The components are connected by a conjunction like "and" or "or," e.g., "Epilogus vnd Weltschluss" (epilogue and end of the world) or "Fratrum vnd Lay-Brüder" (*fratrum* and lay friars); the examples show that the native and non-native element could also be reversed, e.g., "Recht oder Jus" (law or *jus*).

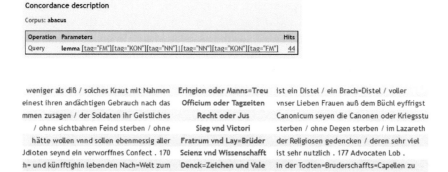

Figure 8. Excerpt from the query for an FM-tag (meaning foreign language element), a coordinating conjunction, and a common noun or vice versa.

The meaning and function of these frequently occurring pair formulas remain questionable. It could be the case that these tautological pairs were worked into the text as a translation for a less educated audience or for didactic reasons. It is more likely, however, that the use of non-native elements was a way for the author(s) to demonstrate erudition and extensive knowledge. Regarding this question, it would be particularly useful to have similar external pieces of literature annotated in the same way, which would allow us to assess how common these pairs were in other text types, and if they were part of every-day speech or only used consciously with a rhetorical intention (a possibility that must not be disregarded for the time being).

Another experiment involving queries for more complex phrases shows that authors like Abraham a Sancta Clara tend to use vivid descriptive language that relies heavily on metaphor and simile, e.g., "sich fürchten wie ein Lambel von den Wölffen" (to be frightened as a lamb among wolves) or "zittern wie ein Laub von der Espen" (tremble like aspen leaves), etc. The excerpt below shows that in the semantic field of death, these comparative phrases are often related to biblical metaphors for transience: e.g., human life disappears like the shadows at the sundial, it peters out like the water sinking into the earth, or it goes by like the flower on the fields.

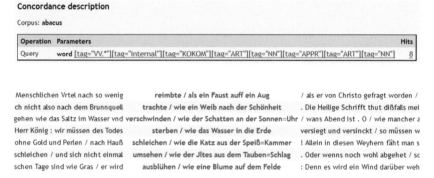

Figure 9. Query for a verb, a comparative conjunction, an article, a noun, a preposition, an article, and a noun.

Another rhetorical figure appearing in the texts under investigation, which can automatically be identified as a recurring pattern, is the serial interlinking of words or phrases with reoccurring elements. The search for a sequence of three nouns separated by a comma (NN / NN / NN), for instance, produces results of compounds ending with the same head, such as "Ertz-Vögel / Spay-Vögel / Spott-Vögel" (scoundrels, jeerers, mockers; literally, arch birds, spy birds, mocking birds) or the same modifier as shown in "Todten-Wägen / Todten-Truhen / Todten-Trag" (hearses, caskets, biers). If we slightly alter the query (NN / NN KON NN) we will get a triad of three matching nouns linked by a conjunction. Examples like "Lieb / Leib vnd Leben" (love, body and life) or "Thron / Cron vnnd Lohn" (throne, crown and reward) show that this kind of construction is often combined with stylistic devices like alliteration or rhyme. Similar queries can also be carried out for other word classes. Searching for adjectives occurring in pairs or in a series of three yields results like "wehrt vnd würdig" (dear and worthy), "künstlich vnd köstlich" (artistic and delicious), "ersahm vnnd tugendsahm" (respectable and virtuous), or "frech / frisch / frey" (bold, fresh, and free). For adjectives in attributive position, we get "Ehr-reiche / Lehr-reiche vnd Gwehr-reiche Statt" (a town full of honor, full of lessons, and full of arms) or "mostige / rostige / tostige Kuchel Diern" (which could be translated as a drunken, rusty, and bloated kitchen maid). All of these original German quotations have something in common: the constructions were not used arbitrarily but had a special, tonal effect and were created to entertain, or at least amuse, their readers. The same was true for the word class of verbs identified in the search query shown below:

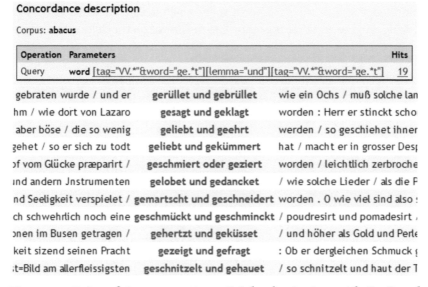

Figure 10. Pairs of German past participles beginning with "ge" and ending with a "t."

In order to detect more of the stylistic peculiarities of "Abrahamic" language, the project group has also experimented with the identification of similarities between words. This can be achieved by segmenting the text into so-called bigrams, that is, sequences of two adjacent characters, which makes it possible to locate forms with a certain number of identical characters. By applying the so-called Dice coefficient, all occurrences of matching strings within a certain span of tokens can be found. Its value gives information about the degree of similarity between the words and ranges from 0 (no similarity) to 1 (identical word forms). The higher the Dice coefficient, the more similar are the two lexemes to each other.

5	0,88	Rundtrincken / Grundtrincken / **Pfundtrincken**
6	0,87	**schandvollen** vnd schadvollen **Mammon** /
7	0,87	**Angster=Freund gibts viel** / **aber** Aengsten=Freund **gar wenig**
8	0,87	**gefährlichen Fall auf eine** gefährliche **Spitz gestellet**
9	0,86	**Ehr=reiche** / Lehr=reiche **vnd Gwehr=reiche**
10	0,86	**himmlische** / **den** himmlischen **werden zugeeignet**
11	0,86	**Federmäus oder** Fledermäuß **ihre Mißgönner**
12	0,86	**Saalbisems oder** Stallbisems . **Mir**

Figure 11. Examples of similar word forms with a Dice coefficient in the range between 0.86 and 0.88.

This kind of bigram-based analysis produces sets of similar word forms that can be found within a specific distance of each other. The above example shows the automatically extracted lists of words that differ in no more than two characters producing pairs such as "Federmäus und Fledermäuß" (mice with feathers/quills, which the author pejoratively uses for writers and bats; in German, literally fluttering mice) and "Saalbisem oder Stallbisem" (musk of a room or musk of a stable). As shown below, the same method can be applied for phrases of two word forms:

276	0,86	**eines Gewichts** / **vnd** eines Gesichts **seyn**
277	0,86	**Placebo Domino , noch** Placebo Dominæ **lesen kan**
278	0,86	**der Chartausen** / **sondern auch viel** / **die von** der Chartaunen **kommen** /
279	0,86	**der Weingarten ist nicht mehr so gut** / **in** dem Weingarten **ist der**
280	0,85	**O allmächtiges Gold** / **als** O allmächtiger **GOtt seuffzen**
281	0,85	**nicht verstunden** / **oder** nicht verstehen **wolten** /
282	0,85	**der Edlgstein** / **in** dem Edlgstein **der Glantz**

Figure 12. Examples of two similar word forms within a certain range of words.

The identification of these similarities does not depend on the annotation and is not limited to a certain word class, but is based on the raw texts automatically divided into bigrams. As not all text passages automatically generated in this way turn up instances of special style, it is necessary to have a closer look at those lists to verify if the examples in question were employed to fulfill a rhetorical function. However, the review of the results has shown that a predominant portion of these sets was indeed used with a rhetorical intention, producing a text peppered with witty word play and entertaining puns.

The above selection of some examples with identified "Abrahamic" features shows the far-reaching potential of using linguistic annotation to analyze textual data from the baroque period. Although we are just at the start, our experiments show that it is possible to detect, measure, and quantify at least some of the significant features of Abraham a Sancta Clara's influential literary style with digital methods. At the same time, it is now evident that a computational approach will not allow us to cover every single peculiarity of his style in the near future. Those who have thoroughly studied Abraham a Sancta Clara's writings and the texts attributed to him may doubt that digital methods are capable of penetrating the linguistic subtleties of "Abrahamic" style with its imaginative and overflowing wit. Our experiments with different text analyzing tools have shown that a computer's rigorous implementation of commands means that researchers have to be very precise and explicit in their instructions. Possible causes of error have to be considered and avoided, which is more easily done with a smaller corpus such as ABaC:us.

Nevertheless, it has become clear that for the evaluation and classification of the results, it would be of enormous help to gather more attested digital data and create more annotated corpora from the same time period. In the coming years, it will be crucial to transform more sources into digital form in order to allow comparisons with other contemporary texts and more general observations on genre and style. This will not only enhance our knowledge about the linguistic and stylistic features under investigation, but will also help to refine our tools. A greater amount of data would also facilitate comparative investigations. Since *memento mori* literature is not a phenomenon limited to the German-speaking area, the source material could also serve cross-linguistic, cross-cultural studies.

Abraham a Sancta Clara is said to be one of the most verbose and magniloquent writers in literary history. A valid and substantiated classification of his style, however, is only admissible if we try to compare his texts with a sufficient amount of other contemporary writings, by means of both qualitative and quantitative corpus-based methods. For literary scholars, the use of such methods would help to get a synoptic view at the literary production of the time, and allow them to assess how unique Abraham was and how outstanding his texts really were in comparison with others.

5. One resource, many purposes: the multi-functionality of ABaC:us

Given the great amount of effort required for building and tagging the corpus, it would be a pity if only literary scholars interested in baroque literature were to make use of it. Therefore, it is absolutely necessary to consider a wider range of usage, not just of the digitized raw texts but of the annotation data in particular. It is quite obvious that the time-consuming annotation process is only justifiable if the results are used not only by the team that carried out the annotation but also by other researchers who may take the tagging as a springboard for their own research and/or those who may find it useful for their own purposes and applications. In creating a publicly accessible online representation of the corpus, the project team strove for maximum reusability and set out to develop a user-friendly, flexible interface that caters to different disciplinary fields and supports various kinds of discoveries and purposes. This is partly achieved by allowing several different methods of approaching the material, such as direct access to the full text, access to and via metadata, and access to and via scanned images. Additionally, there are various ways to query the texts: Users may search for a lemma, a phrase, a word class, or places and personal names, or use all of these search methods in combination. The search bar is also equipped with an auto-complete function. Another interesting feature is the named entity search, which allows the user to search persons occurring in the texts by category (such as biblical, mythological, or historical). The platform also provides clear instructions for the citation of items.

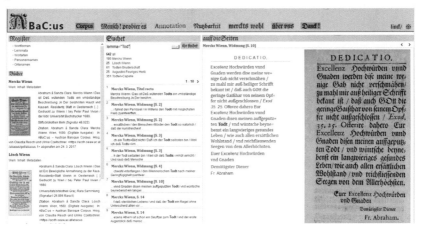

Figure 13. User-friendly interface of the ABaC:us web-application. See https://acdh.oeaw.ac.at/abacus/.

At the moment, ABaC:us is a standalone project lacking "big data" but breaking new ground. While the usefulness of the resource is undeniable, at the moment we may not even recognize the scope of its full potential and cannot anticipate all the questions that could be raised nor the results that could be obtained. The exploitation of the linguistic annotation for literary studies, as shown above, is just one of many potential future uses.

Since the online launch of ABaC:us, reactions from literary scholars, (computer) linguists, religious scholars, and historians have shown how interdisciplinary is the interest in ABaC:us. Researchers from many different fields across the digital humanities hope to benefit from the free availability of the enriched source material:

John Theibault @jtheibault · 13. Jan. 2015
Useful #earlymodern collections online. **Austrian Baroque Corpus** oeaw.ac.at /icltt/sites/de... and 17thC Bruderschaftsdrucke oeaw.ac.at/icltt/node/170

歴史とデジタル @historyanddigi · 4. Juni 2015
The **Austrian Baroque Corpus** "ABaC:us" consists of several texts specific to the memento mori genre. "ABaC:us online

Peeter Tinits @yrgsupp · 8. Mai 2015
Resch & Wohlfarter:The **Austrian Baroque Corpus** ABaC:us: What does the linguistic annotation add? bit.ly/1ceg6QO #whylinguistics

Kat Gupta @mixosaurus · 8. Dez. 2014
Claudia Resch on Memento Mori texts in **Austrian Baroque Corpus** (1650-1750) - lots of annotation & correction work gone into this #nedimah

Martin Wunderlich @martin_wun · 26. Feb. 2015
ABaC:US implements FCS standard so that the data is machine readable for other systems: clarin.eu/content/federa... #dhd2015

Figure 14. Tweets on ABaC:us written by historians, computer linguists, and other researchers.

As its reception in diverse fields shows, the digital *memento mori* corpus may be of value to scholars for a variety of reasons. Some of its value may stem from the fact that it virtually unifies works held in disparate libraries and allows a synoptic look at digital facsimiles as well as a combined query of the full texts. Art historians, in particular, may also find it useful that the corpus includes pictorial elements, such as emblems, that so far have not been published in any other collection. Additionally, theologians or theological historians may utilize the corpus to search all biblical figures mentioned in the texts in order to analyze the sources to which the books refer.

Furthermore, the existence of tagged and annotated full texts allows linguists and philologists to investigate the lexis and morphology of the "Abrahamic" texts and enables the use of concordance tools for historic research. Many other methods of digital text analysis may likewise be tried on the texts, such as a tool for sentiment analysis or topic modeling and/or visualization tools like the ones provided in the Voyant Tool Suite.[16]

Aside from the multi-functionality of the corpus and the re-usability argument, we have to consider whether the practice of digitizing and annotating early modern texts in this way can, in itself, benefit literary and cultural studies. There is no doubt that the annotations enable a whole new range of uses which would not have been otherwise possible.

Additionally, ABaC:us may also be of value as a model for similar projects just starting out. While the corpus is not particularly large, it makes up for its size by displaying a set of standards of good practice, and has established a body of pioneering work for others to build upon within its very specific field. Aspiring to a high level of openness, the project team is eager to share the enriched ABaC:us data with different disciplines. The annotation was carried out in a way that would meet the needs of computer experts and programmers working on text processing tools[17] as well as linguists and literary and cultural scholars. Researchers will now be able to use the enriched resource for many different purposes, using either the web-application (shown in Figure 13) or the xml files to download.

Of course, the value of a resource is always subjective and may evolve over time. While ABaC:us already has a wide variety of areas of relevance and potential utility for the various target groups and audiences listed above, it is quite possible that future researchers of any number of specializations may also find it useful in new, previously unforeseen domains. There is no doubt, however, that ABaC:us can help to enhance our understanding of the early

---

[16] See Voyant in Works Cited under "Software."

[17] The ABaC:us data is also a sound basis for the evaluation and training of tools (such as different taggers) which can be adapted to the specific language material for further annotation procedures. First experiments have shown that using manually corrected data as additional training material had a very positive effect for domain adaptation and significantly improved the performance of our tools. See Resch et al. 2014. The annotations applied in ABaC:us can also contribute to the generation of an expandable computational lexicon for older stages of German, which in turn could improve the performance of existing natural language processing tools and which could be used for studying linguistic variations as well.

modern period and to open up its fascinating literary culture to an international audience of (academic and non-academic) researchers and readers.

WORKS CITED

Digital text archives

Austrian Baroque Corpus (ABaC:us). Austrian Academy of Sciences. Accessed 20 February 2020. https://acdh.oeaw.ac.at/abacus/.

Das Bonner Frühneuhochdeutschkorpus. Accessed 20 February 2020. https://korpora.zim.uni-duisburg-essen.de/FnhdC/.

Deutsches Textarchiv. Berlin Brandenburg Academy of Sciences and Humanities. Accessed 20 February 2020. http://www.deutschestextarchiv.de/.

GerManC Project: A Representative Historical Corpus of German. Manchester: University of Manchester. Accessed 20 February 2020. https://www.alc.manchester.ac.uk/modern-languages/research/german-studies/germanc/.

Wolfenbüttel Digital Library. Herzog August Bibliothek Wolfenbüttel. Accessed 20 February 2020. http://www.hab.de/de/home/bibliothek/digitale-bibliothek-wdb.html.

Printed primary sources

AUGUSTINI Feuriges Hertz Tragt Ein Hertzliches Mitleyden mit den armen im Feeg-Feuer Leydenden Seelen / Das ist / Ein kleiner Haußrath etliche Sentenz auß den Schrifften vnsers Heil. Vatters [. . .] Salzburg: Melchior Haan, 1693.

Besonders meublirt- und gezierte Todten-Capelle / Oder Allgemeiner Todten-Spiegel / Darinnen Alle Menschen / wes Standes sie sind / sich beschauen / an denen mannigfältigen Sinnreichen Gemählden das MEMENTO MORI zu studiren [. . .] Nürnberg: Marrtin [sic] Frantz Hertz, 1710.

Grosse Todten Bruderschaft / Das ist Ein kurtzer Entwurff Deß Sterblichen Lebens / Mit beygefügten CATALOGO, Oder Verzeichnus aller der Jenigen Herren Brüderen / Frauen / und Jungfrauen Schwesteren / welche [. . .] von Anno 1679. biß 1680. gestorben seyn. 1681.

Lösch Wienn / Das ist Ein Bewögliche Anmahnung zu der Kays. Residentz-Statt Wienn in Oesterreich / Was Gestalten / Dieselbige der so viel tausend Verstorbene Bekanten vnd Verwandten nicht wolle vergessen [. . .] Wien: Peter Paul Vivian, 1680.

Mercks Wienn / Das ist Deß wütenden Todts ein vmbständige Beschreibung Jn Der berühmten Haubt vnd Kayserl. Residentz Statt in Oesterreich / Jm sechzehen hundert / vnd neun vnd sibentzigsten Jahr / [. . .] Wien: Peter Paul Vivian, 1680.

Scholarship

Boot, Peter. 2009. *Mesotext: Digitised Emblems, Modelled Annotations and Humanities Scholarship.* Amsterdam: Pallas Publications/Amsterdam University Press.

Eybl, Franz M. 2008. "Abraham a Sancta Clara." In *Killy Literaturlexikon,* edited by v. Wilhelm Kühlmann, 1: 10–14. Berlin: de Gruyter.

———. 1992. *Abraham a Sancta Clara. Vom Prediger zum Schriftsteller.* Tübingen: Max Niemeyer Verlag.

———. 2012. "Wissenslücken um Abraham a Sancta Clara. Zur Problematik populärer Autorschaft." In *Abraham a Sancta Clara. Vom barocken Kanzelstar zum populären Schriftsteller. Beiträge des Kreenheinstetter Symposions anlässlich seines 300. Todestages,* edited by Anton Philipp Knittel, 104–21. Eggingen: Edition Isele.

Hinrichs, Erhard, and Thomas Zastrow. 2012. "Linguistic Annotations for a Diachronic Corpus of German." *Linguistic Issues in Language Technology* 7.7. Accessed 20 February 2020. https://journals.linguisticsociety.org/elanguage/lilt/article/download/2689/2689-5527-1-PB.pdf.

Horber, Ambros. 1929. *Echtheitsfragen bei Abraham a Sancta Clara.* Weimar: Verlag von Alexander Duncker.

Leech, Geoffrey. 2004. "Evaluation of Annotation: Realism, Accuracy and Consistency." *Developing Linguistic Corpora: A Guide to Good Practice,* by Geoffrey Leech, chapter 2. Accessed 20 February 2020. http://users.ox.ac.uk/~martinw/dlc/chapter2.htm.

Resch, Claudia, Thierry Declerck, Barbara Krautgartner, and Ulrike Czeitschner. "ABaC:us Revisited: Extracting Ad Linking Lexical Data

From a Historical Corpus of Sacred Literature." In *Proceedings of the 2nd Workshop on Language Resources and Evaluation for Religious Texts* (LRE-REL 2). This essay is co-located with LREC 2014 Reykjavik, chapter 2.1, "Improvement through Reliable Data." Accessed 20 February 2020. http://www.lrec-conf.org/proceedings/lrec2014/workshops/LREC2014Workshop-LRE-Rel2%20Proceedings.pdf.

Šajda, Peter. 2009. "Abraham a Sancta Clara: An Aphoristic Encyclopedia of Christian Wisdom." In *Kierkegaard and the Renaissance and Modern Traditions – Theology*, edited by Jon Stewart, 1–20. Aldershot: Ashgate.

Wunderlich, Uli. 2000. "Abraham a Sancta Claras Besonders meublirt- und gezierte Todten-Capelle. Der erfolgreichste Totentanz der Barock und seine Rezeptionsgeschichte." In *L'art macabre. Jahrbuch der Europäischen Totentanz-Vereinigung* 1: 191–210.

Software

Sketch Engine. Accessed 20 February 2020. https://www.sketchengine.co.uk/.

Voyant. Accessed 20 February 2020. http://docs.voyant-tools.org/tools/.

Methods and Insights

A Tale of Two Collectors: Using *nodegoat* to Map the Connections between the Manuscript Collections of Thomas Phillipps and Alfred Chester Beatty

Toby Burrows

School of Humanities, University of Western Australia
Oxford e-Research Centre, University of Oxford

Two of the most important manuscript collectors of the nineteenth and twentieth centuries were Thomas Phillipps (1792–1872) and Alfred Chester Beatty (1875–1968).[1] Phillipps's collection was remarkable for its size; he acquired more than forty thousand medieval and early modern manuscripts as well as tens of thousands of books and hundreds of art works. The dispersal of his collection after his death spanned more than a century, and his manuscripts were spread around the world into many institutional and private collections (Munby 1951–60; Burrows 2018b). Beatty's collection, on the other hand, was notable for its selectivity and connoisseurship. Though he owned no more than 190 Western medieval and early modern manuscripts, they were significant as exemplars of outstanding quality in illumination, script, and design (Cleaver 2017). At least sixty of these manuscripts came from the Phillipps collection. Since Beatty's collecting interests and priorities changed over time, only a few are still in the Chester Beatty Library in Dublin; the others were sold on to other collectors and institutions as part of Beatty's extensive sales in 1932/33 and 1968/69.

The intertwined collecting activities of these two men are important for the broader history of manuscript collections since the nineteenth century. They help us to understand what was thought to be worth collecting and how collections were formed and dispersed around the world. The histories of the Phillipps-Beatty manuscripts after they were sold by Beatty also illustrate how and why manuscripts moved between private and public collections. These provenance events are important for their contribution to the wider

---

[1] I am very grateful to Dr. Laura Cleaver (Trinity College Dublin), the staff of the Chester Beatty Library in Dublin, Dr. Mara Hoffman (Sotheby's, London), and Dr. William Stoneman (Harvard University Library) for their assistance and expertise in relation to Alfred Chester Beatty, and to Pim Van Bree and Geert Kessels for their help with *nodegoat*.

ISBN 978-1-64959-016-9 (paper) ISBN 978-1-64959-017-6 (pdf) ISBN 978-1-64959-037-4 (epub)
New Technologies in Medieval and Renaissance Studies 9 (2022) 89–111

picture of the transmission of medieval and early modern manuscripts down to the present day. Without collectors like Phillipps and Beatty, far fewer manuscripts would have survived as witnesses to the variety of medieval and early modern history and society.

In the past, these topics have been explored with the use of lists and tables, or through provenance notes in the descriptions of individual manuscripts. While these histories sometimes have the excitement of a detective story, the results are often anecdotal and hard to aggregate into a larger picture of the history of manuscript collecting (De Ricci 1930; De Hamel 2016). In this essay, I report on a new approach for research into manuscript collections, using the *nodegoat* software developed by Lab1100 in the Netherlands. *nodegoat* is "a Web-based data management, network analysis and visualization environment" (Van Bree and Kessels 2015). It enables the histories and movements of groups of manuscripts to be tracked and visualized, providing a more holistic view of the data and offering a platform for further analysis. It combines flexibility in building data models with a low-tech approach to importing data through CSV files. Individual researchers can request free accounts through the nodegoat. net website, and can set up multiple projects for different datasets. *nodegoat* can also be installed locally or on sites like Amazon Web Services.

Gathering the data

The data relating to the histories of these manuscripts are scattered across various heterogeneous sources. At one extreme is the Schoenberg Database of Manuscripts, in which every record is one piece of evidence relating to the provenance or ownership history of a single manuscript. Of almost 240,000 records, 210 mention both Phillipps and Beatty. Nearly 20,000 records mention Phillipps. The data can be downloaded in the form of CSV files, either for the whole database or for the results of a specific search. CSV files can usually be loaded directly into another database or a visualization engine for analysis. The Schoenberg Database has its own data model, which focuses on the different elements of each provenance event, including seller, buyer, date, previous owners, price, and the contents of the manuscript involved (authors and works).

At the other extreme are unpublished handwritten sources relating to these manuscripts. The most interesting of these is Beatty's notebook in which he recorded his impressions of the Phillipps collection when he went to see it at Thirlestaine House in Cheltenham in the early 1920s.[2] His notes included succinct evaluations of specific manuscripts, such as "Might be worth seeing

---

[2] This notebook is now owned by the Chester Beatty Library in Dublin, Ireland.

again. Doubtful" (in relation to Phillipps MS 9592), as well as estimated prices suggested to him by the owner: "F. asked £3000 at first but far too high" (Phillipps MS 3633). While digital images can be made of the notebook, data from it can only be extracted and captured by manual transcription.

The other data sources fall somewhere between these two extremes. Printed volumes can be scanned and the OCR version of the text extracted for transformation into a format like CSV. But this is heavily dependent on the nature and quality of the printed pages; Phillipps's own printed catalog of his manuscripts (which covers little more than half of his collection) produces relatively poor results in the version scanned by Google Books (Phillipps 1837–71). Library catalog databases are another important source, usually in the MARC format, but it can be surprisingly difficult to download groups of records from them in a format suitable for reuse. Library manuscript catalogs encoded using the Text Encoding Initiative (TEI) specifications are even more difficult to reuse, since they exist as XML documents rather than database records. The recent "Library Collections as Data" program is a welcome initiative aimed at persuading libraries to re-think the way they make their digital data (including catalog data) available for reuse by researchers.[3]

Digital environment

The provenance histories of manuscripts are difficult to model in a computational setting, given the variety of different approaches adopted by libraries and museums (Burrows 2018a). Bringing such heterogeneous sources together in a single environment requires a unifying data model as well as suitable software for managing and combining the data. My requirements for identifying such software included:

- Flexible and adaptable data modeling.
- Ability to ingest data manually and through spreadsheets.
- Capacity to reconcile with external Linked Data vocabularies.
- Ability to produce visualizations of geographical and temporal relationships and of social networks.
- Web-based, with low data storage needs.
- Relatively easy to learn.
- Capacity for browsing and searching the data in a variety of ways.

After ruling out wiki-style environments like Confluence, I investigated the Neo4j graph database software (Van Bruggen 2014). While it met several of

---

[3] Always Already Computational: Collections as Data. https://collectionsasdata. github.io (accessed 1 September 2019).

my requirements (especially for data modeling and ingest), it was not web-based and had a fairly steep learning curve. Its visualization capabilities were relatively limited, and most users built a more sophisticated environment on top of Neo4j itself.

nodegoat, on the other hand, met all my requirements. Its flexible approach provides a good way of aggregating data with a customized data model, using a structure based on objects and attached sub-objects. In simple terms, "objects" represent entities and "sub-objects" represent events or changes of state affecting these entities. In the context of my data model, a "Manuscript" object can have sub-objects for transactions such as "Sold" and "Owned," and these sub-objects can contain links to the Persons and Organizations participating in each transaction, as well as the times and places where the transaction occurred.

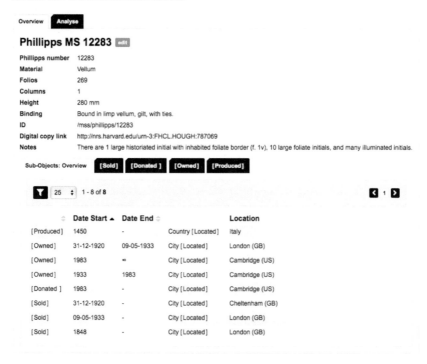

Figure 1. *nodegoat* record for Phillipps manuscript 12283.

The sub-objects attached to each manuscript record can provide a summary of the known events in its provenance history. Figure 1 shows the *nodegoat* record for Phillipps MS 12283, one of the Italian manuscripts owned by Phillipps and later by Beatty, which is now in the Harvard University Library. The

"Object" record, which contains a physical description of the manuscript, is accompanied by a series of "Sub-objects" which show different events in its history: Produced, Owned, and Sold. Three of these "Sold" sub-objects appear in Figure 2, showing the places, persons, and organizations linked into each event.

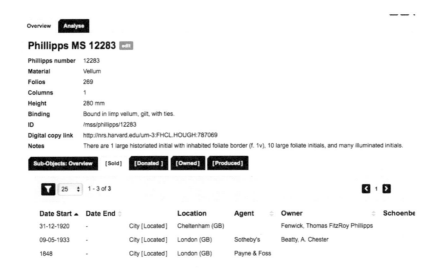

Figure 2. "Sold" sub-objects for Phillipps manuscript 12283.

Within the *nodegoat* database, two different types of vocabulary can be deployed: those inherent in *nodegoat* itself and those chosen by the creator of the database. The Geonames ontology for place-names is incorporated into individual projects hosted on the *nodegoat* site. While this makes geographical visualizations of the data relatively easy, it also has the limitations associated with only recognizing contemporary countries and cities. Personal names in *nodegoat* can be matched against Wikidata and the Virtual International Authority File (VIAF). Other types of classifications can be created specifically, including those for languages, currencies, and materials.

Data can be entered manually in *nodegoat*, but it is generally more efficient to import data in bulk through CSV files. An Import Template must be created for each unique CSV format by mapping the CSV columns to objects and sub-objects. The import routine consists of loading the CSV file to *nodegoat*, choosing the appropriate Import Template, and running the import process. Various parameters can be set for this process, such as whether to create new objects automatically as part of the data load or to hold each object for manual review against possible matches.

The major difficulties in the import process are likely to arise from mapping the source data to the *nodegoat* data model. This is especially so when multiple pieces of information are conflated into a single column in the CSV file, or into a single field in the source database. A person's dates of birth and death may be included in the same column as their name, for example, or the names of multiple previous owners may be included in a single provenance field. Alternatively, a field may be given in a narrative or note format, containing multiple pieces of information. In these cases, the source data are likely to require extensive editing with a tool like OpenRefine before they can be loaded to *nodegoat* (Verborgh and De Wilde 2013).

Identifying and recording Beatty's Phillipps manuscripts can be done by means of a spreadsheet or table (as in Appendix 1), but only up to the point where the complexity of the data relating to each manuscript becomes difficult to manage. A software environment like *nodegoat* makes it possible to record and collate a large number of data points for each manuscript, together with the interconnections between them. The *nodegoat* database used to record, identify, and analyze the Phillipps-Beatty manuscripts is actually designed for a much larger purpose: recording the Phillipps manuscripts and their histories. It is still very much work-in-progress, given the scale of the Phillipps collection and of the very large body of evidence relating to it. The pilot version of this database covers more than 1,600 former Phillipps manuscripts, and has been populated with a selection of data from the Schoenberg Database of Manuscripts, several library catalogs, the printed Phillipps catalog, and archival sources like the Beatty notebook. It can be explored at http://personal-research-domain-burrows.nodegoat.net/.

Exploring the data

Beatty's acquisitions of former Phillipps manuscripts were discussed by Christopher de Hamel in a *Book Collector* article in 1991, but his list of fifty-one is incomplete (De Hamel 1991). Based on a fuller range of sources, the actual number seems to have been at least sixty. A summary list of these is given in Appendix 1. My *nodegoat* database contains records for all sixty of these manuscripts, but these represent the data gathered from other sources. The database cannot currently be used to determine whether any other Phillipps manuscripts were later owned by Beatty; it would have to contain all the records of all the histories of all the Phillipps manuscripts to make this possible. No other current manuscript database can meet this requirement, either. Sources like the Schoenberg Database of Manuscripts tell only part of the story. But the *nodegoat* database can serve as the means of collating relevant data from various sources and making them available for exploration and analysis, within the context of the broader Phillipps database.

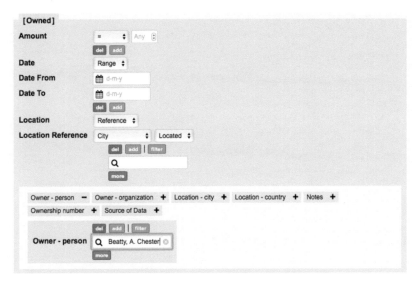

Figure 3. Records filtered for Chester Beatty as owner.

The *nodegoat* data can be searched and browsed in various ways. The records in the database can be filtered to show those which meet a specific criterion or a combination of criteria. This is the way to identify those Phillipps manuscripts in the database which have Alfred Chester Beatty recorded as an owner, as shown in Figure 3. By contrast, Figure 4 shows the filter for finding manuscripts that have been located in Cambridge, Massachusetts at some point in their history. These filters can be combined to show those manuscripts, once owned by Beatty, which also have a connection to Cambridge.

Figure 4. Records filtered for Cambridge, Massachusetts as location.

Where *nodegoat* comes into its own is with visualizations of the history and movement of these manuscripts. Figure 5 shows a geographical visualization of the history of a single manuscript (Phillipps MS 12283). This is a fifteenth-century Italian copy of the Patristic writer Lactantius, which had been acquired by Phillipps in 1848 from the booksellers Payne and Foss. It was one of a batch of twenty-seven manuscripts bought directly by Beatty from Phillipps's grandson, Thomas FitzRoy Fenwick, in December 1920. This purchase included one manuscript (Phillipps MS 14122), which was bought by Beatty's wife Edith. The total amount paid was £12,454 (including £500 for Mrs. Beatty's manuscript).

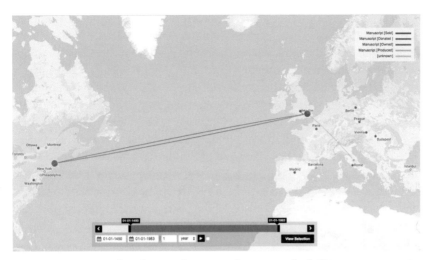

Figure 5. Geographical visualization: history of Phillipps manuscript 12283.

There were three other batches of manuscripts bought directly from Fenwick by Beatty: eight in February 1923 for a total price of £3,320, and nine in August 1924 for a further £5,105. The final batch, consisting of eight manuscripts acquired from Fenwick by Edith Beatty in November 1925 for the huge amount of £21,800, as a gift for her husband, is the most interesting. They included three of the top fifteen manuscripts listed in Beatty's earlier notes on the "order in which Mr F places manuscripts":[4]

- #2. Statius, *Thebaid* (Phillipps MS 1798) – bought for £7,000 (and earlier described by Beatty as "a beautiful book . . . of uniformly high grade – The book is not for sale except at a high price £3000 – £5000");
- #6. *Dictys Cretensis* (Phillipps MS 3502) – bought for £7,000 (despite Beatty's earlier comment: "1st Visit talked about £5000"); and,
- #13. "Ferdinand, Italy XV" [i.e., the *Epistolae* of Francesco Barbaro, once in the Aragonese Royal Library] (Phillipps MS 6640) – bought for £3,000.

In total, these fifty-two manuscripts cost the Beattys £42,679. Mrs. Beatty paid far higher prices than her husband; his most expensive purchases (all in 1920) were £2,000 each for Phillipps MSS 4259 and 4769, and £1,500 for Phillipps MS 2165.

---

[4] In Beatty's notebook on Phillipps manuscripts, now owned by Sotheby's.

Beatty also owned a further eight manuscripts which were not acquired directly from Fenwick. Three of these (Phillipps MSS 3734, 21163, and 21642) were bought from the book dealer Quaritch in late 1912, and one (Phillipps MS 2803) was bought at a Sotheby's auction in July 1921. They had originally been sold by Fenwick at Sotheby's auctions in 1896, 1898, and 1903. For three other manuscripts (Phillipps MSS 345, 629, and 3726), the method and date of acquisition remain unknown. One (Phillipps MS 345) was in Beatty's hands by 1928 at the latest, and another (Phillipps MS 3726) at some time before 1933. Beatty's final purchase was one of Phillipps's greatest treasures: the Armenian Gospel Book (Phillipps MS 15364) with which Phillipps had been photographed in 1860. It was bought in 1948 from the Robinson brothers, the London book dealers who had acquired the residue of the Phillipps collection in 1945.

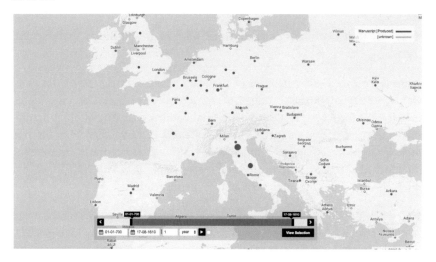

Figure 6. Geographical visualization: Phillipps-Beatty manuscripts to 1610.

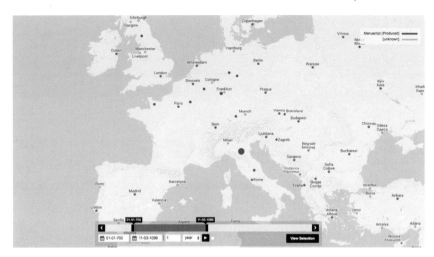

Figure 7. Geographical visualization: Phillipps-Beatty manuscripts before 1100.

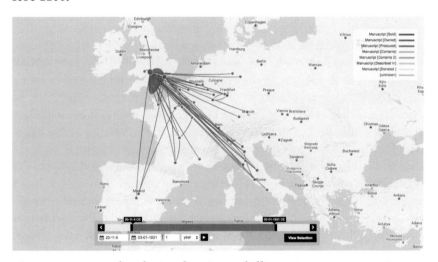

Figure 8. Geographical visualization: Phillipps-Beatty manuscripts to 1931.

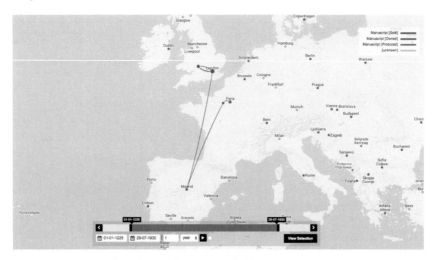

Figure 9. Geographical visualization: Phillipps manuscript 4259 to 1931.

The *nodegoat* visualizations can be extended to show the data relating to the provenance of all sixty manuscripts. Figure 6 shows their places of production, where this can be localized. They came from all over Western Europe, but mainly from Italy, Germany, and France, with only a few from Britain and Spain. The time-slider at the bottom of the map can be used to refine this information further. Figure 7 shows the places of production for those manuscripts originating from before 1100; the geographical distribution is generally similar to that of the later manuscripts. Figure 8 shows the histories of the Phillipps-Beatty manuscripts up to 1931, after Beatty had acquired almost all of them but before the first of his major sales in 1932. Most of the movement is towards England, reflecting the nineteenth-century purchases by Phillipps and the twentieth-century sales by Fenwick to Beatty. There are a small number of other movements around Europe, but for most manuscripts their history before Phillipps acquired them is largely unrecorded. An exception is Phillipps MS 4259, the so-called Duprat Bible; produced in the earlier thirteenth century, it had successive owners in France and Spain before travelling to England in the nineteenth century, as shown in Figure 9 (Kidd 2015).

Beatty was not the kind of collector who kept everything he acquired. He preferred a continual reappraisal of his collections, partly for financial reasons, partly because he was keen to improve their overall quality, and partly because his tastes and interests changed over time (Horton 2000). Relatively few of his Western manuscripts remain in the Chester Beatty Library today. It was in this context that he eventually disposed of most of his Phillipps manuscripts. Twenty-four of them were offered for sale at Sotheby's as part of his two great auctions of 1932 and 1933. Ten were offered in the 1932 sale; two of these failed to sell. A further fourteen were offered and sold in the 1933 auction. Three other manuscripts were exchanged with, or sold to, the collector A. S. Yahuda in the 1920s and 1930s (Phillipps MSS 345, 385, and 437). Edith Beatty sold at least two manuscripts in 1952, to the Morgan Library and the Walters Art Museum (Phillipps MSS 2165 and 14122). The time and method of disposal of three other manuscripts remain unknown (Phillipps MSS 629, 3734, and 21642).

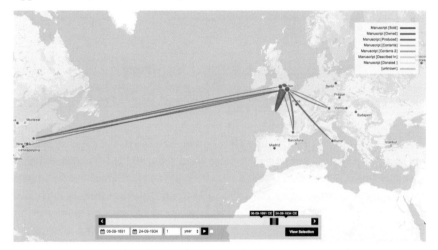

Figure 10. Geographical visualization: Phillipps-Beatty sales to 1933.

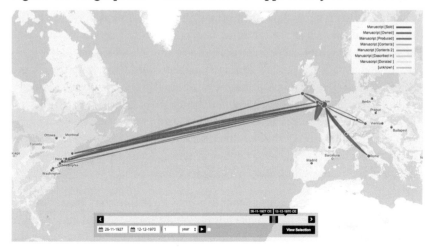

Figure 11. Geographical visualization: Phillipps-Beatty sales to 1969.

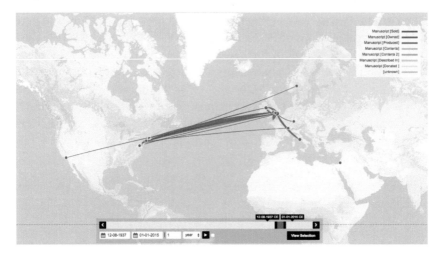

Figure 12. Geographical visualization: Phillipps-Beatty current locations.

In the initial sales of 1932–33, most of the buyers were European or English, as shown in Figure 10. Only three manuscripts are shown as traveling to the United States. In fact, these sales were regarded as a relative failure, with the Great Depression blamed for the poor market conditions (Cleaver and Magnusson 2018). After the sales in 1968 and 1969, as well as in earlier years, the picture was rather different, as seen as Figure 11; the migration of manuscripts to North America substantially increased. Since then, they have spread even farther around the world, as Figure 12 shows. The current locations of forty-seven of these manuscripts are known. There are eighteen in public institutional collections in the United States, six in Italy, six in the United Kingdom, two in Switzerland, and one each in Germany and Israel. The known owners of these manuscripts are the Biblioteca nazionale centrale di Roma (six), the British Library (four), Harvard University (four), the Morgan Library (four), the Walters Art Museum (three), the Bodmer Library in Geneva (two), the New York Public Library (two), Yale University (two), the Getty Museum in Los Angeles (one), the Boston Public Library (one), Lincoln College Oxford (one), the National Library of Israel (one), Princeton University (one), the Sir Paul Getty Library at Wormsley in the United Kingdom (one), and the Landesbibliothek in Stuttgart (one).

Today, thirteen former Phillipps manuscripts are still in the Chester Beatty Library in Dublin. Twelve of these appear on a list of Western manuscripts exhibited at the Chester Beatty Library in November 1967. These were the same manuscripts that remained in the library after Beatty's death, in accordance with his will—as set out in the typewritten list certified by his librarian

Richard James Hayes, dated 22 April 1968.[5] The other is the Armenian Gospels bought in 1948. One of the two manuscripts left unsold at the 1932 sale is still in the Chester Beatty Library today (Phillipps MS 132). Of these manuscripts, six had been bought from Fenwick in 1920, six from Fenwick in 1925 by Edith Beatty, and one from the Robinson brothers in 1948 (the Armenian Gospels). This is a substantial reduction from the thirty- to thirty-four Phillipps manuscripts which must have been in the Chester Beatty Library when it first opened to the public in Dublin in 1953. Seventeen of these were then offered for sale in the two Sotheby's auctions held after Beatty's death—eight in the 1968 sale, and nine in the 1969 sale. The latter group included one of the manuscripts left unsold thirty-seven years earlier (Phillipps MS 10190).

The current location of fourteen of the manuscripts remains unknown. They include one (Phillipps MS 2251) which is known to have been exported to France for a private owner after its sale in 1975. Another manuscript (Phillipps MS 2506) was broken up after it was sold in 1969. At least sixteen individual leaves from it have passed through the sale rooms in the last forty-five years, including three which were bought back by the Chester Beatty Library and two which are now in the University of Melbourne, Australia.

Figure 13. Geographical visualization: British Library and Biblioteca nazionale centrale di Roma.

If the first group of research questions around the Phillipps-Beatty manuscripts relates to their histories, their sales, and their current locations, the second relates to their various owners. The map-based visualizations may

---

[5] Copy in Bodleian Library, R.Pal.6.6a.

reveal some features of the institutional owners. Figure 13 shows the histories of the ten manuscripts now owned by either the British Library or the Biblioteca nazionale centrale di Roma. All but one of the latter's holdings are of manuscripts originating from Nonantola Abbey in Northern Italy—probably a sufficient explanation for their acquisition by that library. But only one of the British Library's four manuscripts has a British origin (Phillipps MS 12200), so the reasons for their acquisition have to be sought in factors other than their geographical histories.

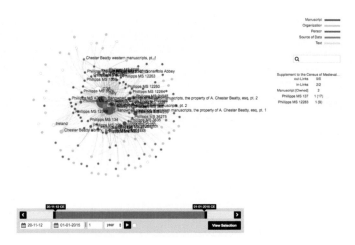

Figure 14. Network graph: Phillipps-Beatty manuscripts.

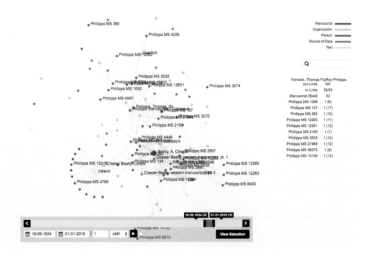

Figure 15. Network graph: Phillipps-Beatty manuscripts since 1934.

More applicable to the analysis of ownership is the other kind of visualization in *nodegoat*, which takes the form of a "social visualization" or network graph, showing the connections between manuscripts, persons, and organizations. The network graph for the Phillipps-Beatty manuscripts is shown in Figure 14. Unsurprisingly, the predominant entities are Beatty (who owned all these manuscripts), Fenwick (who sold most of them), and Sotheby's (where many of the later sales took place). A time-slider can be used here too, with Figure 15 showing the network graph for these manuscripts since 1934. The social networks of individual owners of manuscripts can also be visualized; Figure 16 shows the network graph for the Biblioteca nazionale central di Roma.

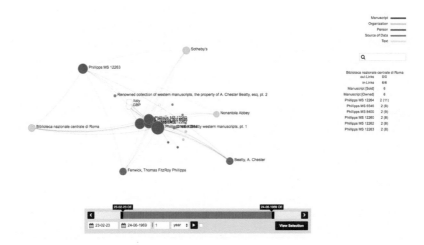

Figure 16. Network graph: Biblioteca nazionale centrale di Roma.

In its current state, however, the database does not contain enough contextual data about persons and organizations to make quantitative network analysis feasible. The evidence shows, for example, that a number of other well-known private collectors owned at least one of these manuscripts at some stage after they were sold by Beatty. Their names are a roll-call of many important European and American collectors of the twentieth century: St. John Hornby, Major J. R. Abbey, Philip Hofer, Eric Millar, William Scheide, Martin Schøyen, Peter Ludwig, A. S. Yahuda, and André De Coppet. In all cases, these collectors either donated their manuscripts to a public institution or sold them at auction, sometimes posthumously as part of their estate. The involvement of this group of collectors reflects the value and significance of the manuscripts themselves, as well as the taste and judgment of Beatty and Phillipps. But without much fuller data about the social networks of these people, and about their entire manuscript collections, quantitative analysis of their networks is not realistic. Data can always be exported from *nodegoat* as CSV files or as JSON objects via an API for possible reuse and analysis in another software environment. In any case, because the *nodegoat* database produces a complex, multimodal graph with both directed and undirected edges, the reservations about applying analytical measures expressed by an expert like Scott Weingart are very relevant (Weingart 2011).

Conclusion

The data relating to the individual histories of cultural objects like medieval and Renaissance manuscripts can be complex and difficult to manage. *nodegoat* is particularly suitable as a digital environment for this purpose. It can gather and store large quantities of data in a flexible but consistent format, and present it for exploration by the researcher. As well as answering straightforward quantitative research questions (such as, how many manuscripts did Phillipps and Beatty both own?), it can also provide answers to questions involving more complex combinations of criteria: which manuscripts originated in Italy, were owned by both Phillipps and Beatty, and are now located in Italy again? The geographical and network visualizations built into *nodegoat* are a particularly helpful way of enabling researchers to conceptualize a whole body of interrelated data, and provide a valuable diagnostic tool for exploring relationships and linkages within an entire dataset.

These visualizations are not, in themselves, explanations of the data, and the relationships they reveal between entities and events are not necessarily causal ones. As Johanna Drucker reminds us, visualizations tend to gloss over uncertainties, ambiguities, and gaps in the evidence—and almost inevitably simplify the picture (Drucker 2014). Nevertheless, they are very helpful summaries of a complex body of data, which may serve as useful indicators and diagnostic tools for thinking about the dataset in a holistic way. In the context of manuscript histories, these visualizations can point out factors and connections which may be significant: trends in geographical movement over time (to the United States, in the case of the Phillipps-Beatty manuscripts); the distribution of places of origin of the manuscripts; the extent and nature of connections between particular collectors or groups of collectors.

nodegoat has in-built strategies for coping with uncertainty and ambiguity, and with variations in terminology over time, though the geographical visualizations work best when specific places and years can be associated with specific events. Regions can be used, as long as they are associated with a geographical polygon. The data model is flexible enough to incorporate indicators for levels of certainty and uncertainty, and these can be used to filter the display of information in the visualizations. Nevertheless, these images cannot be taken as aggregations of *all* the data in the dataset; rather, they are aggregations only of those data which are sufficiently precise and specific to be mapped or linked.

As well as recording, analyzing, and displaying complex data relating to the histories of the Phillipps-Beatty manuscripts, *nodegoat* can also help to put these manuscripts into a broader context. Adding data relating to the wider activities of these two collectors, and to their relationships with other people and institutions in the manuscript trade in the nineteenth and twentieth centuries, is readily done. This expansion of the networks of relationships can be visualized at an increasing density and scale. In this way, *nodegoat* can serve as the digital environment not just for a specific investigation, but for a broader set of research questions across an expanding dataset.

Appendix 1: The Phillipps-Beatty manuscripts – a summary list

Phillipps MS no.	Beatty no.	Current location	Other owners
125	W.M.S.66	Chester Beatty Library	
134 / 3948	W.M.S.80	Chester Beatty Library	
137	W.M.S.110	Getty Museum	Marston, Ludwig
240	W.M.S.125	Unknown	
250	W.M.S.99	Chester Beatty Library	
345		Yale University	Yahuda
385	W.M.S.33	British Library	Yahuda
389	W.M.S.13	Bodmer Collection	
390	W.M.S.14	Princeton University	Scheide
437		National Library of Israel	Yahuda
447	W.M.S.57	Unknown	
629	W.M.S.179	Unknown	Abbey
934 / 2708	W.M.S.18	Unknown	Abbey
1036	W.M.S.46	Walters Art Museum	
1092	W.M.S.31	Harvard University	
1798	W.M.S.76	Chester Beatty Library	
2165 / 21787	W.M.S.9	Morgan Library	
2251	W.M.S.102	Unknown	Hornby, Abbey
2506	W.M.S.173	*Broken up by 1975*	
2803	W.M.S.123	Unknown	
3009	W.M.S.120	Unknown	
3010	W.M.S.112	New York Public Library	
3075	W.M.S.15	Unknown	Schøyen, Bodmer
3339	W.M.S.67	Unknown	Hornby, Abbey
3344	W.M.S.29	Chester Beatty Library	
3383	W.M.S.65	Unknown	
3502	W.M.S.122	Chester Beatty Library	
3535	W.M.S.23	Morgan Library	Millar
3674	W.M.S.16	British Library	
3726	W.M.S.35	Harvard University	
3734	W.M.S.36	Walters Art Museum	

Phillipps MS no.	Beatty no.	Current location	Other owners
3897	W.M.S.70	Sir Paul Getty Library	
4259	W.M.S.54	Boston Public Library	
4448	W.M.S.58	Lincoln College Oxford	
4597	W.M.S.32	Stuttgart Landesbibliothek	
4600	W.M.S.68	Harvard	Hofer
4769	W.M.S.22	Chester Beatty Library	
6546	W.M.S.12	Biblioteca nazionale centrale di Roma	
6640	W.M.S.113	Chester Beatty Library	
6659	W.M.S.110	Bodmer Collection	
6972	W.M.S.114	New York Public Library	
7084	W.M.S.108	Chester Beatty Library	
8400	W.M.S.2	Biblioteca nazionale centrale di Roma	
10190	W.M.S.11	Yale University	
12200	W.M.S.59	British Library	
12260	W.M.S.4	Biblioteca nazionale centrale di Roma	
12261	W.M.S.3	British Library	Wilfrid Merton
12262	W.M.S.7	Biblioteca nazionale centrale di Roma	
12263	W.M.S.6	Biblioteca nazionale centrale di Roma	
12264	W.M.S.5	Biblioteca nazionale centrale di Roma	
12269	W.M.S.43	Chester Beatty Library	
12283	W.M.S.104	Harvard University	
12348	W.M.S.17	Chester Beatty Library	
14122	W.M.S.10	Walters Art Museum	
15364	Armenian Ms 558	Chester Beatty Library	
17364	W.M.S.167	Chester Beatty Library	
21163	W.M.S.105	Unknown	

Phillipps MS no.	Beatty no.	Current location	Other owners
21642	W.M.S.191	Unknown	De Coppet
21948	W.M.S.24	Morgan Library	Hornby, Abbey
36275	W.M.S.1	Morgan Library	

WORKS CITED

Burrows, Toby. 2018a. "Digital Representations of the Provenance of Medieval Manuscripts." In *Meeting the Medieval in a Digital World*, edited by Matthew Evan Davis, Tamsyn Mahoney-Steel, and Ece Turnator, 203–22. Leeds: Arc Humanities Press.

———. 2018b. "'There never was such a collector since the world began': A New Look at Sir Thomas Phillipps." In *Collecting the Past*, edited by Toby Burrows and Cynthia Johnston, 45–62. London: Routledge.

Cleaver, Laura. 2017. "The Western Manuscript Collection of Alfred Chester Beatty (ca. 1915–1930)." *Manuscript Studies: A Journal of the Schoenberg Institute for Manuscript Studies* 2.2: 445–82.

Cleaver, Laura, and Danielle Magnusson. 2018. "American Collectors and the Trade in Medieval Illuminated Manuscripts in London, 1919–1939: J. P. Morgan Junior, A. Chester Beatty and Bernard Quaritch Ltd." In *Collecting the Past*, edited by Toby Burrows and Cynthia Johnston, 63–78. London: Routledge.

Collections as Data Initiative. 2016–18. *Always Already Computational: Collections as Data*. Accessed 31 October 2018. https://collectionsasdata.github.io.

De Hamel, Christopher. 1991. "Chester Beatty and the Phillipps Manuscripts." *Book Collector* 40: 358–70.

———. 2016. *Meetings with Remarkable Manuscripts*. London: Allen Lane.

De Ricci, Seymour. 1930. *English Collectors of Books and Manuscripts (1530–1930) and Their Marks of Ownership*. Cambridge: Cambridge University Press.

Drucker, Joanna. 2014. *Graphesis: Visual Forms of Knowledge Production*. Cambridge, MA: Harvard University Press.

Horton, Charles. 2000. "'It was all a great adventure': Sir Alfred Chester Beatty and the formation of his Library." *History Ireland* 8: 37–42.

Kidd, Peter. 2015. "The Duprat Bible [Part 1]" *Medieval Manuscripts Provenance.* Blog, 1 August 2015. Accessed 31 October 2018. http://mssprovenance. blogspot.co.uk/2015/08/the-duprat-bible-part-i.html.

Munby, Alan Noel Latimer. 1951–1960. *Phillipps Studies*, 5 vols. Cambridge: Cambridge University Press.

Phillipps, Thomas. 1837–1871. *Catalogus librorum manuscriptorum in bibliotheca D. Thomæ Phillipps, Bart.* Middle Hill and Cheltenham: Middle Hill Press. Accessed 31 October 2018. https://archive.org/details/ CatalogusLibrorumManuscriptorum1837.

Van Bree, Pim, and Geert Kessels. 2015. "Mapping Memory Landscapes in *nodegoat.*" In *Social Informatics*, edited by L. M. Aiello and D. McFarland, 274–78. Lecture Notes in Computer Science 8852. Berlin: Springer International Publishing.

Van Bruggen, Rik. 2014. *Learning Neo4j.* Birmingham, UK: Packt Publishing.

Verborgh, Ruben, and Max De Wilde. 2013. *Using OpenRefine.* Birmingham, UK: Packt Publishing.

Weingart, Scott. 2011. "Demystifying networks, Parts I & II." *Journal of Digital Humanities* 1.1. Accessed 31 October 2018. http:// journalofdigitalhumanities.org/1-1/demystifying-networks-by-scott-weingart/.

TL;DR[1]: An Experimental Application of Text Analysis and Network Analysis to the Study of Historical Library Collections, in Particular the Title Catalogs of Four Libraries in the Western Holy Roman Empire in the Period 1606–1796, Accompanied by Some Methodological Speculations and Ideas for Further Research

Colin Wilder

Department of History, University of South Carolina

This essay is an experiment in applying some techniques from text analysis and network analysis to book history, specifically to the study of the title catalogs of four libraries in Germany in the seventeenth and eighteenth centuries. My goal is to make empirical discoveries about the collections that would be difficult or impossible to do through purely reading and studying the 1,296 titles contained in the four collections. For example, can we say what many of the books in the collections were *about*, at least based on their titles? Two of the four collections were law libraries and, as we will see, law books made up a surprising portion of the other libraries as well. First, I briefly discuss the domain of work—in time and space, and the model of library collections used here. Second, I account for the methods I employ and introduce the theory of distant reading that informs the study. Third, I present findings, in several areas—general findings, findings about law libraries in Marburg, and findings about the city library of Frankfurt. I contend that, despite the limitations of the methods, some real contributions to our knowledge about these collections and perhaps others like them can be made with these methods.[2]

---

[1] *TL;DR* is internet slang for *too long, didn't read*. It is often used to signal that the writer is going to give a very short synopsis of something that others are likely to find so long (or implicitly so boring) that they are unlikely to read much of it.

[2] An early, shorter version of this study was given as a paper at the conference Digitizing Enlightenment 2, held at Radboud University in Nijmegen (Netherlands). I am grateful to Alicia Montoya for her encouragement and for her support in helping me attend the conference. I am also grateful to the conference participants (especially Robert Morrissey, Katharine McDonough, Charles van den Heuvel, Dirk van Miert,

ISBN 978-1-64959-016-9 (paper) ISBN 978-1-64959-017-6 (pdf) ISBN 978-1-64959-037-4 (epub)

New Technologies in Medieval and Renaissance Studies 9 (2022) 113–156

A library is a world of potential knowledge. This is a common idea, almost a cliché, but nevertheless a valuable basic premise. More specifically, we can say that the books of a library give possibilities for understanding, and therefore of acting. If we consider the specific context of, for instance, a law library, we can discover a clear application: law books give judges ways of producing court decisions; jurists, ways of writing treatises; professors, ways of training students, and so on. Similar if perhaps not as acutely practical accounts can be given for the other kinds of libraries studied here. By extension, a library catalog is therefore one (if a crude) measure of the intellectual horizon of its patrons.[3]

Scope and object of study

The period studied is 1606–1796. A time span of 190 years is long for any study, much less for a single essay. But I think that a view of library collections in a *longue durée* is justified because collections changed slowly, though punctuated by sharp occasional change, as in wars or natural disasters. A metaphor from physics maybe useful: book collections housed in institutional settings are like *masses* of intellectual capital, persisting over a long period and undergoing only slow change, with *high inertia* and *strong gravitational pull* toward them. They tend to change more slowly than regimes or even political boundaries. For instance, one of the libraries studied here—the library of the University of Marburg—began with the expropriation of nineteen volumes from the monastic library of Alsfeld in 1527. It grew over the centuries, with no significant diminution. Through acquisitions including bequests it had grown to over one thousand volumes by 1610. The nine-thousand-volume Estoriana (library of Johann Georg Estor) was added to it by bequest in 1773. At my best guess, and according to the finding aids (*Findbücher*) at the university today, this collection is substantially still intact (Zedler 1896, 7, 28–31). By the metaphor of gravitational pull, I mean to suggest both the way in

and Lucas van der Deijl) for many helpful suggestions and further encouragement. The research on which this essay is based has been supported at times by grants from the University of South Carolina Office of the Vice President for Research and Office of the Provost. Research assistance in 2013 was performed by Axton Crolley. I presented a revised version of this essay at the Sixteenth Century Society and Conference in Milwaukee in October 2017. I am grateful for my fellow panelists and the audience members at that event for the feedback and suggestions.

[3] Obviously, a person might patronize more than one library, might own books as well as borrow them, and might receive intellectual influence from other sources than books. Detecting and rigorously measuring influence is notoriously difficult.

which large collections attract accession of other collections to them and the fact that people come from far and wide to read books in those collections.

The geographical scope of the present study is a region rather than an empire, a nation, a state, a city, or a single institution. I have chosen this geographical limiting unit because, in earlier research in the history of natural and civil law ideas in Germany, I have seen in great detail how schools and courts constituted a kind of regional network which professionals such as jurists traversed throughout their careers.[4] Concomitantly, a degree of regionalism is also apparent in legal scholarship, with jurists using a combination of important national (imperial) historical materials and materials of local origin that reflect local events and customs.[5]

Four book collections are studied in this essay, held at libraries in Marburg, Hanau, and Frankfurt, all in the Hessian and Rhine-Main region of Germany. The great majority of the books in the collections are in Latin.[6] Let me emphasize again that there was a strong connection binding many of the jurists, courts, and law schools around the region, despite the political separation of Marburg (in Hesse), the principality of Hanau (incorporated into Hesse in the late eighteenth century) and the free city of Frankfurt am Main. The first library was that of the Marburg Collective High Court (*Samthofgericht*, hereafter abbreviated S), in a manuscript dated 1705.[7] The Hessian principalities for several centuries were ruled by parallel major and cadet lines of the House of Brabant. From the sixteenth to the early eighteenth century, enough solidarity subsisted in the house to maintain the *Samthofgericht*, an old institution established to settle disputes ranging across the *Land* among nobles and to some extent between princes (Bettenhäuser 1964). S was a small collection, containing twenty-six books. The second library was that of the law faculty of the Marburg University Library (hereafter U), as given in a manuscript dated 1606.[8] U and S would have been closely linked since they significantly

---

[4] The European term *jurists* basically comprises private lawyers, government attorneys, professors, and judges.

[5] For an example of this, see the vita of Johann Georg Estor (1699–1773), professor of the University of Marburg and chancellor of the princely Hessian regime there (Wilder 2010, 167–68).

[6] About 80–90% of the texts in the four libraries are Latin. The remainder are German, French, and English in decreasing frequency.

[7] See Samthofgericht Catalogus librorum 1705.

[8] The eighty-seven books in U's law collection were cataloged by Hermann Vultejus (Professor and regime vice chancellor) and Johann Hartmann (MD, professor, librarian) on 9 September 1606. See Vultejus and Hartmann 1606.

shared personnel, with professors often serving as chancellors, vice chancellors, regents, assessors, or other high judicial roles in the princely regime, including sitting on high courts. U was a slightly larger collection, containing eighty-seven books. The third library was the Hanau Leihbibliothek or lending library (hereafter H), whose collection was cataloged in lists dated 1755, 1765, 1787, and 1796.[9] H was larger still than S or U, containing 350 books. Finally comes the largest collection, that of the Frankfurt Stadtbibliothek (city library, hereafter F), in a manuscript catalog dated 1691–1701. F is by far the largest, at 833 volumes.[10]

Simon Burrows makes a useful fourfold classification of types of historical bibliometric scholarship, that is, scholarship which uses quantitative or other technical methods to write the history of the book. The four types of scholarship are those investigating the *quantification of book production*; *reception studies* about readership, including book borrowing; projects which seek to *map* where printers, publishers, booksellers, were located; and *literary mapping projects* ("to understand, reinterpret, and analyze fictional literary texts through mapping their geographical settings") (Burrows 2015, 7, including notes 29–34).

My purpose in this essay is to do something seemingly simpler and more basic than any of these: to use quantitative methods to reconstruct the content of books, specifically large numbers of books grouped together in library collections. What were they about? In substance, this effort belongs to the earlier form of book history scholarship, represented in works by authors like Otto Brunner or Robert Darnton,[11] though in method and especially in tools this effort is a highly modern.

There are a number of empirical questions that we would like to be able to answer about historical library collections. First, we would ask about domain, scale, and contents: Which books were held in the libraries? What were they about? Do some genres, such as *dissertationes* or handbooks, appear with unusual frequency? Second, book historians are also very interested in

---

[9] See "Bücherverzeichnisse der Regierungsbibliothek zu Hanau" 1787–1836.

[10] The catalog of F was gathered by the librarian, Johann Martin Waldschmidt, in two manuscript catalogs, dated 1691–1701 and 1701–04. See Waldschmiedt 1691–1701. On the history of F, there are a number of works. The earliest scientific one was Nathusius-Neinstedt 1896. Most recently, see Allwörden 2006.

[11] Consider for instance Brunner's reconstruction of the intellectual horizon of Wolf Helmhard von Hohberg by way of the latter's library (Brunner 1949). For Darnton one may think of his genre or subgenre studies, such as Darnton 1971.

provenance: Where do books in a collection come from? What is the distribution of certain books—that is to say, where are certain important books held? Third: When were books acquired? Can we reconstruct longitudinal trends? Finally, what could be said about whole collections, parts of collections, and peer collections? Could we compare two collections, such as the two Marburg law libraries? Could we compare a given library to some other metric of collective book activity, e.g., book production and sales? Could we compare a library to the notional master set of period books produced by the magic of WorldCat? Building on answers to all of these questions, we might wish to pose further, interpretive questions: for instance, were some books more important than others?

Methodology

Dear reader, I want to let you down easy, up front. The most that I am going to be able to do in the rest of this essay is to apply a set of methods to try to answer the first and second questions just posed: which books were held and what they were about. If the results I present are persuasive, there is room for a great deal of further work to refine and extend these methods in pursuit of more elusive quarry in the future.

A number of quantitative methods for the study of textual sources have been adopted or developed by humanities scholars. Approaches of this sort have sometime been dubbed *distant reading*, a term coined by Franco Moretti in 2000. Moretti employed several basic quantitative methods, including mapping locations of scenes in stories and graphing various literary phenomena such as the number of various kinds of books published per year (Moretti 2005, 3–66). Matt Jockers has similarly applied methods like these via a database constructed by himself and Moretti dedicated to twentieth-century Irish-American literature (Jockers 2013, 35–62). In subsequent work, Moretti has experimented with using other quantitative methods for the study of texts in the humanities, such as creating network graphs to explore plot relations in drama (Moretti 2015, 211–40).

Critics of digital humanities and distant reading have sometimes assumed that such approaches implicitly displace close reading, the regnant method of humanities source interpretation. Is distant reading in fact reading at all? Whether this criticism is fair or accurate, the usual counter held up against it is that distant reading should be paired with close reading. That is what I will try to do here.[12]

---

[12] I tend to use the terms *distant reading* and *macroanalysis* interchangeably, since I am

There have been a few applications of distant reading methods and theory to the study of historical library collections. One example is Jockers's study of book titles, mentioned above. Jockers focuses principally on the measure of lexical richness, essentially the type-diversity of words in a given book title.[13] Another is recent work by scholars affiliated with the Digitizing Enlightenment project based at Radboud University.[14]

Like the latter work, my study of library collections focuses naturally on book *titles*. This requires an important assumption that should be formally stated at the outset: the title of a book approximates its content. When stated baldly like that, all kinds of red flags fly. But given the present state of digital archives, the size of historical collections, and the ambiguity of many cataloged titles, I believe that for the immediate future, using book titles for a "macroanalysis" offers the best balance for accuracy and scale—that is, an accurate calculation of what books were about with the possibility of doing analysis on a large scale.

For each library catalog, the following data preparation and analysis steps were taken: preprocessing/data normalization; creation of types and n-grams; and tabulation, graphing, and miscellaneous analysis.

The preprocessing stage involves several steps. One basic task to prepare a text for any kind of computational analysis is to clean and normalize it. That

hard-pressed to say how they substantively differ. A signal critic of digital humanities and distant reading from the side of philology has been Stanley Fish. See Fish 2012.

[13] By this measure, "it is possible to examine the degree to which the 'title lexicon' of a given period is or is not homogenous. Using title data, we can approximate the lexical variety of titles in the marketplace at any given time. . . . In the early years of the corpus, there is greater heterogeneity among the titles; that is, there is a higher percentage of unique words than in later periods. In practical terms, what this means is that the potential reader browsing titles in the 1820s would have found them very diverse (in terms of their vocabularies—and, by extension, their presumed subjects), whereas a reader of more recently published texts would find greater similarity among the titles available on this hypothetical bookshelf" (Jockers 2013, 55–56). Such an approach is not rigorously applicable to the study of library collections in this essay, however, since publication dates for titles in the catalogs were only available for two of the four collections. Making an analysis like this will have to wait for further source and data acquisition in the future.

[14] For instance, a paper by Simon Burrow at the conference Digitizing Enlightenment 2 (organized by Alicia Montoya) analyzed the holdings and circulation patterns of books in England during the Enlightenment.

means to transform all inflections of a word into a single form of the "head word," usually the nominative form. This is called *lemmatization*, meaning changing a given instance (token) of a word into its "head" form (type). For instance, we would transform *runs*, *run*, and *ran* all into run, or *theoretica* and *theoretico* into *theoreticus*. The other major preprocessing task is to remove "stop words," that is, articles, pronouns, numbers, most common verbs (like *be* or *go*), and so on. For instance, normalization changes *Decisiones Sev Diffinitiones Cavsarum Pervsinarum & Prouinciae Umbriae* [Decisions or rulings of disputes in Perugia and the Province of Umbria] (Frankfurt am Main: 1573)), edited by Giuseppe Ludovisi (found in U), to simply *decisio diffinitio causa perusia provincia umbria*.

The basis of the lemmatization was done with the Classical Language Toolkit (CLTK) developed by Luke Hollis, Kyle P. Johnson, and Patrick J. Burns (Hollis et al. 2014–17). CLTK uses a built-in Latin dictionary. I found that it gave accurate or appropriate results on only about half of the tokens, however—obviously a very low success rate. CLTK permits you to pass it a custom dictionary, which I used to both lemmatize the non-Latin titles (French and German, with one English periodical thrown in) and get the software to swallow the considerable amount of non-standard spelling used in early modern writing. On account of these adversities, my custom dictionary ultimately grew to 2,444 tokens, out of a total of 2,794 total unique tokens and 5,718 total non-unique tokens in all titles in all libraries.[15] In order to process large numbers of book titles in multiple library catalogs, I incorporated the CLTK and code from the Programming Historian into a new suite of modules, which have been made freely available on GitHub (Wilder 2017a).

The basic method used in this study is network analysis, specifically the application of network analysis to the distant reading of texts.[16] Several intuitions lie behind this application. First, we might treat a given set of texts (the four catalogs) as constituting a synchronic pool of language or ideas,

---

[15] Thus, the CLTK had a success rate on my data of about 13%. I do not regard this relatively low rate as a major failure of CLTK. I am indebted to its developers for producing a very useful tool that made my work much easier. I regard the low rate as chiefly a result of the dirtiness of my catalogs' titles, the presence of a lot of non-Latin, and the general inconstancy of early modern spelling.

[16] The phrases *network analysis* and *social network analysis* are often used interchangeably in scholarly and popular contexts. This seems to be true even when the kind of analysis being done is not about people primarily ("social") but about something else, as in the application to words in book titles, in this essay.

embodied in the texts (the titles of the 1,296 titles held by the four libraries). Second, words are close to one another in a text because they are semantically linked, meaning that they go together to describe the same thing, to approach the same topic. Third, the proximities of words as just described can be tallied and counted in order to produce subsequent metrics which will help us understand all of the language in all of the texts together. For books in libraries held in states in the Holy Roman Empire, we will find *Holy* and *Roman* linked by proximity, and *Roman* and *Empire* linked, and *Holy* and *Empire* close together as well. The reason for this is that they are often referring to the Holy Roman Empire, whether the language is English, French, German, or Latin. The farther apart we find the words *Holy*, *Roman*, and *Empire* in a text, the less likely they are referring together to the Holy Roman Empire.

This is not the first such application of network analysis to the study of texts, but seems to be unique in certain ways. In the past, network analysis has been used in three ways to study texts. First, it has been used to model exchange of information or things among people. The network model has been applied loosely as a tool of conceptualization for the exchange of information (as in correspondence networks, networks of circulation of objects, putative networks of knowledge transmission via printers).[17] Other applications of network analysis to humanities research model real-world actors as nodes, representing connections between the actors as edges. Thus, edges represent routes of interaction or information-sharing. Second, network analysis has been used to model the plot of narrative works (Moretti 2013, 211–40). Finally, network analysis has been used to model social relations among *people*, based on co-occurrence of names in *textual* materials. This is the approach taken in scholarly projects such as *Six Degrees of Francis Bacon*, which uses co-occurrence of names on pages of the *Oxford Dictionary of National Biography* (*ODNB*).[18]

After preprocessing, the next step I have taken is to produce synthetic objects for computational analysis: n-grams. *N-grams* are the collective name for combinations of *n* words which are immediately adjacent to one another. Bigrams are two-word combinations, trigrams are three-word combinations, and so on. The procedure of making bigrams can be easily illustrated. In the

[17] See for instance the project Circulation of Knowledge at the Huygens Institute, Netherlands, under the leadership of Charles van den Heuvel.

[18] The Six Degrees of Francis Bacon, directed by Christopher Warren, hosted by the Carnegie Mellon University Libraries. Accessed 30 October 2017. http://www.sixdegreesoffrancisbacon.com.

nursery rhyme *The cow jumped over the moon*, here are the bigrams: *the cow, cow jumped, jumped over, over the*, and *the moon*.

Since word order is not strictly required for meaning in Latin, two words may mean the same thing whether they are neighbors or are separated from one another by one or more other words. N-grams can capture the former situation, but since they only count immediate adjacency, they cannot capture the latter. Fortunately, linguists have devised a variant of n-grams that can collect word pairs that are not immediate neighbors: *skip-grams* (short for *k skip n-grams*). For instance, a k skip bigram or skip two-gram is a form of bigram that may represent two words that sit adjacent to one another in a text *or* may be separated from each other by as many as *k* other tokens. Thus, in the example text of *The cow jumped over the moon*, both *cow-jumped* and *cow-over* would be one-skip bigrams, or k skip bigrams where k=1. But *cow-over* would not be a *normal* bigram because *cow* and *over* are not adjacent to one another.[19]

The reason it is useful to deconstruct a text into bigrams in particular is that a bigram is a pair of linked words. Two linked words can be straightforwardly modeled as a pair of nodes in a network linked by an edge. Thus, the n-gram *cow jumped* can be modeled as two linked nodes, *cow* and *jumped*.[20]

While working to find and apply methods appropriate to the computational study of my texts, I came to the conclusion that several of the commonly used metrics in network analysis seem to have less utility when applied to texts. In network analysis, *node degree* is usually considered to be one of the most important network measures. Node degree refers to the number of edges connecting a given node to other nodes. In network analysis, degree is considered to be a chief indicator of a node's importance. However, I reason that node degree is actually an unimportant or even misleading metric in text networks. Thus, a high node degree indicates that the node is found in bigrams with many different word types. Which really means that it does not have a particularly strong semantic attractiveness (i.e., it is not drawn to a few things in particular, but rather equally to many). *Node weight* reflects frequency of the appearance of a given word type. *Edge weight* reflects frequency of the appearance of a given bigram type. These will be similar but not the same, since there are some isolate word types (e.g., a book whose title is simply *Opera*) that may appear several times (thus have a high node weight) but

---

[19] For discussion of skip-grams, see Guthrie et al. 2006.

[20] In this essay I often use the terms *n-grams* and *edges* interchangeably.

connect to other words seldom because they usually are the sole title word (thus have low-weight or few edges extending from them).

One typical measure of network topology is to detect *communities*. As the term implies, communities in networks are supposed to model various concrete, natural, social associations, such as friendships, exchange patterns, or influence. In network analysis, the technical methods for detecting communities, such as clustering algorithms, use *network density* as their basis.[21] That is, these methods depend on relatively low graph density to be effective—basically, the idea is that you can only detect meaningful communities if there are not nominal connections between everything. As word distance is increased, median node degree increases and density increases, so that more and more nodes connect to one another. As all nodes increasingly connect to each other, discrete communities of difference and separation disappear. If everyone says they are friends with everyone else, you have no good data about what the actual friendship cliques are. In the application to text analysis, the implication would be that you could only usefully apply community detection in situations where there is low density, meaning that not every word is associated with every other. But since we are using skip-grams (for good reason), the number of connections is somewhat arbitrary. This implies to me that it may not be appropriate to apply clustering algorithms to word networks, at least where Latin texts predominate.[22]

To detect semantic communities in this essay, I instead apply to text networks a network technique called *triangles*. Triangles may be thought of as the smallest possible community of words—a triangle is any three words that are found together (given a certain rule to govern what does and does not count as association, e.g., word distance or collocation). Triangles may be ranked based on the weights of the three edges that make them up, possibly either summing them or averaging them.[23] Triangles that are ranked high represent frequent co-occurrence of three words, such as *corpus-iuris-civilis* or *corpus-iuris-canonicus*.[24] I will explain the method of constructing triangles

---

[21] One such algorithm is the Louvain method.

[22] The way that the "skip" distance affects density is depicted in Graph 6, discussed below.

[23] For sum of edge weights in network triangles, see Gupta et al. 2016.

[24] Triangles are similar to but not the same as either trigrams or k-skip trigrams. A trigram is a sequence that actually exists in a text in which three words, A B C, are found together. Triangle D-E-F is an artifact created through synopsis of all bigrams taken together; the bigram D E may actually be found together, likewise bigram E F

in greater detail when reporting the first set of results, those for the Marburg libraries, in the next section.

In the following study, simple software written in Python has been used to create usable lists of tokens, types, and skip-grams. The code for this has been made freely available at GitHub (Wilder 2017b).[25] Graphs were constructed using the software Gephi (Bastian et al. 2009).

Limitations and risks of the methods employed

Before proceeding to the results of the study, I would like to foreground the limitations of using these methods. I must admit at the outset that, generally, it can seem like computational text analysis has (only) retrodictive validity; perhaps we only see what we already knew, and therefore do not learn much that is new. The reader will have to judge.

More specifically, I think that use of the above methods may invite three misfortunes: removal of words (preprocessing to remove stop words), simplification of language (in lemmatization), and breaking up of sense (via bigrams and network analysis).

Removal of words distorts word proximity. Thus, words that are not very close to one another in an original text may become close after preprocessing, and get made into bigrams.[26]

Lemmatization reduces the number of distinct symbols in a text, to some extent transforming diversity into sameness (e.g., both *gratiam* and *gratias* are reduced to gratias). It seems logical that this problem would be more acute in a small language like Latin.

---

and bigram D F, but the trigram D E F need not actually exist.

[25] I would like to note that there is an unintended resemblance between the title "Text Networks" for my software and that of recent scholarship by a colleague of mine at the University of South Carolina (see Gavin 2016). It is possible that the name for the software occurred to me in conversations with him, although I do not believe that there is much similarity between the analyses undertaken in his work and in my essay.

[26] Consider the following example: the preprocessing transformation of Laude 1550 (in U), whose full title is *Consilia : aurea quidem sunt haec ac pene divina responsa*. After preprocessing, the title becomes *consilium aureus pene divinus responsum*. The underlined tokens are all removed as stop words from the original title. This excision makes *aurea* appear to be immediately adjacent to *pene* and one stop from *divina*.

The very use of bigrams as a way of reconstructing text is also ambiguous. While it enables us to measure word proximity, and thus approach measuring meaning itself, it terribly lames the meaning of text at the same time. The verb is the life of the sentence, and most verbs are either transformed into a meaningless uninflected form or removed altogether respectively by lemmatization and the removal of stop words.[27] The former also makes word order and noun case unintelligible. Without directional word order or inflections, the sense of titles is lost. (In the case of nouns alone, consider the difference in meaning of *origin of species* and *species of origin*—which produce one and the same bigram!)

The methods employed here also treat all titles as equally important, whether long or short. This seems like a potentially bad idea. There are a lot of titles that are something like "On Possession" or "Royal *Consilia*." These will produce few bigrams and thus little text-network information compared with long titles. Thus, one book (with a short title) can produce perhaps a single data point (one bigram) while another book (with a long title) can produce many data points (and thus many bigrams). Yet I intuit that each book should be permitted to contribute only as much data as any other book.

With all of these risks, I believe that the results and interpretation offered in what follows should be taken with a grain of salt.

Results for the two Marburg libraries

The rest of this essay presents the results of the application of the methods above to the 1,296 book titles contained in S, U, H, and F.

In the four catalogs, there are a total of 1,296 titles. See Table 1 for a grand summary of the results of constructing n-grams for the four libraries, as well as the number of titles in each library. The average original title length was 5.8 words, the median 4.0 words. After preprocessing and lemmatization, the average was 4.4 and the median 3.0. This means that 1.4 words in the average title are what can be considered insignificant or "stop" words, such as numbers (decem), "no" (ne, non), etc.—about one in four words of the title.[28]

---

[27] The notion that "the verb is the life of the sentence" comes from the work of Irad Kimhi. See Kimhi 2018.

[28] Here is an example of before and after that processing: *Tractatus de commissariis et commissionibus camera imperiali* (seven tokens) becomes *tractatus commissarus commissio cammer imperium* (five tokens).

The more specific findings that follow fall in two areas. The first is a report on the two law library collections. This (a) reveals things not previously known about such libraries while also (b) implicitly demonstrating the efficacy of the suite of methods used. I then make a similar examination of the Frankfurt city library, the largest collection in my set of four sources.

S and U were both law libraries, with catalogs of respectively twenty-six and eighty-seven books. In the titles of the 113 books held in the two Marburg law library collections, there were 417 distinct words (types) amid 726 word tokens.

Table 2 depicts the frequencies of all word types which appear five or more times in the two libraries' cataloged titles. The most frequently appearing terms are law words, unsurprisingly, with terms like *jus* (law), appearing twenty-seven times (3.7% of all tokens), and *consilium* and *opus* appearing with great frequency as well (respectively 2.6% and 2.3%). (As Graph 1 and Graph 2 show, the great majority of words [again, types] appear only once.)

We could generalize to say that typical titles in law libraries describe themselves as *books or works of law, decisions, counsels, commentaries,* etc. This may seem obvious and unsurprising.

The way that *law* appears and connects with other words can be seen via skip-gram analysis. Making and then ranking one-skip bigrams (i.e., bigrams permitting a word distance of two) shows that by far the most commonly associated pair of words across all 113 titles in the two libraries is *jus-civile*, civil law.[29] This reflects the predominance of civil law over other kinds of law (canon law, ecclesiastical law, natural law, etc.). The most frequently appearing bigrams are given in Table 3. Other frequently occurring pairings are about the body of one or another kind of law, such as the body of canon law or the *body* of civil law. These refer to the major, canonical ancient and medieval source collections for civil and canon law.

A graph of the most frequently appearing skip-grams in S and U is shown in Graph 3. The large interconnected swarm shape on the right is the graph's *giant connected component*, or largest subgraph of the whole.[30] The center of this central component is clearly *jus*, law. This graph gives an adequate picture of the major semantic links in the set of law titles, showing the centrality of

---

[29] one-skip bigrams are even more greatly stacked toward unique appearances than the ordinary bigrams we made first, with 1,455 out of the total of 1,510 bigram types appearing only once.

[30] For giant connected components, see Caldarelli and Catanzaro 2012, 42–45.

terms like law, counsel (*consilium*), the *Digest of Roman Law*, civil law, the Holy Roman Empire (in the lower left), and other terms.

As discussed above in the Methodology, I believe that the method of constructing triangles makes more sense for detecting meaningful "communities" of words in texts than do clustering algorithms based on subnetwork density. The triangles of a graph are all *complete triads* in the graph, that is, the set of all sets of any three nodes where all three nodes are connected by edges. In part, I was guided by the idea that many associations appear once and never again, even in a large set of texts. Therefore, when constructing the triangles here, I decided to treat bigrams with frequency = 1 as "noise" and exclude them from the construction process. Specifically, I removed all edges with a weight of (only) 1, since the vast majority of nodes have a degree of 1 (the word type appears once) and the vast majority of n-grams have a weight of 1 (the n-gram type appears once). In this essay, I hope to convince the reader that triangles help us detect communities of nodes in a more meaningful way in text analysis than do other kinds of community detection.

Preliminary examination of triangles for S and U (taken together[31]) appear to confirm that the method detects meaningful communities of words—that is, we see in the triangles what we would expect to see, do not see anything that seems unlikely, and *prima facie* nothing seems missing. See Table 4 and Graph 4. The graph represents all triangles, whose edges all have a weight of 2 or more, for the two Marburg law libraries together (113 books total between them). This graph strikes me as a satisfying result: it shows connected legal terms which all make perfect sense given the context. I cannot say offhand that any concepts seem missing. (Note that there is no particular meaning to the arrangement of nodes and edges: above, below, left, right, etc.) In Graph 4, we see *heilig-roma-reich*; the *Heiliges Römisches Reich* (Holy Roman Empire) is a set of three word types that appear frequently together. Likewise, *recessus-imperium-cameralis* (recess-imperial-chamber). *Herr Land Graf Hesse* refers to the prince of the largest territory in the region, which both Marburg libraries belonged to: the landgrave of Hesse. Similarly, in the bigger subnetwork to the right in Graph 4, several standard pieces from the law of the period can be seen: *jus-consilium-responsum* (counsels and responses of law), *corpus juris canonici, corpus iuris civilis*, the pandects (of civil law), and so on.[32]

---

[31] That is, all titles in both libraries were combined and preprocessed; edges were constructed and weighed, and then triangles were constructed and ranked by total triangle weight.

[32] Books in S whose titles would generate these triangles include Stucke 1666, Seiler 1572, and *Aller deß Heiligen Römischen Reichs* [. . .] 1660.

To repeat for clarity: the edges in Graph 4 are a subset of all of the n-grams found collectively in S and U. But in a graph of triangles like Graph 4, only those edges are shown which form complete, closed triangles. Rather than simply rank the triangles by frequency, I experimented with a different way of ranking them: total edge weight. (See caption to Table 4.) This preserves the role of the triangles as a filtering mechanism to show only those relationships which reflect substantial communities of words, while still allowing edge weight (= skip-gram frequency) to provide rich information about significance.

To test the triangle approach further, I have also calculated all of the n-grams for the two Marburg law libraries using a higher word distance of four. The resulting triangles for n-grams calculated with word distance = 4 are graphed in Graph 5. Increasing the word distance to four means that k skip bigrams (i.e., four-skip bigrams) can be formed from a pair of words that can be separated from one another by as many as four other words. Doing this produces a larger number of bigrams than using word distance = 2. (Graph 6 shows results of a testing the number of n-grams produced for word distances between one and one hundred. Obviously, the number of n-grams increases rapidly, but plateaus after word distance gets to about twenty.) The same triangles found in Graph 4 are of course present here, but so are other ones: *abschied* is connected by its own triangle to the Holy Roman Empire triangle found earlier: This refers to an imperial resolution made at the diet, probably the Diet of Regensburg (depending on the year). We also find new language connected to *ius*, with triangles referring to things such as a commentary on the civil law, book (*tomus*) of civil law, and *locuples* (*rich*: perhaps a rich or high-quality summary). In the bottom right we find something like "new and old decisions," probably of a specific court. Thus, this variant set of triangles based on skip-grams of a higher word distance produces new results that seem correct. Based on this and the lower-k triangle set, the triangle method seems to acquit itself well as a technique of distant reading.

I elected to introduce the triangle construction method on a relatively small scale and in a context that we would expect to have a closed set of semantics (law, which has a controlled, recurring set of terms). In the remainder of this study, I will expand the use of triangles to explore larger, less closed title sets. The above demonstrations with word distance 2 and 4 (represented in Graph 4 and Graph 5) showed the soundness of the method: the libraries were small enough, and they and their titles and the work done by the jurists connected to them were familiar enough to me, that I was comfortable making certain judgment calls in writing the algorithms to create the triangles, such as removing edges with a weight of only 1. The triangle method applied to texts of this kind should obviously be vetted in other contexts and on other data sets, but this is a promising start.

In the two Marburg libraries, there is a mystery of a dog that doesn't bark: we find little indication of feudalism in the book titles. Specifically, there are no n-grams involving the language of feudalism in U or S. Further, feudalist terms only barely make it into the word distribution presented above.[33] This does not reflect a lack of feudalist terms in book titles of the era. I think instead that it reflects the famous reception of Roman law in Germany, the process by which ancient Roman sources and commentary on them attained a position of strength (hegemony, in the eyes of some) in German legal practice until well into the modern era (Wieacker 1995, 132–42). But the scarcity of feudalist sources in these libraries is nevertheless surprising because the study of feudal legal sources, the collecting and editing of them, and the comparison of them with Roman civil sources were very common forms of scholarship for jurists including many of the members of the Marburg law faculty and those who sat on the *Samthofgericht*. I think that this mystery is solved by considering the difference between book titles and book contents. Fief real estate and real rights were the almost universal norm, and the terms *fief*, *feudal*, etc., are strewn frequently throughout both legal primary sources (e.g., estate custumals) and interpretive works (e.g., treatises, court decisions). However, feudalist terminology is much less common in book titles, which were usually in Latin and thus tended overwhelmingly to use Roman legal terms—largely to the exclusion of feudal and customary terms.[34]

By contrast to the missing feudalism, the importance of authority and expertise comes through clearly in the book titles. A form of precedent was

---

[33] *Lehn* (fief) and *germanicus* (etc.) can sometimes be used as proxies for feudal law, at least for heuristic purposes. But only one book in the two libraries has *Germany* in its title and none mentions fiefs.

[34] Consider the example of Senckenberg 1735, held in H. With a general Latin title indicating "select bits of law and history, rare but now edited," nothing would nominally indicate elements of feudal or customary law. But the chapters of the volume contain contributions to German and French history on the origin of the House of Brabant; the Nivellensis genealogical chronicle; the clan history of the Salic (German) Emperor Conrad II; local legal customs from Hesse in the sixteenth century; a chronicle of the town of Amoeneburg in the environs of Marburg in Hesse up to 1479; and two others. The local legal customs were later printed as "Stadt- und Landesbrauch" 1749.

operative in the German civil law context, albeit not as precise and binding as in the unified royal common law system that developed in England.[35] In imperial and princely courts, there was a great deal of reverence for expert opinion represented in the decisions of other courts (most especially imperial, Saxon, and Italian) and the expert opinions of law faculties, individual law professors, and other jurists. In the first category (decisions) you find a lot of books in the two collections typified by the likes of David Mevius's *Decisiones super causis praecipuis ad summum tribunal regium Vismariense delatis* (in the edition of Frankfurt am Main: s.d.) (S) or Johann Meichsnerus et al., eds., *Decisiones Diversarvm Cavsarvm In Camera Imperiali Ivdicatarvm Adivnctis Relationibus Actorum* (Frankfurt am Main: 1604) (S). In this category it is particularly worth noting the prominence of books representing the decisions of the imperial chamber court (*Reichskammergericht*), which represented the highest formal level of juridical and jurisprudential authority in the empire.[36] In the category of books of expert counsels and responses to inquiries belong works like *Consilia feudalia ex vaiorum scriptis diligentissime collecta* (Leiden: 1570) (U) or Pier Filippo Corneo, ed., *Consilia* (Venice: 1572) (U). A complementary point is that the law libraries contain very few titles indicating studies of specific legal problems or concepts. Most use general language ("all the decisions of the royal council," etc.).[37] A specific finding that runs contrary to conventional narratives of legal history is the presence of a surprising number of works of canon law in the two law libraries. Canon law is the general term used to describe all forms of law created and applied by episcopal (and in some cases monastic) authorities, beginning in about the tenth century, though with earlier biblical and patristic sources as well.[38] Typical materials of the *Corpus Iuris Canonici* or body of canon law are, for example, decisions of clerical courts and decrees by popes and bishops.[39] Canon law makes up a significant part of the two law library collections—four of the twenty-six titles

---

[35] On precedent in civil law countries, see for instance Baade 2002 and Silving 1996.

[36] I write *formal* because it would probably be correct to say that other jurists, like Hugo Grotius and Samuel Pufendorf in the seventeenth century or Chancellor Ludewig or Christian Thomasius in the eighteenth century, were more highly revered for their jurisprudence. Of course, formal authority and expertise are not the same thing.

[37] Exceptions that prove the rule are works like Angelo Gambiglioni et al., *De maleficiis . . . de inquirendis animadvertendisque criminibus opus . . .* (Leiden: 1551) (U) on combatting witchcraft or Bartholomaeus Blarer, *Repetitio solemnis L. diffamari cod. de ingen. manumiss. et commendatio in eandem Joh. Bendorpii* (Basel: 1579) (U) on slander.

[38] For an accessible overview of medieval canon law, see Berman 1983, 1–272.

[39] The *Corpus Iuris Canonici* may be thought of as the supertitle for all law of all Western Christian churches under the authority of the papacy.

of the *Samthofgericht* and nine of the eighty-seven titles of the law faculty, respectively about 15% and 10% of their collections.[40] This was established by counting all titles containing types which are firm markers of canon law: *canon**, *decretum*, *decretale*, and *utriusque*.

In Protestant Northern Germany, why do the law libraries have so many works of canon law—heavily identified with the medieval Catholic Church? Martin Luther famously burned books of canon law in a bonfire on December 20, 1520. I imagine that the answer is twofold. Some of the books probably represented legacy works—donated, inherited, or otherwise acquired without significant meaning, or even holdovers from before the anti-canonistic furor of the Reformation Era. This probably explains the presence of volumes such as Gratian's *Decretum* and the *Decretals* of Pope Gregory IX, both published in Leiden in 1528. But on the other hand, much legal learning was quietly retained and incorporated into the law reformations and new civil and criminal codes of Protestant states in Germany.[41] This was a matter both of the retention of specific books and of their substantial incorporation into cutting-edge jurisprudence. In the catalogs here, examples of this are editions of Gratian's *Decretum* and the *Decretals* of Pope Gregory IX, both published in Leiden in 1528. But other, new editions of canon law were created or acquired later, such as Giovanni Paolo Lancelotti's edition of Pope Gregory XIII's *Corpus juris canonici emendatum et illustratum* (Cologne: 1696) or Hermann Vultejus et al., *Tractatus de judiciis, in libros IV divisus : Quo judiciorum natura in genere & processus judiciarius in specie accuratißime ex Jure Civili, Canonico, Receßibus Imperii & moribus hodiernis traditur & explicatur* (Cassel: 1654). Some, like the last-named work by Vultejus et al., are clearly modern works that incorporate earlier canon law. The reason for this can only be that these uniformly Protestant jurists, in securely Protestant (Reformed) Hesse, had a quiet reverence for the rules, institutions, and ideas of earlier ecclesiastics, notwithstanding modern bloody religious conflict. Vultejus's book was about courts and court procedures, including ecclesiastical. In fact, Protestant jurists since the heyday of the Reformation had been writing treatises on subjects originally native to canon law. Examples of this include the work of Johann Oldendorp (on equity, 1541) and famously that of Hugo Grotius (on natural rights, 1625).[42]

---

[40] By contrast, there is very little canon law in the other two larger libraries H and F. Respectively, canon law makes up six books out of a total 350 at H, and four books out of a total 833 at F.

[41] See for instance Berman 2003, 100–75.

[42] Brian Tierney makes just such an argument about Grotius's incorporation of Span-

But the limits of the canon law texts in the two libraries should also be noted. These limits can be quickly appreciated by examining the four (only four) triangles produced from these canon law titles (see Table 4): (1) *canonicus - corpus - jus,* (2) *corpus - glossa - jus,* (3) *canonicus - corpus - glossa,* and (4) *canonicus - glossa - jus.* They all basically add up to "body of the canon law" and glosses on the body of law. There is little more detail than this, which reflects the fact that, while we see books like Vultejus's in the collection making use of canon law in a more specialized study (of procedure), most of the works are just general collections of canon sources. This suggests to me that while jurists liked to make comparative reference or generic accounts of legal institution—including earlier canon law forms and ideas—they had little interest in doing deep studies of special areas of canon law.

A rough comparison of the holdings of the two law libraries S and U and the other two libraries H and F can be made by comparing overall appearance of words that are clear markers of law. Data for such a comparison are given in Table 5, showing the most frequent twenty word types in S and U (taken together), F, and H. *Jus* is commonly found in the titles of all the libraries, indicating that a large number of law books are found in all the collections—making up an astounding 7.6–12.2% of all words in all titles in all catalogs. Further, the Hanau catalog actually exhibits a higher overall incidence of certain characteristic law words, such as *corpus, imperium,* and *ius,* in several cases marginally higher than even that of the two law libraries. But for all of this evidence of a general cross-library interest in law, it remains at a very general level in H and F. The more specialized terminology—such as *canonicus, decretum, glossa,* or *utriusque*—appears far less frequently in H and F. Most books in H that pertain to law are not much more specialized than collections of imperial or princely edicts (e.g., *Hanauische Verordnungen 1566–1793* (2 vols., n.d., n.p.) and general works such as Denis Godefroy's edition of the *Corpus Iuris Civlis* (Frankfurt am Main: 1587). Infrequent or altogether absent are more specialized works like those of Lancelotti or Vultejus, mentioned above.

Results for the Frankfurt library

Moving on from the law libraries, I would now like to briefly present a study of the contents of the Frankfurt city library (F). While it may be impossible to construct an ideal type of the contents of an early modern city library, owing to inevitable diversity, a few remarks can be made about the Frankfurt city library—especially in comparison to the other three libraries, close as they are to one another in region and time.

---

ish scholastic sources (Tierney 1997, 316–42).

As with the Marburg library studies, I began with a word frequency ranking of the 833 titles in F. The thirty-six words that appear nine or more times are given in Table 6. Table 6 conveys some sense of the importance of words connected to Germany, Catholicism, and history. My initial supposition based only on the table therefore was that German, Catholic, and history books might be important clusters of meaning. I proceeded next to make the triangles, the ones with the highest total weight being given in Table 7.

The interconnections among words in the Frankfurt library titles—and their separations—are vividly revealed in Graph 7. French title words about the Catholic faith, church, and clergy appear in two distinct clusters toward the left.[43] Greek and Hebrew philology appear on the top, the Frankfurt law reformation of 1578 in the center left,[44] and so on. But the graphing is particularly valuable for revealing the interconnectedness of terms relating to history, law (*jus*), and German things in the book titles. These and many other words connect to one another like a clique in the giant connected component on the right side. This giant component is also the site of the heaviest nodes and edges, reflecting their relative frequency among all nodes and edges. In order to examine this giant component better, I isolated and loosened the graph up a little, as shown in Graph 8.[45] Graph 8 really helps illustrate the prominence and connectedness of history terminology in the F titles. Further investigation and calculations reveal just how significant history is in the collection. As can be seen in Table 6, *history* words are the most frequently used words in the Frankfurt city library title: cognates and inflections of *history* such as *historia*, *historicus*, and *histoire*) appear eighty-nine times in the library of 833 titles, or in 10.7% of the book titles.[46] I propose that two other words, which most often signal history books, be added to this, namely *scriptor* (nineteen times) and *chronicon* (fifteen times).[47] If all of these are aggregated, the total

---

[43] There is far more Catholic material in this library than in S or U. Of the eighty-seven significant triangles, seven (about 8%) represent trifold Catholic semantics, such as "catholicus eglise foy." Other Catholic triangles express such relationships as "catholicus foy touchant" or "catholicus foy perpetuite." Notably, the Catholic works are almost all in French.

[44] F held the important codification of this law reformation: Fichard 1578.

[45] It should be borne in mind that the position of nodes is a meaningless feature of graphs.

[46] This is calculated by adding up the appearances of *historia* (fifty-four times), *historicus* (eighteen times), and *histoire* (seventeen times).

[47] *Scriptor* means *writer*, but in the context of the period the word is very often used to mean a writer of history, secondarily ancient religious writers such as the apostles

appearance of history books weighs in at 123 appearances, or 14.8% of all words in all titles, and in fact in 104 out of those 833 titles (12.5% of them)— basically, about one in eight books in F was a history book. This is the largest plurality of any semantic marker I have sought or found in the book titles. For comparison, in the other non-specialized library here studied, H, *historia* words including *chronicon* appear a total of sixteen times in the tokens of the 350 titles, or 4.6% (only twenty out of 350 titles, or 5.7%). It seems pretty straightforward to conjecture that history books made up a large part of the Frankfurt city library, at least in comparison to other semantic markers and to one other significant, non-specialized regional library.[48]

The graph also helps us see easily what these history books were about, through direct edges between the history words and other words—*kirche* and *eccelsiastes* (church), *ketzer* (heretics), *franc* (the Franks), works of history, *old-history-church,* historical matter (*res*), writer of history, and so forth. Examples of history titles held in F include Johannes Isacius Pontanus's *Rerum Danicarum historia* (Amsterdam: 1631), Gebhard Florian's *Chronica der Handelstadt Frankfurt am Mayn* (Frankfurt am Main: 1664), and Gilbert Burnet's *Historia Reformationis ecclesiae Anglicanae* (Geneva: 1689).

The triangle analysis also helps us detect what could be called a "Germanistic" theme. By this I mean a special interest in what the Germans call *Germanistik*, that is, study of Germanic culture, ancient sources, and so on. Six of the eighty-seven significant triangles (6.9%) express distinctly Germanic associations, e.g., *germanus-res-vetus* or *germanus imperium romanus*—ancient Germanic matters and the German-Roman Empire. The prominence of Germanistics is also attested by the fact that the tokens *German** and *Deutsch/ Teutsch*, taken together, appear forty times in the titles, when the average type frequency is 2.13 and the median is 1. Germanistic n-grams, also thus identified, likewise are among the most frequent. There are twenty-six appearances of such n-grams, when the mean is 1.1 and median 1.0. Some examples of books in F matching this description include works examining the German historical aspect of the Holy Roman Empire (e.g., Hermann Conring, *De Finibus Imperii Germanici* (1654), studies of medieval German manuscripts and insignias (e.g., Marquard Freher *Germanicarum rerum* (1600), and histories of institutions denoted as German (rather than non-national or

---

or other church fathers.

[48] There were far more history books in F than in H, S, or U. The paucity in S and U is not prima facie surprising though since the two Marburg libraries were special law collections.

other-national) (e.g., Kaspar Brusch, *Monasteriorum Germaniae praecipuorum chronologia* (1551). Prominence of Germanistics in F is particularly surprising to me for two reasons. First, marker words for it were fleeting in S and U.[49] Second, as in the case of feudalistic topics, I would expect that the incidence of Germanistic title elements would be higher in law libraries than in other, non-specialized libraries. My belief is that Germanistic titles are sublimated into the other law library titles, so they go hidden.

Summary

It sometimes seems that distant reading has only retrodictive validity, telling us things that we more or less already knew, or could more or less have come up with by close reading and thoughtful reflection. But I think this is unfair. As with automation in many fields, from industrial production to GPS-aided car navigation, one of the valuable things that computational analysis can do for the reading of texts is to take some of the tedium out. Reading the 1,296 titles held collectively in the four libraries in Marburg, Hanau, and Frankfurt would be exceedingly tedious. But aside from reducing labor, these techniques can also help us to achieve a kind of objectivity. By this I do *not* mean that we can achieve some kind of perfect encapsulation or accurate metaphysical representation of a thing, but rather just that we can measure all parts of it the same way. By contrast, if we read long lists of things, trying to find patterns and interesting phenomena, it is very likely that we will change our criteria as we go.

I contend that despite limitations of my methods, use of them permits us to accomplish two difficult things. First, we can generalize with more confidence about the contents of library collections and similarly can confirm general assumptions about habits of reading and collection. For instance, the studies above show that law (*jus*) is astonishingly highly represented in all four libraries—two law libraries to be sure (S, U), but also in the regime's "lending library" in Hanau (H) and the "city library" in Frankfurt (F). The difference seems to be that H and F hold general or, so to speak, universal law titles—the corpus of civil law, all the decrees of the local princely regime, etc. The law libraries hold multiple versions of these as well as more unusual works important to the legal profession, such as collections of authoritative rulings and technical specialized works. The importance of authority and expertise really comes through. Second, the distant reading techniques employed here also helped us notice some unexpected presences and absences. Certain

---

[49] I say surprising because, as explained above, I had expected to find many law books in S and U identifying their content to include "Germanic" law in various forms.

kinds of canon law book show up with surprising prominence in S and U. On the other hand, feudal law and Germanistics are almost absent or invisible in the law libraries, which was surprising on the face of it. Likewise, history works make up a large part of F. I think this would be hard to discern by merely reading F—either reading F on its own or reading F and then the other catalogs, H, S, and U. Similarly, the number and character of Catholic and explicitly Germanistic material in F is also significant. As above, I also doubt that this could be discerned except with some luck by just reading the catalog lists.[50]

WORKS CITED

Manuscript sources

"Bücherverzeichnisse der Regierungsbibliothek zu Hanau." 1787–1836. Held at Staatsarchiv Marburg (StAMa). StAMa B86#26130.

"Samthofgericht. Catalogus librorum." 1705. Held at Staatsarchiv Marburg (StAMa). StAMa b5 10412.

Vultejus, Hermann, and Johannes Hartmann. 1606. "Catalogi librorum, qui in bibliotheca academica Marpurgensi anno MDCVI mense Septembri noviter inventi et recensiti fuerunt." Held at Universitätsbibliothek Giessen. HS 28 UB Giessen.

Waldschmiedt, J. Martin. 1691–1701. "Rechnung über Einnahme und Ausgabe der Stadtbibliothek, Verzeichnisse der dieser zugewendete Geschenke, der Ablieferungen von Bücher seitens städtischer Ämter, der Verwerffung von Dubletten, der Büchbinderausgaben." Held at Institute für Stadtgeschichte Frankfurt am Main. IfStG Best. Stadtbibliothek, Nr. 2.

---

[50] Moving forward, I intend to make a number of improvements to the Python code that embodies the network analysis and text analysis methods employed in this study. I am also working to acquire more library catalogs, beginning with those of the Hohe Schule Herborn (seventeenth century), the gymnasium in Hersfeld (1600), the other faculty libraries of the University of Marburg as cataloged in 1606, and finally the short but important catalog of the first books acquired by the University of Marburg in 1527.

Printed sources

Aller deß Heiligen Römischen Reichs gehaltene Reichstäge, Abschiede und Satzunge,
   sambt andern Kayserlichen und Königlichen Constitutionen als Gülden Bull
   (Lateinisch u. Teutsch) . . . Nunmehr auß den Originalien von newen coll . . .
   mit . . . Kaisers Caroli V. peinlichen Halßgerichts-Ordnung verm. 1660. Mainz:
   Schönwetter.

Brusch, Kaspar. 1551. *Monasteriorum Germaniae praecipuorum chronologia.*
   Ingolstadt: Vueyssenhornios fratres.

Burnet, Gilbert. 1689. *Historia Reformationis ecclesiae Anglicanae : in duas partes*
   diuisa : continentes : exordia & progressvsejusdem sub regnis Henrici VIII.
   Edvvardi VI. & Elizabethae cum iconibus personarumillustrivm. Geneva:
   Duilleriana.

Conring, Hermann. 1654. *De Finibus Imperii Germanici Liber II, Hoc Ed. adornata*
   est Tractatus de Germanorum Imperio Romano Liber unus. Helmstedt:
   Müller.

Consilia feudalia, ex variorum doctorum scriptis diligentissime collecta. 1570.
   Leiden: Iunta.

Corneo, Pier Filippo. 1502. *Consilia.* Perugia: Francisci Baldasaris.

Fichard, Joannes. 1578. *Der Statt Franckenfurt am Mayn ernewerte Reformation.*
   Frankfurt am Main: Sigismund Feyerabend; Georg Raben.

Florian, Gebhard. 1664. *Chronica der weltberühmten freyen Reichs-Wahl-u.*
   Handelstadt Frankfurt am Mayn etc. An den Tag gegeben durch Gebhard
   Florian der Historien Liebhaber. Frankfurt am Main: Georg Fickwirdt.

Freher, Marquard, ed. 1600. *Germanicarum rerum scriptores aliquot insignes, :*
   hactenus incogniti qui gesta sub regis et imperator. Teuton. inde a Karolo M.
   usque ad Karolo V perpetua fere serie litt. mand. reliquerunt. Frankfurt am
   Main: Andrea Wechelius.

Godefroy, Denis, ed. 1587. *Corpus iuris civilis in IIII partes distinctum : quibus quae*
   contineantur proxima à praefatione ostendit pagina his omnibus adiectus est
   commentarius. Frankfurt am Main: Ex officina Ioannis Wecheli.

Grotius, Hugo. 1625. *De jure belli ac pacis libri tres.* Paris.

Hanauische Verordnungen 1566-1793. Mentioned in catalog but no details of date, publisher, or publisher location given.

Lancelotti, Giovanni Paulo, ed. 1591. *Corpus Juris Canonici emendatum et notis illustratum Gregorii XIII Pont. Max. jussu editum*. Leiden.

de Laude, Oldradus de Ponte, ed. 1550. *Consilia : aurea quidem sunt haec ac pene divina responsa*. Leiden: Jacob Juncta's heirs.

Ludovisi, Giuseppe, ed. 1573. *Decisiones Sev Diffinitiones Cavsarum Pervsinarum & Prouinciae Vmbriae*. Frankfurt am Main: Feirabend: Petrus Fabricius.

Meichsner, Johannes, ed. 1604. *Decisiones Diversarvm Cavsarvm In Camera Imperiali Ivdicatarvm Adivnctis Relationibus Actorum*. 3 vols. Frankfurt am Main: Richterus.

Mevius, David, ed. 1698. *Decisiones Super Causis Praecipuis Ad Summum Tribunal Regium Vismariense Delatis : Quibus Praeter priores Decisionum ac rerum indices Accessit Repertorium, Quo Dictae Decisione iuxta ordinem Pandectarum exhibentur*. Frankfurt am Main.

Oldendorp, Johann. 1541. *De iure et aequitate forensis disputatio*. Cologne: Johannes Gymnicus.

Pontanus, Johannes Isacius. 1631. *Rerum Danicarum historia : Libris X. Vonoq[ue] Tomo . . . deducta. Accedit Chorographica Regni Daniae tractatusq[ue] eius universi borealis Urbiumq[ue] Descriptio eodem Authore*. Amsterdam: Hondius.

Rulant, Rutger. 1604. *Tractatus, de commissariis, et commissionibus Camerae Imperialis, quadripartitus. Rutgeri Rulant Aquisgranensis, D. . . . Pars 1. [-4.]. 4, 4.* Frankfurt am Main: Ex officina typographica Ioannis Saurii, sumptibus Rulandiorum.

Seiler, Raphael, ed. 1572. *Cammergerichts- Bei- u. Endurthail. Selectissimarum sententiarum in imp. camarae iudicio . . .* 2 vols. Frankfurt am Main.

Senckenberg, Heinrich Christian, ed. 1735. *Selecta iuris et historiarum*. Vol. 3. Frankfurt am Main: Johann Friedrich Fleischer.

"Stadt- und Landesbrauch des Oberfürstenthums Marburg." (1572) 1749. In *Marburgische Beyträge zur Gelehrsamkeit*, Vol. 3, edited by Johann Georg Estor. Marburg. Citation refers to the 1749 edition.

Stucke, Johann. 1666. *Consiliorum Sive Juris Responsorum, Tum Collegii in dicta Academia Helmstadiensi, tum ab ipso privato nomine elaboratorum ac partim a nobilioribus Germaniae Collegiis Juridicis subscriptorum, partim etiam ab ipsis Consiliariis Caesareis Aulicis approbatorum Volumen; In Quo Insigniores Tam Publici, Quam Privati Iuris Materiae accurate, & plene disceptatae, maturo eoque gravissimo judicio discutiuntur*, edited by Johann Justus Stucke and Christian Daniel Stucke. Bremen: Kohler.

Vultejus, Hermann. 1654. *Tractatus de iudiciis in libros IV divisus, quo iudiciorum natura in genere et processus iudiciarius in specie . . . explicatur*, edited by Johannes Vultejus. Cassel: Köhler.

Modern scholarship

Allwörden, Hubertus von. 2006. *Die Geschichte der Stadtbibliothek in Frankfurt am Main*. Frankfurt am Main: Literaturhaus.

Baade, Hans W. 2002. "*Stare Decisis* in Civil-Law Countries: The Last Bastion." In *Themes in Comparative Law: In Honour of Bernard Rudden*, edited by Peter Birks and Arianna Pretto-Sakmann, 3–20. Oxford: Oxford University Press.

Berman, Harold. 1983. *Law and Revolution: The Formation of the Western Legal Tradition*. Cambridge: Harvard University Press.

———. 2003. *Law and Revolution II: The Impact of the Protestant Reformations on the Western Legal Tradition*. Cambridge: Belknap Press.

Bettenhäuser, Erwin. 1964. "Die Entwicklung des Gerichtswesens in Hessen." *Justiz-Ministerial-Blatt für Hessen* 16.7: 51–62.

Brunner, Otto. 1949. *Adeliges Landleben und europäischer Geist: Leben und Werk Wolf Helmhards von Hohberg, 1612-1688*. Salzburg: Otto Müller.

Burrows, Simon. 2015. "Locating the Minister's Looted Books: From Provenance and Library History to the Digital Reconstruction of Print Culture." *Library & Information History* 31.1: 1–17.

Caldarelli, Guido, and Michele Catanzaro. 2012. *Networks: A Very Short Introduction*. Oxford: Oxford University Press.

Darnton, Robert. 1971. "The High Enlightenment and the Low-Life of Literature in Pre-Revolutionary France." *Past and Present* 51: 81–115.

Fish, Stanley. 2012. "Mind Your P's and B's: The Digital Humanities and Interpretation." *New York Times Opinionator Blog.* Blog post. 23 January 2012. Accessed 21 April 2016. https://opinionator.blogs.nytimes.com/2012/01/23/mind-your-ps-and-bs-the-digital-humanities-and-interpretation/.

Gavin, Michael. 2016. "Historical Text Networks: The Sociology of Early English Criticism." *Eighteenth-Century Studies* 50.1: 53–80.

Gupta, Rishi, Tim Roughgarden, and C. Seshadhri. 2016. "Decompositions of Triangle-Dense Graphs." *Society for Industrial and Applied Mathematics (SIAM)Journal on Computing* 45.2: 197–215.

Guthrie, David, Ben Allison, Wei Liu, Louise Guthrie, and Yorick Wilks. 2006. "A Closer Look at Skip-Gram Modelling." *Proceedings of the 5th International Conference on Language Resources and Evaluation*, Vol. L06-121-. pp. 1222–1225. Accessed 22 August 2019. http://www.lrec-conf.org/proceedings/lrec2006/pdf/357_pdf.

Jockers, Matthew Lee. 2013. *Macroanalysis: Digital Methods and Literary History.* Champaign: University of Illinois Press.

Kimhi, Irad. 2018. *Thinking and Being.* Cambridge, MA: Harvard University Press.

Moretti, Franco. 2005. *Graphs, Maps, Trees: Abstract Models for a Literary History.* London and New York: Verso.

———. (2013) 2015. *Distant Reading.* London: Verso. Citation refers to the 2015 edition.

Nathusius-Neinstedt, Heinrich von. "Die beiden ältesten Kataloge der Stadtbibliothek." In *Die Stadtbibliothek in Frankfurt am Main; im Auftrage der städtischen Behörden aus Anlass der Vollendung des Erweiterungsbaues,* edited by Friedrich Clemens Ebrard, 137–53. Frankfurt am Main: Gebrüder Knauer.

Silving, Helen. "*Stare Decisis* in the Civil and in the Common Law." *Revista juridica de la Universidad de Puerto Rico* (1966): 194–242.

Tierney, Brian. 1997. *The Idea of Natural Rights: Studies on Natural Rights, Natural Law, and Church Law, 1150-1625.* Emory University Studies in Law and Religion 5. Atlanta: Scholars Press.

Wieacker, Franz. (1952) 1995. *A History of Private Law in Europe with Particular Reference to Germany.* Translated by Tony Weir. Oxford: Clarendon Press. Citation refers to the 1995 edition.

Wilder, Colin F. 2010. "Property, Possession and Prescription: The Rule of Law in the Hessian and Rhine-Main Region of Germany, 1648–1776." PhD thesis. University of Chicago.

Zedler, Gottfried. 1896. *Geschichte der Universitätsbibliothek zu Marburg von 1527-1887.* Marburg: Elwert'sche Verlagsbuchhandlung.

Software

Bastian, Mathieu, Sebastien Heymann, and Mathieu Jacomy. Gephi: An Open Source Software for Exploring and Manipulating Networks. Software released 2009. Accessed 2017. https://www.aaai.org/ocs/index.php/ICWSM/09/paper/view/154.

Hollis, Luke, Kyle P. Johnson, and Patrick J. Burns. CLTK: The Classical Language Toolkit. Software released 2014-17. Accessed 28 August 2017. http://cltk.org/.

Wilder, Colin F. Latin Phrase Processor. Software released 2017. Accessed 31 October 2017. https://github.com/ColinWilder/latinPhraseProcessor. Cited as Wilder 2017a.

———. Text Networks. Software released 2017. Accessed 31 October 2017. https://github.com/ColinWilder/textNetworks. Cited as Wilder 2017b.

Number of titles, word tokens, word types, and n-grams in each of the 4 libraries

Library name		Abbrev.	Books total (titles)	Words				N-grams	
				Tokens	Avg. tokens per title	Types	Avg. types per title (lexical richness)	Tokens	Types
Samthofgericht Marburg	Institutional library of the Collective High Court of Marburg	S	26	239	9.2	174	6.7	563	535
Universitätsbibliothek Marburg	The library of the University of Marburg	U	87	487	5.6	301	3.5	1,032	988
Leihebibliothek Hanau	Lending library of Hanau	H	350	2,239	6.4	1,029	2.9	4,720	4,183
Stadtbibliothek Frankfurt	Public City Library of Frankfurt	F	833	2,753	3.3	1,290	1.5	3,661	3,305
Total	Total		1,296	5,718	4.4	2,139	1.7	9,976	8,521

Table 1. Tokens of words means how many separate, non-unique words are found in all the book titles for a given library, taken together. Types of words means how many distinct, unique words are in those titles taken together. Similarly, tokens of n-grams means how many n-grams can be made from all those titles. Types of n-gram means how many unique n-grams there are. All counts are based on data status *after* pre-processing.

Word types in S and U appearing 5+ times

Word (type)	Translation	Frequency	Frequency as a percentage of all tokens
jus	law	27	3.7%
consilium	counsel	19	2.6%
opus1	work	17	2.3%
civilis1	civil	10	1.4%
decisio	decision	10	1.4%
decretum	decree	9	1.2%
tractatus	treatise	9	1.2%
responsum	response	8	1.1%
corpus	body (sc. of law)	7	1.0%
decretales	decrees	7	1.0%
imperium	empire	7	1.0%
cammer	chamber	6	0.8%
codex	book	6	0.8%
digestum	digest	6	0.8%
glossa	gloss	6	0.8%
liber4	book	6	0.8%
novus	new	6	0.8%
omne	all	6	0.8%
causa	matter	5	0.7%
commentarius	commentary	5	0.7%
communis	common	5	0.7%
feudal*	feudal	5	0.7%
judicium	court	5	0.7%

Table 2. This is a list of those words (word types) which appear most in S and U, ranked by frequency of appearance. The right-hand column shows what overall share tokens of that type make up in all the titles of S and U. Thus, tokens meaning *law* (*jus, juris, jura*, etc.) make up 3.7% of all tokens in all the titles in S and U.

Distribution of word types in S and U

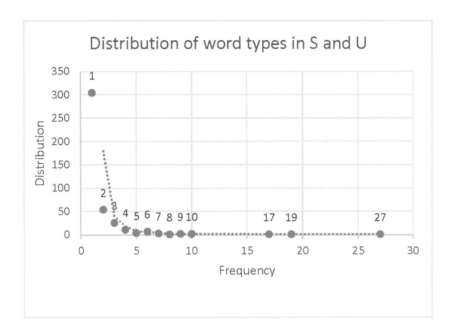

Graph 1. The vertical axis shows how many times a given word type appears. The horizontal axis shows how many word types appear that many times. Thus there is but one single word (=type, jus) which appears about 300 times (top left), while there are 27 words which appear only 1-2 times each (bottom right). The language of describing distribution and frequency is unfortunately ambiguous.

Distribution of word types in S and U, considered as portions of total appearance

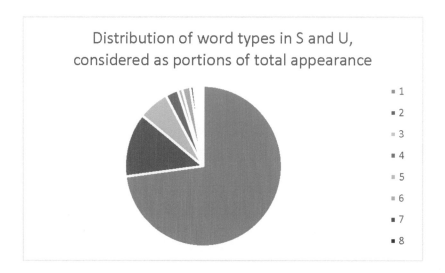

Graph 2. This graph is similar to Graph 1 but depicts the share which each given frequency level has in the total. Thus, frequency level 1 (word types which appear but once) accounts for almost ¾ of all appearances. Frequency level 2 accounts for about 1/8. And so on.

Bigrams in S and U, ranked by frequency

Bigram (type)		Translation	Frequency
jus	civilis1	civil law	10
consilium	responsum	counsel response	6
jus	corpus	body of law	6
decisio	causa	decision & matter under dispute	4
jus	responsum	law response	4
jus	consilium	law counsel	3
corpus	canonicus	body of canon (sc. law)	3
corpus	civilis1	body of civil (sc. law)	3
corpus	glossa	body – gloss	3
jus	glossa	law – gloss	3
land	graf	landgrave (the prince of Hesse)	3
opus1	omne	all work(s)	3
primus	secundus1	primary secondary	3
roma	reich	Roman Empire	3
jus	utriusque	both kinds of law (civil and canon)	3

Table 3. This table gives the 15 bigrams which appear most in titles in S and U, ranked by their frequency. Clearly *civil law* appears the most.

Skip grams in S and U

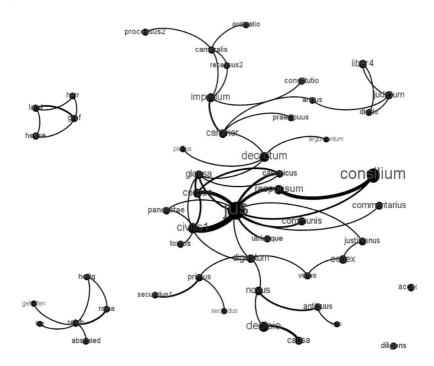

Graph 3. The large interconnected swarm shape on the right is the graph's giant connected component, or largest subgraph of the whole. Law (jus) is clearly the most important word in this central component. This graph gives an adequate picture of the major semantic links in the set of law titles: Words like law and counsel (consilium) are each prominent in that they appear a lot. But counsel is not central in that it only connects usually to two other words. Other terms like civil and gloss are central in that they connect to lots of other important words, but they themselves are not as prominent. The Digest of Roman Law appears under various synonyms of course. The Holy Roman Empire appears in the lower left.

Triangles in S and U, ranked by total edge weight of each

Triangle	Rough meaning	Triangle weight	Average edge weight
civilis1 - corpus - jus	the body of civil law	19	6.3
civilis1 - glossa - jus	gloss on the civil law	15	5.0
civilis1 - jus - pandectae	pandects of the civil law	14	4.7
consilium - jus - responsum	counsels and responses of law	13	4.3
corpus - glossa - jus	gloss on the canon law	12	4.0
canonicus - corpus - jus	the body of canon law	11	3.7
canonicus - corpus - glossa	gloss - canon – body	8	2.7
civilis1 - corpus - glossa	gloss on the body of law	8	2.7
canonicus - glossa - jus	gloss on the canon law	7	2.3
graf - herr - land	the lord landgrave	7	2.3
graf - hesse - land	the landgrave of Hesse	7	2.3
heilig - reich - roma	the Holy Roman Empire	7	2.3
cameralis - imperium - recessus2	imperial chamber recess	6	2.0

word distance = 2

Table 4. This table shows the triangles in S and U which have the greatest total edge weight. That is, all triangles in S and U were calculated. The total of the 3 edge weights for each was then calculated. The triangles were then ranked by total edge weight. Table 4 is the basis for Graph 4. Compare with Table 7.

Most important triangles in S and U

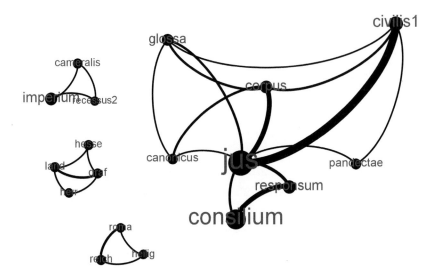

Graph 4. This is a graph of the 13 triangles which appear most frequently in S and U. Node size and node label size represent the frequency of the nodes (that is word types) themselves. Edge weight represents the frequency with which that edge (skip gram) appears in S and U. Graph 4 is based on the data in Table 4. Compare with Graph 7.

Tringles in S and U based on word distance of 4

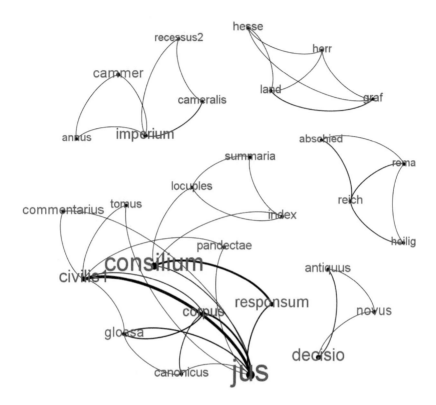

Graph 5. This graph may be considered a variant of Graph 4, but using a higher word distance (k) threshold.

Relationship between word distance and total number of k-skip bigrams

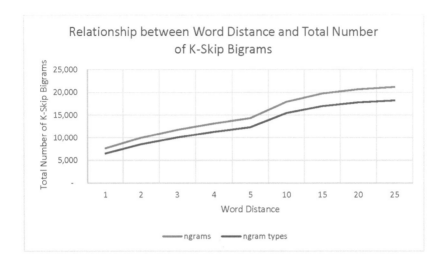

Graph 6. The idea here is to see how the number of k skip bigrams grows as we permit higher word distances. The data is from S and U. There is clearly a positive direct relationship. A word distance of 1 produces 7,638 n-gram tokens (blue, lower left) and 6,497 n-gram types (red, lower left). As we move to the right and permit ever greater word distance, the number of skip gram tokens and skip gram types increase. But as we permit word distances past about 20 (!) the number of n-gram tokens and types plateaus. This is because old book titles, while long, are not often longer than 20-30 words.

The 20 most frequently appearing words in S–U, F, and H

S and U taken together			Frankfurt			Hanau		
Label	Weight	Overall frequency	Label	Weight	Overall frequency	Label	Weight	Overall frequency
adicio	2	3.3%	biblia	15	3.1%	abschied	17	3.7%
cammeralis	2	3.3%	chronicon	15	3.1%	commentarius	15	3.3%
cammer	2	3.3%	commen-tarius	24	4.9%	consilium	18	3.9%
canonicus	4	6.6%	deutsch	13	2.7%	corpus	19	4.1%
communis	2	3.3%	ecclesiastes	17	3.5%	criminalis	16	3.5%
corpus	3	4.9%	german*	27	5.6%	decisio	24	5.2%
decretum	9	14.8%	graecus	14	2.9%	deutsch	32	7.0%
explico	2	3.3%	histoire	17	3.5%	german*	20	4.3%
glossa	4	6.6%	historia	54	11.1%	heilig	14	3.0%
gratianus	2	3.3%	historicus	18	3.7%	imperium	19	4.1%
imperium	2	3.3%	jus	37	7.6%	jus	56	12.2%
judicium	3	4.9%	liber4	21	4.3%	kaiser	14	3.0%
jus	7	11.5%	omne	22	4.5%	land	27	5.9%
matthaeus	2	3.3%	opus1	46	9.5%	omne	14	3.0%

neapolitanus	2	3.3%	res	47	9.7%	ordnung	17	3.7%
omne	2	3.3%	roma	25	5.1%	recht	27	5.9%
processus2	2	3.3%	sacer	17	3.5%	reich	52	11.3%
summa	3	4.9%	scriptor	19	3.9%	roma	22	4.8%
totus1	3	4.9%	tractatus	17	3.5%	staat	17	3.7%
utriusque	3	4.9%	vetus	21	4.3%	tractatus	20	4.3%

Table 5. As explained above, this table reveals some interesting things. law (jus) is common in all of the libraries titles, indeed actually more common in the Hanau "lending library" than in the two Marburg law libraries! But all law words taken together are ultimately far more common in S and U than in the other libraries. The main law words in each title catalog are highlighted in yellow.

Words which appear 9 or more times in the F catalog

Label	Frequency	Label	Frequency
historia	54	graecus	14
res	47	deutsch	13
opus1	46	hebraeus	13
jus	37	imperium	13
german*	27	novus	13
roma	25	annalis	12
commentarius	24	ecclesia	12
omne	22	epistula	12
liber4	21	antiquitas	11
vetus	21	antiquus	11
scriptor	19	bibliotheca	11
historicus	18	actum	10
ecclesiastes	17	publicus	10
histoire	17	thesaurus	10
sacer	17	consilium	9
tractatus	17	dissertatio	9
biblia	15	latinus	9
chronicon	15	obseruatio	9

Table 6. As mentioned above, words relating to history, the (Catholic) church, and Germany are particularly prominent in this title catalog. Words representing those three semantic areas are highlighted in yellow.

Triangles in F, ranked by total edge weight of each

Triangle	Approximate, generic translation	Triangle weight	Average weight per side of triangle
german* res scriptor	writer of about German matters	16	5.3
historia res scriptor	writer of history	15	5
alemanni res scriptor	writer about Alemannic [German] matters	14	4.7
res scriptor sicula	writer about Sicilian matters	14	4.7
institutio jus publicus	institutes of public law	13	4.3
german* jus publicus	German public law	11	3.7
historia ketzer kirche	history of heretics, church	10	3.3
historia scriptor vetus	writer of ancient history	10	3.3
catholicus eglise foy	church, Catholic faith	9	3
catholicus eglise perpetuite	perpetual Catholic Church	9	3
catholicus foy perpetuite	perpetual Catholic faith	9	3
deutsch kaiser krieg	German emperor, war	9	3
deutsch kaiser ursache	German emperor, cause	9	3
deutsch krieg ursache	cause of the German war	9	3
eglise foy perpetuite	faith, perpetual Church	9	3
franc historia vetus	history of the ancient Franks	9	3
german* res ueters	ancient German matters	9	3
german* res vis	(too ambiguous)	9	3
german* ueters vis	(too ambiguous)	9	3
historia ketzer un-parteyisch	non-partisan history of heresy	9	3
historia opus1 tempus	a work of history of the time	9	3
kaiser krieg ursache	emperor-war-cause	9	3
res ueters vis	(too ambiguous)	9	3

Table 7. Compare with Table 4.

Triangles in F

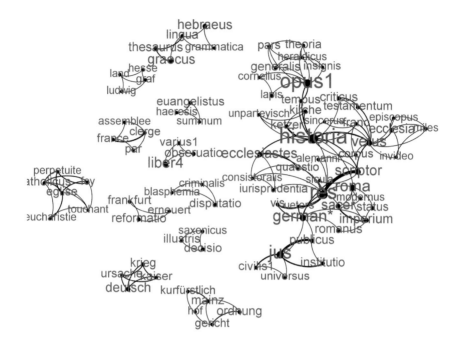

Graph 7. Compare to Graph 4 and Graph 5.

Triangles in F – detail: Giant connected component

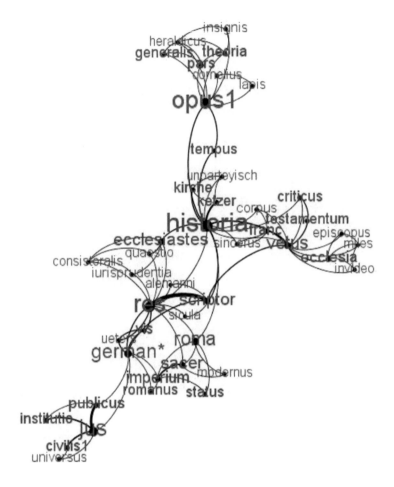

Graph 8. This graph uses the same triangle data as Graph 7. But I cropped out the small triangle subgraphs on the left side of Graph 7, leaving only the giant interconnected component from the right side of Graph 7. Then I loosened out its layout on the graph space manually to make it easier for the reader to see the different parts of the graph.

The Implications of Image Manipulation Tools for Petrarch's Philology[1]

Alessandro Zammataro
Oxford University

This essay is focused on the development of new digital paleographical methods to support the study of medieval and modern manuscripts. The potential of image manipulation software such as Adobe Photoshop has not yet been entirely explored, especially if we consider the constant improvements and new features that are offered by continual software updates. Compared to traditional (human eye on the page) manuscript reading, digital imaging processing offers many tools for the analysis of script from several different paleographical perspectives: for instance, close reading of the external shape of words or single letters as well as overlaying letter comparison to define commonalities and differences via accurate pixel computation. In addition, features of this software can be used to enhance readings and build knowledge by restoring effaced, discolored, or corrupted parchment without affecting the original document.

The poetic corpus written by Italian poet Francesco Petrarca (Petrarch) during the thirteenth century, entitled *Rerum vulgarium fragmenta*, also known as the *Canzoniere*, serves as a case study here. This corpus is fascinating in part because it is extremely rare in medieval literature to be able to trace the process of author revision from first draft (MS Vat. Lat. 3196) through definitive final copy (MS Vat. Lat. 3195: Figure 1). Petrarch is in fact the only medieval poet for whom we have the original autograph manuscript. In composing the *Canzoniere*, Petrarch transcribed poems previously written in Vat. Lat. 3196, also known as the *Codice degli abbozzi*, to Vat. Lat. 3195. Since an autograph always provides invaluable insight into a text's genesis and creation, these two codices remain at the center of a long hermeneutical and philological debate.

---

[1] My thanks to Dr. Amyrose McCue Gill of TextFormations for her assistance in editing the text and revising translations.

ISBN 978-1-64959-016-9 (paper) ISBN 978-1-64959-017-6 (pdf) ISBN 978-1-64959-037-4 (epub)

New Technologies in Medieval and Renaissance Studies 9 (2022) 157–194

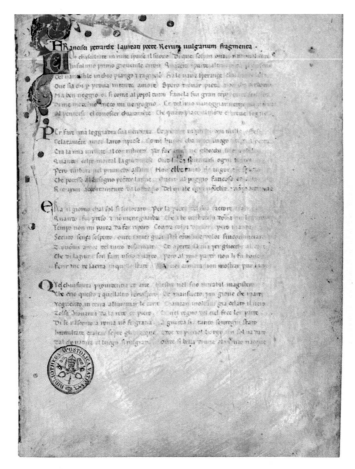

Figure 1. Vat. Lat. 3195, f. 1r.

Thanks to a series of techniques developed using digital image processing software, it is now possible to offer a new contribution to this long debate—and, at the same time, to shed light on specific readings that are still the subject of animated discussion among scholars. The following pages report the key results of several practical applications of these methodologies to Petrarch's manuscripts. I first proceed to analyze line 9 of sonnet 179, "Geri, quando talor meco s'adira," focusing on restoring original text that has been corrupted by physical damage in order to give Petrarch's original voice back to the reader. I then analyze sonnet 321, "È questo 'l nido in che la mia fenice," where image processing tools give us significant insights into how Petrarch revised his *Canzoniere*. Finally, I digitally reconstruct the colors of

Antonio Grifo's illuminations of the *editio princeps* of the *Canzoniere*, shedding light on possible interpretations of these illuminations.

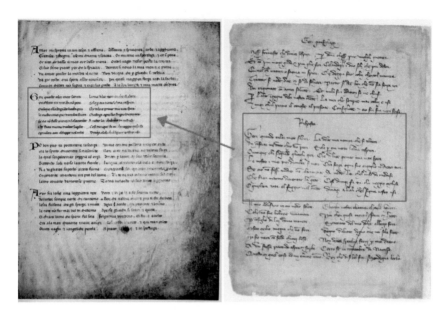

Figure 2. Vat. Lat. 3195, f. 37r; Vat. Lat. 3196, f. 8v.

Petrarch transcribed the still debated *Canzoniere* sonnet 179 from Vat. Lat. 3196 to Vat. Lat. 3195 (Figure 2), so two different autograph versions of this sonnet are extant. I focus specifically on line 9 in order to address the assumptions responsible for the different readings of editors and commentators. The controversy that the sonnet has inspired concerns the conditional *Se* (if) at the beginning of the line (Figure 3): "[S]e ciò non fusse, andrei non altramente / a veder lei che 'l volto di Medusa, / che facea marmo diventar la gente" (And [if] that were not so, I would not go to see her otherwise than to see the face of Medusa, which made people become marble).[2] A corruption of the manuscript has been interpreted by modern editors and scholars as an erasure made by Petrarch himself to change *Se ciò* (if) into *E ciò* (and). These commentators suggest the following reading, which has been adopted by almost all modern editions: "E ciò non fusse, andrei non altramente" (with *E ciò* alternating with *Et ciò* and *Eccio*). In order to be syntactically legitimate, this reading requires either interpreting the conjunction *e* as a conditional *se* or assuming an ellipsis of the conditional *se*. Scholars who agree on this reading include Giovanni Mestica, Giosuè Carducci and Severino Ferrari, Salvo Cozzo, Ettore Modigliani, Gianfranco Contini, Livio Petrucci, Marco Santagata, and

---

[2] All translations of Petrarch's poem are from Durling 1976.

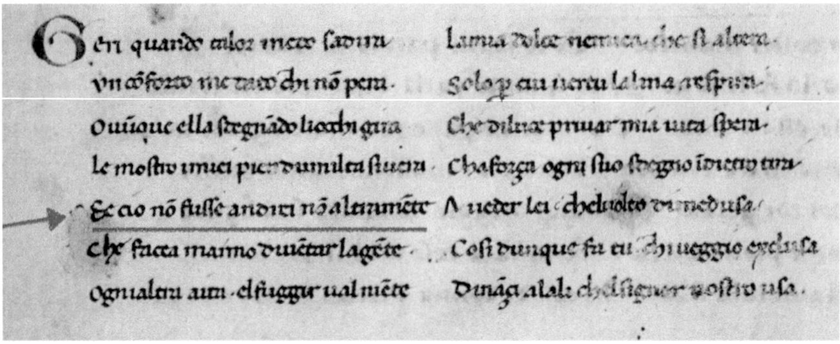

1   Geri, quando talor meco s'adira / La mia dolce nemica, ch'e` sı` altera,
3   Un conforto m'e` dato ch'i' non pera, / Solo per cui vertu` l'alma respira.
5   Ovunque ella sdegnando li occhi gira, / Che di luce privar mia vita spera,
7   Le mostro i miei pien d'umilta` sı` vera, / Ch'a forza ogni suo sdegno indietro tira.
9   Se ciò non fusse andrei non altramente / A veder lei, che 'l volto di Medusa,
11   Che facea marmo diventar la gente. / Così dunque fa' tu, ch'i' veggio exclusa
13   Ogni altra aita. E 'l fuggir val niente / Dinanzi a l'ali che 'l signor nostro usa.

Figure 3. Vat. Lat. 3195, f. 37r, sonnet 321.

Rosanna Bettarini; only Wayne Storey and Giuseppe Savoca disagree. Storey argues that "though tampered by later hands, the legitimate *lectio* is the one we find in MS Vat. Lat. 3195, and throughout the traditions of the manuscript and early printed editions of the *Fragmenta*: 'Se ciò'."[3] Nearly all other scholars have instead followed the original reading by Mestica that appears in his annotations to Vat. Lat. 3195:

> Ecciò non fusse, dove le prime due lettere di Ecciò sono scritte con inchiostro nero … dalla mano del Petrarca anch'esse, sopra un'abrasione, mediante la quale fu fatto sparire probabilissimamente il Se, che perciò dovrebbe dirsi scartato dal poeta. Ad ogni modo, questo è certo che egli volle qui la lezione Ecciò (cioè Et ciò, cangiata per assimilazione la t in c); e ne viene una locuzione dello stesso significato, ma più intensiva e, nella sua singolarità, più efficace, che vuol dire: "E sia pure che ciò non fosse;" costrutto simile a quello che ricorre nei vv. 79, 80 della Canz. LXXIII, dove invece di E v'è solamente la congiunzione E nel senso di Se, posto che è registrata anche nel Vocabolario della Crusca (Quinta Impressione) al § XXIII della E congiunzione. (Petrarca 1896, 258)

---

[3] Storey 2007, p. 85. See also Savoca's comments in Petrarca 2008.

"Ecciò non fusse" [And were it not thus], where the first two letters of *Ecciò* are written in black ink . . . also in Petrarch's hand on top of a scraping by which the *Se* was very likely made to disappear—and thus, one should say, was eliminated by the poet. In any case, this is certain: that here he wanted the reading *Ecciò* (that is, *Et ciò*, the *t* transformed to a *c* by assimilation); and this is an expression with the same meaning, though one more decisive—and, because of its rarity, more incisive—that means: "And may it indeed be that it were not thus," a construction similar to that which appears in lines 79 and 80 of *Canzoniere* LXXIII, where instead of *e* there is "solamente" [only]. The conjunction *e* in the sense of *se* has an established meaning that is even recorded in the *Vocabolario della Crusca* (5th printing) in section XXIII of the *e* conjunction.[4]

Mestica's argument, which influenced the entire twentieth-century tradition, is that in the definitive copy of the manuscript (Vat. Lat. 3195), the *S* of the word *Se* in line 9 was erased by Petrarch, who replaced it purposefully with an *E*. This reading, however, implies a syntactical anomaly—the ellipsis of the conditional *se*, which does not appear anywhere else in Petrarch's *Canzoniere*—which proponents of the *E ciò* reading address by observing that the use of the conjunction *e* in place of the conditional *se* occurs in some instances in medieval Italian literature. For instance, Carducci comments, in his edition of Petrarch, that

> Di e nel senso di condizionale *se*, posto che, la nuova Crusca cita parecchi esempi ma non certissimi: Cf. Fra Giordano da Rivalto dell'Ordine dei predicatori: "I Pagani hanno voluto dare ai Santi, e agli Apostoli oro ed argento e farli Segnori, e impromesso loro grandi cose, ed eglino lascino la fede." (Petrarca 1975, 265)

> Concerning *and* in the sense of the conditional *se*, there is an established meaning for which the new *Crusca* cites a few examples, though not entirely certain ones: Cf. Fra Giordano da Rivalto of the Order of Preachers: "The Pagans wanted to give to the Saints and to the Apostles gold and silver and to make them Lords, and they promised them great things, were they to leave the faith."

According to Carducci, we should read the alleged *e* at the beginning of sonnet 179, line 9, in a similar way: as if it were the conditional *se*. While Carducci accepts Mestica's reading, it is worth mentioning that he is the only

---

[4] All translations from Italian into English are mine, unless otherwise indicated.

commentator who shows some hesitation regarding a syntactical claim that requires an understood ellipsis of the conditional *se*. The reading proposed by Bettarini is similar, but for the fact that she shows no hesitation in the interpretation:

> Et ciò non fusse — in questo luogo Petrarca di sua mano corregge la precedente lezione Se ciò, già attestata dagli scartafacci, talché nel manoscritto in questo punto autografo si legge Ee ciò no(n). (Petrarca 2005, xxxiv)

> "Et ciò non fusse"—here Petrarch, in his own hand, corrects the earlier reading *Se ciò* that already appeared in the drafts, such that in the manuscript, which is autograph at this point, one reads "Ee ciò no(n)."

According to the quoted note of Bettarini, Contini adopts Modigliani's reading:

> "La E iniziale, di cui la parte superiore è formata di ciò che resta di una S rasa inferiormente, è con inchiostro più scuro, su rasura. Il Petrarca volle mutare *Se ciò* in Eccio, ma lasciò intatta (forse volutamente, per la somiglianza della e con la c) la e di Se [. . .]». (Modigliani 1904, 89)

> "The initial *E*—the upper part of which is formed by what remains of a poorly scraped away *S*—is in a darker ink on top of the erasure. Petrarch wished to transform *Se ciò* into *Eccio* but he left intact (perhaps intentionally, given the resemblance of the *e* with the *c*) the *e* of *Se*. . . .

In order to support her choise of "Et ciò", Bettarini adds that:

> Per la rarità nel Libro del raddoppiamento fonosintattico, è più probabile che l'autore abbia omesso di correggere Ee così ottenuto in Et (suggerimento di Livio Petrucci, già adottato da Santagata) o di eradere la seconda e." (Petrarca 2005, xxxiv)

> Given the rarity of phonological reduplication in the Book, it is more likely that the author may have neglected to correct the *Ee* thus obtained to *Et* (a suggestion by Livio Petrucci that has already been adopted by Santagata) or to scrape away the second *e*.

I argue that this reading, which is accepted by nearly all modern editors, is based upon a misreading of the original manuscript. I will support this statement by analyzing the syntactic aspect of the text and by providing codicological and paleographic details revealed by the close analysis of ultraviolet scans enhanced by digital tools.

Other than in this disputed instance, the ellipsis of the conjunction *se* occurs only once in Petrarch's *Canzoniere*, in sonnet 73, lines 79–84:[5]

> Solamente quel nodo
> Ch'amor cerconda a la mia lingua, quando
> L'umana vista il troppo lume avanza,
> Fosse disciolto, i' prenderei baldanza
> Di dir parole in quel punto sì nove
> Che farina lagrimar chi le 'ntendesse.

> If only that knot
> which Love ties around my tongue when
> the excess of light overpowers my mortal sight
> were loosened, I would take boldness
> to speak words at that moment so strange
> that they would make all who heard them weep.

Line 82 should be read as follows: "[Se] fosse disciolto, i' prenderei baldanza," with the ellipsis of *se* at the beginning of the line. I argue that the syntactical structure employed in these lines is not comparable, however, to the structure of the widely accepted reading of "E ciò non fusse" because here there is a passive construction that mimics the Latin ablative absolute, in which an independent phrase with a noun in the ablative case has a participle, expressed or implied, which agrees with it in gender, number, and case. Such ablatives are only loosely connected grammatically to the rest of the sentence, hence their name "absolute" (*absolūtus* = free or unconnected). A similar structure can naturally be interpreted as the protasis of a conditional, so the conjunction *se* is not needed.

In his *Prose della vulgar lingua*, Pietro Bembo dedicates a chapter to the ellipsis of the conjunction *se* followed by the verb *fosse*, in which he lists some

---

[5] These lines are mentioned by Pietro Bembo, in *Prose della vulgar lingua*, book III: *Leggesi la particella* Se non, *che si pone condizionalmente*. The aforementioned text is quoted from the critical edition of the *Editio Princeps* printed in 1525.

examples from Italian poets who employed this structure in their poems, for instance Bonagiunta da Lucca:

> E tanto gli agradisce il vostro regno,
> che mai da voi partir non potrebb'ello,
> non fosse da la morte a voi furato

> And your kingdom so pleased him
> that never from you could he part,
> not if by death were he stolen from you;

Lapo Gianni:

> Amor, poiché tu se' del tutto ignudo,
> non fossi alato, morresti di freddo,

> Love, since you are entirely naked,
> if you were not wingèd, you would die of cold;

and Francesco Ismera:

> Non fosse colpa, non saria perdono

> If there were no fault, there would be no pardon. (Bembo 2001, 246)

These examples likewise fail to provide a good comparison for Petrarch's sonnet 179 because their conditional sentences do not begin with the conjunction *e*. I argue, therefore, that neither they nor Petrarch's isolated case of conditional *se* ellipsis in sonnet 73 are sufficient to support Mestica's reading of line 9, which proposes an apparently unique case in Petrarch's *usus scribendi*. Indeed, it is crucial to underline that the *Canzoniere* includes several instances in which Petrarch uses both *et* and *se* together, which demonstrates that he is not in the habit of omitting *se* after the conjunction *et*:

CP 191 009	Et se non fusse il suo fuggir sì ratto,
CP 259 005	Et se mia voglia in ciò fusse compita,
CM 267 008	Se non fossi fra noi scesa sì tardo.
CM 271 009	Et se non fosse experientia molta
CP 331 049	Se stato fusse il mio poco intellecto
CP 345 004	Quel che se fusse ver torto sarebbe.
CP 358 010	Et se non fusse, e' fu 'l tempo in quel punto

(Savoca and Calderone 2011)
And if its fleeing were not so swift
And if my wishes in this were fulfilled
If you had not come down among us so late
And if it had not been for much experience
If my little intellect had been
That which, if it were true, would be wrong
And if it were not, it was time in that instant

Debates about an author's *usus scribendi* in attempts to emend a text always entail a certain degree of risk because it is easy to suppress an innovation thereby, as well as to invest established occurrences with an authority that may not be highly relevant. In this case, I support my considerations of *usus scribendi* by looking at Petrarch's original manuscript. I argue that what has always been considered an erasure by scholars is actually a stain that corrupted Petrarch's original handwriting and compelled an unknown reader to correct the text, by retracing the original handwriting.[6]

I support this theory with an analysis of the codicological features of the alleged erasure on folio 37r using both regular color scanning and ultraviolet digital reproduction. The ultraviolet scanning technique uses an ultraviolet light set to a stable frequency as well as a high-resolution camera; the technique takes advantage of the fluorescence property of some substances to absorb ultraviolet light and reissue it at a higher visible frequency range. This property is made possible by the chemical compounds—such as the ligand and pigments—of which ink is made, and by their reciprocal interactions. The Vat. Lat. 3195 ultraviolet digital scan was made using a high-resolution camera equipped with a Wratten Kodak ultraviolet spectrum filter and with a fluorescent ultraviolet light set at 254 nm, making it capable of penetrating the parchment's inner layer and bringing the erased writing, or *scriptio inferior*, back into view (Schuler 2009).

Compared to the other poems copied by Francesco Malpaghini on folio 37r, the sonnet transcribed by Petrarch is easily discernible because of the remarkable difference in the *ductus* of the handwriting and in the poem's layout—that is, the text is aligned along the left margin of each line.

---

[6] According to Savoca (Petrarca 2008), the erasure is a mirrored stain. Although Storey (2007, 85) agrees to the reading "Se ciò," he argues that there is an erasure at the beginning of line 9: "Unfortunately, we cannot identify as Petrarca's the hand that erase and rewrite the 'E,' and later the 'Che'."

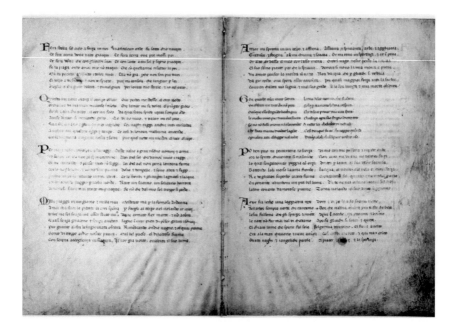

Figure 4. Vat. Lat. 3195, f. 36v – 37r. Digital color scan.

If we look at Figure 4, images of the two consecutive folios 36v and 37r that belong to the central *bifolium* of the fifth quaternion of the codex, we can see that there is a stain on folio 36v that mirrors perfectly the area affected by the alleged erasure on folio 37r. The ultraviolet digital scan shows a clearer picture of the two stains and allows us to measure the distance of each stain from the central fold of the *bifolium*. This distance appears to be the same on both folios. To confirm that the stains are mirror images of one another, we can use a 3D-modeled reconstruction of the two stained folios (Figure 5). Using the video editing software Adobe Premiere, I simulated how folio 36v turns over onto folio 37r while remaining anchored to the codex binding. This simulation was created by importing the image files of the two folios to two different video tracks and by using the "motion effect" to position, scale, and rotate the two pages within the video frame. I created the animations by directly manipulating the two image files in the "program monitor" and setting "keyframes" for the "motion effect" in order to rotate folio 36v from left to right until it entirely overlapped folio 37r. By adjusting the transparency of the two files in the option tab, it is possible to make visible the actual position of the two stains when the two pages are superimposed. The result of this 3D animation shows clearly that the stains match perfectly in terms of shape, size, and absolute position when the codex is closed. Obviously, it is impossible for

Figure 5. Vat. Lat. 3195, f. 36v – 37r. Ultra violet scan.

an erasure to mark other folios by contact: erasure on parchment is a dry procedure that does not involve other substances. The different color of the parchment at the beginning of line 9, therefore, is caused not by an erasure but by a stain (probably caused by oil or wax) that also corrupted the opposite page. Hundreds of similar marks were left involuntarily by Petrarch and his copyist on the manuscript's folios as well as by later owners and readers of the codex. Given that the text of the *Codice degli abbozzi* (Vat. Lat. 3196) is *Se ciò*—with the initial *S*—we can say with a high level of certainty that no change was intended on Petrarch's part (Figure 6).

Supporting this hypothesis is the fact that, until the sixteenth century, many texts—both manuscripts and printed editions—clearly preserved the *Se ciò* form. These include mss. Laur. Red. 118 and Parisinus it. 551[7] (which were both directly transcribed from Vat. Lat. 3195); the *editio princeps* printed by Vindelino da Spira in Venice in 1470; the Valdezoco edition printed in 1472; and, last but not least, Bembo's own manuscript (Vat. Lat. 3197, which was

---

[7] For a detailed reconstruction of the history of the codex and for additional philological analysis, see Pulsoni and Cursi 2009.

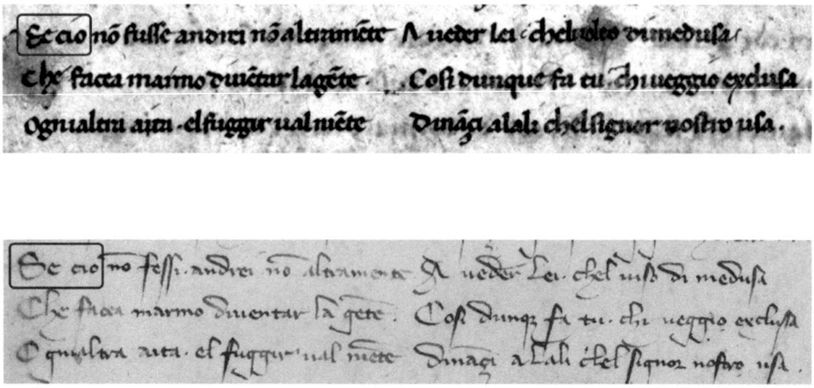

9   **Se** ciò non fusse andrei non altramente / A veder lei, che 'l volto di Medusa,
11   Che facea marmo diventar la gente.

Figure 6. Vat. Lat. 3195, f. 37v, 179, vv. 9–14; Vat. Lat. 3196, f. 8v, vv. 9–14.

copied directly from Vat. Lat. 3195; see Figure 7) as well as his printed edition, the so-called *Aldina*. Based on evidence from these early texts, therefore, it seems convincing that the stain was made by accident after the sixteenth century, and that before the manuscript was damaged anyone could clearly read *Se*.

If the initial letter of line 9 really is an *S*, one might argue that it has a very strange shape. The first letter (also *S*) of line 4 in the same sonnet, in comparison, is characterized by a more open stroke and by an oblique rather than a horizontal median line (Fig 8). I argue, however, that in Petrarch's Vat. Lat. 3195 semi-Gothic script it is possible to find an *S* similar to the *S* used on line 9 in other occurrences of the word *Se*—even if the form is less common. It may be that the horizontal median stroke of this unusual *S* is what is responsible for the misreading of *S* as *E*. In what follows, I will demonstrate that we can find this specific capital *S* shape elsewhere in Petrarch's script so as to support the claim that the letter is not an intentional authorial *E* written on top of the original *S*.

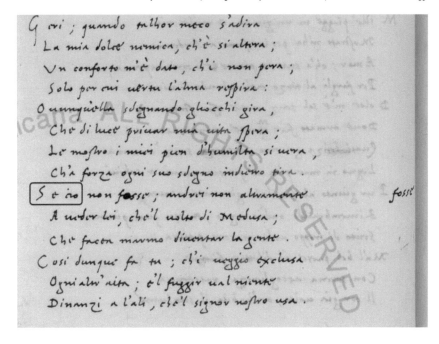

Figure 7. Vat. Lat. 3197, f. 74v, sonnet 321 (Vat. Lat. 3195 numeration). Here, the "Se ciò" form is clearly readable.

Figure 8. Vat. Lat. 3195, c. 37r, sonnet 179. Comparison of the two capital Ss. Vat. Lat. 3195, f. 37r, sonnet 321: capital S, line 9. Vat. Lat. 3195, f. 37r, sonnet 321: capital S, line 4.

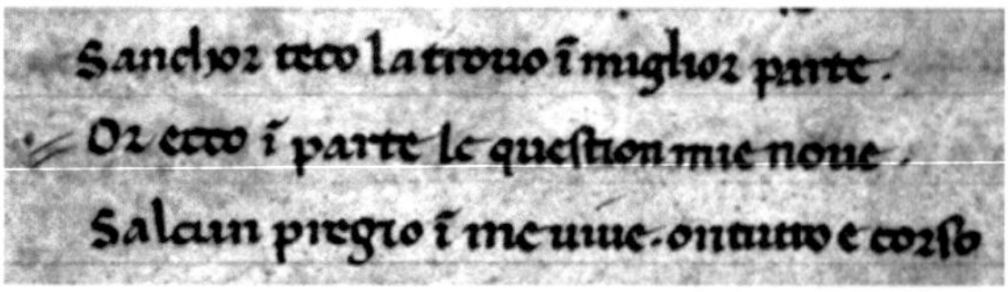

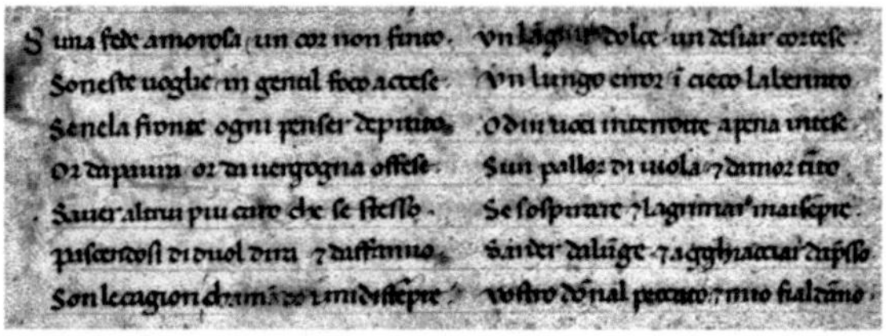

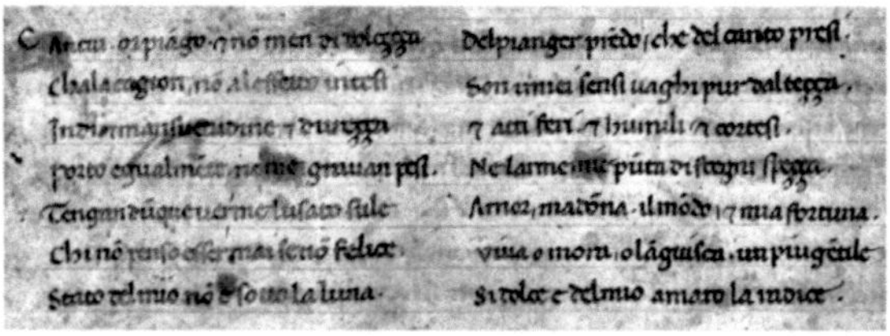

Figure 9. Vat. Lat. 3195, comparison of capital *S*s. Vat. Lat. 3195, c. 42*v*; Vat. Lat. 3195, c. 44*r*; Vat. Lat. 3195, c. 44*v*.

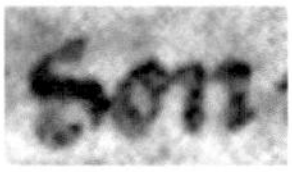

Vat. Lat. 3195,
c. 44*v*, *original*

Vat. Lat. 3195,
c. 44*v*, *restored*

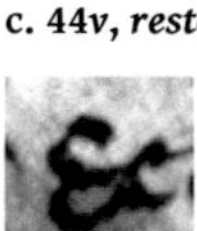

Vat. Lat. 3195,
c. 37*r*

Vat. Lat. 3195, c. 44*v*.

Figure 10. Vat. Lat. 3195, comparison of capital *S*s. Vat. Lat. 3195, c. 44*v*, *original*; Vat. Lat. 3195, c. 44*v*, *restored*; Vat. Lat. 3195, c. 37*r*; Vat. Lat. 3195, c. 44*v*.

As we can see in Figures 9–10, some more open *S*s were made by Petrarch with a similar horizontal median stroke. This specific kind of S, though different from Petrarch's usual semi-Gothic *S* (Petrucci 1967, 71–86), is very close to the chancery script style used by Petrarch in Vat. Lat. 3196 (Petrucci 1967, 107–10). This is a crucial point because the line 9 initial *S*s in Vat. Lat. 3195 and Vat. Lat. 3196 match almost perfectly when overlapped. We can compare the two letters not only by looking at manuscript scans but also by using the Photoshop tools "lasso" (both the free hand and magnetic lasso) and "magic wand" to compare their shapes (Figure 11). These tools permit us to select the boundaries of each character and to crop it from its background to better compare the characters' common aspects and differences. We can even try to overlap the isolated characters so as to visualize their degree of similarity, defined primarily by tolerance for areas that do not match. This technique reveals the *S*s in Vat. Lat. 3195 and Vat. Lat. 3196 to be very similar, though distinct from Petrarch's usual semi-Gothic *S*. This last point should be relatively unsurprising since, as alluded to above, Petrarch used two different scripts: a chancery script for the draft (Vat. Lat. 3196) and a semi-Gothic script for the final copy (Vat. Lat. 3196). There are many instances, however, where the chancery script style appears in Vat. Lat. 3195: two different realizations of *f* and *s* are used by Petrarch in Vat. Lat. 3195—one with a vertical stroke that descends only slightly below the baseline and another (inspired by the Vat. Lat. 3196 chancery hand) with a longer vertical stroke (Belloni et. al 2004).

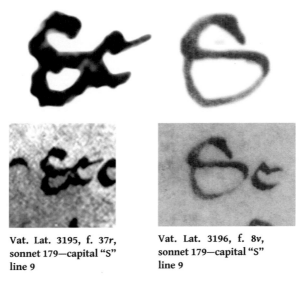

Vat. Lat. 3195, f. 37r,
sonnet 179—capital "S"
line 9

Vat. Lat. 3196, f. 8v,
sonnet 179—capital "S"
line 9

Figure 11. Comparison of capital *S*s between Vat. Lat. 3195 and Vat. Lat. 3196.

Chancery hand of *s* in *al signor* (*folio* 63r, line 22), of *f* in *fatto* (*folio* 63r, line 23), of *p* and *s* in *passato* (*folio* 41r, line 1), of *s* in *stella* (*folio* 40v, line 3).

disfaccio (Vat. Lat. 3195 *folio* 40r, 1.2) *s* and *f* are made with a vertical stroke that descends slightly below the baseline.

f. 63r, line 22   f. 63r, line 23   f. 41r, line 1   f. 40v, line 3   f. 40r, line 2

The list of lemmata above follows the examples offered by Zamponi et Alii, (Zamponi 2004, *tavola* 7).

The long s in the word *signor* reproduced above from Vat. Lat. 3195 is very close to the same one appearing in Vat. Lat. 3196 in a chancery hand:

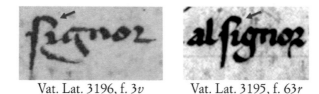

Vat. Lat. 3196, f. *3v*   Vat. Lat. 3195, f. *63r*

The overall similarity of the *ductus* of these two long *S*s is undeniable.

Another significant example of fluctuation in terms of handwriting style is offered by the different versions of Petrarch's *g* in Vat. Lat. 3195:

f. 40r, line 23   f. 41r, line 20   f. 41v, line 11   f. 41v, line 24   f. 42r, line 25   f. 42r, line 25   f. 42r, line 25

The list of lemmata above follows the examples offered by Zamponi et Alii, (Zamponi 2004, *tavola* 7).

Here Petrarch alternates a more gothic style marked by the interchange of thick and thin strokes (see *raggio*, *largo*) with a very cursive *ductus* characterized by long emphasis strokes and a more rounded style. Given these variations, we can state that expecting fluctuations in Petrarch's script style should be more or less a rule of thumb; thus, it stands to reason that stylistic variation can occur even within the same sonnet.

I argue, therefore, that the *S* of "*Se ciò* non fusse" was probably made with a horizontal median stroke that resembles the chancery version used in Vat. Lat. 3196. The letter was copied almost identically by the poet, perhaps in a moment of a less controlled writing in which he simply followed the same cursive style he saw in the draft as if he were copying a drawing more than writing a letter. When that part of the page was accidentally stained, it probably became unreadable and for this reason was repainted with a darker ink by a different hand and with a different-sized quill. I believe that this repainting procedure was responsible for having emphasized the close orientation of the lower stroke, which is the one actually affected by the stain.

My proposed reconstruction of events is confirmed by the singular aspect of the letters *C*, *h*, and *e* in the word *Che* on line 11, which appear immediately under line 9. When we look at this unique *C* in detail, we note that it is made with only one semi-circular stroke (Figure 12).

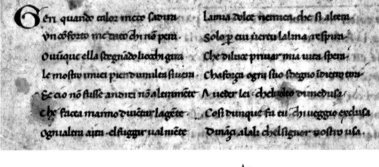

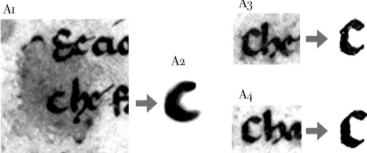

Figure 12. A: Vat. Lat. 3195, f. 37*r*, sonnet 179 (ultra violet reproduction); A1: Detail of the stain on "Se" (beginning of line n. 9) and "Che" (beginning of line n. 11); A2: detail of the cropped capital letter "C" of "Che," beginning of line n. 11; A3: detail of capital letter "C" of "Che," line n. 6; A4: detail of capital letter "C" of "Che," line n. 8.

All of Petrarch's other *C*s follow a strict standard procedure in which we can distinguish three different strokes that alternate thick and thin lines of the quill and an extremely regular vertical line in place of the semi-circular one. The line 11, *C* in contrast is fashioned in a more cursive script and by a later hand that does not belong to Petrarch—the same hand, I would argue, that repainted the *S*. Close analysis of the letter *h* in the relative pronoun *Che* reveals its features to not reflect Petrarch's *ductus*: the starting point of the h is made by a different stroke here, and the final emphasis stroke is longer and more open compared to that of Petrarch's usual *h*. Furthermore, the final dot of the emphasis stroke does not appear elsewhere in Petrarch's writing; his *h* is characterized by a highly regular shape that is only marginally subjected to graphical variants. Again, therefore, I suggest that the line 11 *h* was written in a different hand by someone trying to emulate Petrarch's style. As Storey, in answer to Modigliani, wrote in his commented edition of Vat. Lat. 3195 (Belloni et. al 2004, 389):

> Egli [Modigliani] indica, però "volto" e "Che" (vv. 10 e 11) quali interventi della stessa mano con inchiostro più scuro su rasura: al contrario, l'inchiostro e la mano di "volto" risultano diversi rispetto alla mano e all'inchiostro degli interventi di "E" e "Che"; sia "E" che "C" e "h" non paiono infatti rispecchiare il *ductus* petrarchesco (essendo lo svolazzo tipicamente petrarchesco della "e" di "Che" il residuo di una "e" fuori dallo spazio della rasura). Per quanto riguarda la tradizione di questo sonetto, la lezione "Eccio" non è inoltre attestata né dai codici trecenteschi, né dall'edizione Valdezoco (1472).

> He [Modigliani], however, points to "volto" and "Che" (lines 10 and 11) as interventions in the same hand with a darker ink on top of the erasure: on the contrary, the ink and the hand of "volto" are distinct from the hand and the ink of the interventions of "E" and "Che"; in fact, neither "E" nor "C" and "h" seem to reflect the Petrarchan *ductus* (the typical Petrarchan flourish of the "e" of "Che" being the remainder of an "e" outside the space of the erasure). As regards the tradition of this sonnet, moreover, the reading "Eccio" is documented neither in fourteenth-century codices nor in the 1472 Valdezoco edition.

According to Storey, neither the line 9 *E* nor the line 11 *Ch* can be attributed to Petrarch because they do not reflect his *ductus*. In disagreement with Modigliani, Storey argues that *volto* and *Che* are emendations made by different hands with different inks. I agree with Storey that *volto* and *Che* are made by two different hands and that *volto* was probably written in a different ink by Petrarch himself, as its letters still preserve the same semi-Gothic features that belong to his usual writing style, despite the fact that the letters are horizontally scaled narrowly due to lack of space. However, I do wish to highlight that the oblique flourish of the *e* of *Che* is not typical of Petrarch's style but was made by the same non-authorial hand responsible for the retracing of *S* and *Che*. Instead, the only sign of the original *e* flourish that remains visible is in the ultraviolet digital reproductions; it has the same horizontal orientation that is used regularly by the poet and was probably made almost invisible by the stain. Figure 13 shows how the Photoshop "lasso" tool can identify the shape of this horizontal stroke and then fill the selected area using the "clone" tool to sample the original ink color.

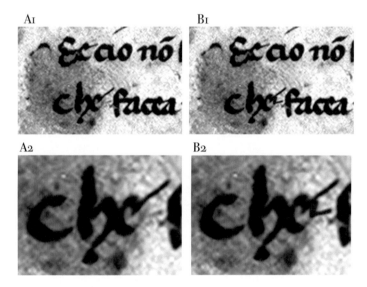

Figure 13. A1-A2: Detail of sonnet 179, beginning of line n. 9 and 11 (ultra violet reproduction). B1-B2: Detail of Sonnet 179, beginning of line n. 9 and 11 with the restored ending stroke of the original petrarchan's "e" of "Che" (ultra violet reproduction).

The results of using this technique make implausible what scholars including Mestica, Modigliani, and Bettarini state in order to support their reading of the beginning of line 9: that Petrarch's distraction caused him to forget to emend the lower case *e* of *Se* while he was erasing the capital *S*. Indeed, according to their own reconstruction, in the specific moment of revision the conditional word *Se* should have been under the watchful eye of the author, were he emending and not simply copying from a draft source. It seems highly unlikely that he could have forgotten to correct the *e*: first, because during an erasure process an author would normally be extremely vigilant; and second, because we are certain that Petrarch was a relentless editor of his *Canzoniere*, always focused on a constant *labor lime* on all poems. Vat. Lat. 3195 itself demonstrates this with its numerous still-visible authorial corrections. To stand by the Mestica reading, we would also need to agree implicitly that Petrarch would have never read back over the sonnet after his alleged emendation, a notion that seems profoundly unlikely considering Petrarch's authorial *modus operandi*. Instead, codicological, palaeographical, and historical evidence suggests that the words at the beginning of lines 9 and 11 were manipulated by a non-authorial hand in order to repair them following staining of the parchment. During this operation, Petrarch's original script was partially impacted, causing a misreading not only of the text but also of the author's intention.

A second case in which imaging manipulation tools can help us to read and interpret Petrarch's text is sonnet 321, "È quest 'l nido in che la mia fenice." (Figure 14).

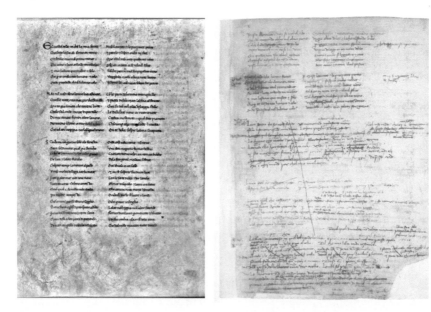

Figure 14. Vatican City, Biblioteca Apostolia Vaticana, Vat. Lat. 3195, c. 62v; Vatican City, Biblioteca Apostolica Vaticana, Vat. Lat. 3196, c. 2r.

In this sonnet, the memory of Laura arises from the ashes of the previous poem to create an image of the phoenix, which constitutes one of the most significant and innovative metaphors used by Petrarch to depict his deceased beloved. I will focus specifically on line 8 in order to discuss the assumptions behind the disparate readings of commentators. The controversy that the sonnet has inspired concerns the first word of the line "Sol eri in terra, or se' nel ciel felice." Two readings have been proposed: the first interprets the word *Sol* as the adjective *sola* (alone) and is supported by the majority of scholars: Giosuè Carducci and Severino Ferrari (Petrarca 1899), Gianfranco Contini and Daniele Ponchiroli (Petrarca 1992), and Rosanna Bettarini (Bettarini 1998); others, including Cozzo G. Salvo (Petrarca 1904a) and Savoca, propose a second reading—*Sol* as the noun *sole* (sun). In both interpretations, the word is subject to apocope. Proponents of *sola* cite as evidence the fact that in the definitive copy (Vat. Lat. 3195) an effaced *a* is still visible and that in the draft codex (Vat. Lat. 3196) the entire word *Sola* appears (Figure 15). Cozzo argues, however, that Petrarch's erasure of the final vowel of *Sola* reflects a change of mind on the part of the author, who felt a new need to address Laura using a metaphor.

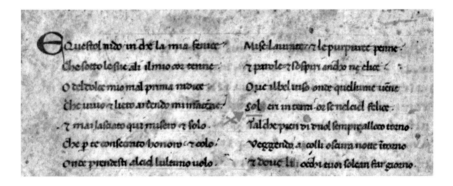

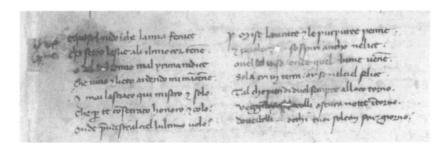

Figure 15. Vat. Lat. 3195, c. 62v; Vat. Lat. 3196, c. 2r.

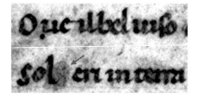 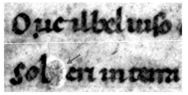

Figure 16. Vat. Lat. 3195, f. 62v, detail of sonnet 321. Before applying enhancement filter / After applying enhancement filter.

The *Canzoniere* is replete with instances where Laura is identified as the sun (e.g., "Almo Sol, quella fronde ch'io sola amo" in *canzone* 87) and where she is considered unique, the only woman who can inspire the poet (*sola*). Readers are thus accustomed to bestowing both these attributes upon Laura. This controversy, in other words, is based on evidence not of an ambiguity that must be resolved but of an ambiguity that readers have always experienced in the text.[8] Indeed, all of the metaphoric codes adopted by Petrarch are based on ambiguity and antithesis. For example, his writings fuse Christian and pagan symbols in order to generate a new semantic code in which the world of classical literature can coexist with—rather than be opposed to— Holy Scripture. Even the phoenix, a pagan symbol, is used by Petrarch to allude to Christian resurrection (Van den Broek 1971).

Stepping away from the metaphorical to the physical, I want to now focus on the physical area where scholars anticipate the letter *a* as the last letter of *Sola*. By applying a filter to enhance the image level, it is possible to see a multitude of different cursive *a* letters, all placed in the space between the words *Sol* and *eri* (Figure 16). We can restore the faded ink of these letters using Photoshop, though since we want to restore only what is missing in the heavy erasure patch, we cannot apply a global level adjustment to the whole image. Fortunately, the division between the erasure area and the rest of the page is clear enough to permit the use of the "magnetic lasso" tool for selecting out the bits of the image that we are going to edit. Once the boundaries of the erasure are selected, we can use the "exposure" and "tonal curve" tools to brighten the area and to emphasize the contrast between the background and the effaced text. Because we have already performed a level adjust on

---

[8] For a similar approach, see Stanley E. Fish: "What I would like to argue is that they [matters of pronoun referents, lexical ambiguities, punctuation] are not *meant* to be solved, but to be experienced (they signify), and that consequently any procedure that attempts to determine which of a number of readings is correct will necessarily fail" (Fish 1976, p. 476).

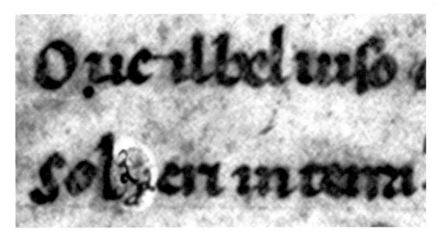

Figure 17. Vat. Lat. 3195, f. 62v, sonnet 321, line 8—restored a into the area of erasure.

The deleted material recovered using this technique (i.e., the multiple letter *a*'s) confirms that Petrarch changed his mind many times,[9] suggesting that he was not sure whether to retain the ambiguity (letting the word *Sol*, with the apocope of the final *a* stand) or whether to clarify the meaning by writing out the entire word *Sola* (Figure 17). His decision to leave the word without the final *a* keeps the word open to both interpretations. In order to support this reading more strongly, we must delve into Petrarch's poetics and *modus operandi*, focusing our analysis on the draft that appears in Vat. Lat. 3196 on folio 2r. Next to the sonnet are two marginalia: the first, to the left of the first line: "tr(anscriptum) p(er) me" (transcribed by me); the second, to the right of first two lines: "at(tende) in h(oc) repetit(i)o(nem) u(er)bor(um) n(on) s(e) n(tent)iar(um)" (pay attention to the repetition of words not of sentences). This second marginalia is crossed out; some scholars (e.g., Santagata) argue this indicates that Petrarch changed his mind about paying attention to the repetition of words over concepts. However, since the word *solo* is repeated on the following line ("et m'hai lasciato qui misero, et solo"), I argue that Petrarch actually did as the marginalia suggested by erasing the *a* from *Sola* in the Vat. Lat. 3195 copy, thereby avoiding repetition of the same adjective.

---

[9] I agree entirely with Storey (2007, 74–78), who advocates for a shift in Vat. Lat. 3195 from "fair copy" to "service copy" as confirmed by a much higher occurrence of erasure in the sections copied by Petrarch. The presence of many *a*'s written and subsequently erased by Petrarch confirms that the poet used the manuscript to experiment with and change his text.

After making this erasure, he likely crossed out the corresponding marginalia in Vat. Lat. 3196 to remind himself that he had done what it said (Figure 18).

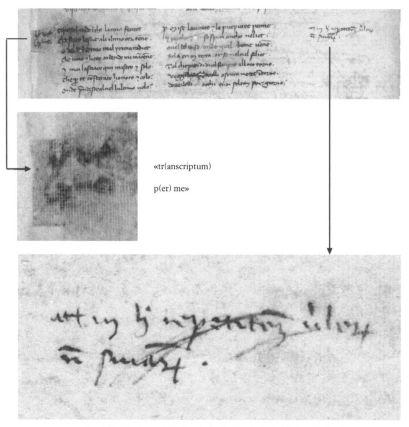

«tr(anscriptum)

p(er) me»

«at(tende) in h(oc) repetit(i)o(nem) u(er)bor(um) n(on) s(e)n(tent)iar(um)»
(pay attention to the repetition of words, not to the repetition of concepts)

Figure 18. Vat. Lat. 3196, f. 2r.

The paleographical features of these *a*'s indicate that they were written using the same script adopted by Petrarch for his marginal gloss and note. According to one of the most important paleographical essays on Petrarch (Petrucci 1967), we can legitimately state that each different *a* shape belongs to specific period of time, demonstrating that Petrarch worked on this sonnet for a long period of time during which he wavered between the two variants (Figure 19).

Before 1325-1335

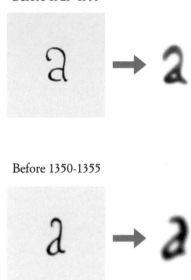

Before 1350-1355

Figure 19. The classification above follows the results of the paleo-graphical essay written by Armando Petrucci (Petrucci 1975) related to Petrarch's marginalia script.

Another productive experiment that we can conduct is to select the final *a* from other occurrences of the word *Sola* in Petrarch's hand and to digitally move them into the area of erasure to confirm whether or not there was enough space for Petrarch to include the final *a*. In order to be sure of an exact match, the selection is limited to *Sola* appearing with a capital *S* at the beginning of a line; we of course cannot ignore variations in Petrarch's handwriting according to the letter's specific position within the word. To simulate similar scenarios digitally, we can crop the final *a* of selected words employing the same technique already adopted and export each letter into a separate layer to be moved manually to the end of the word *Sol* and manipulated individually. As we can see from the two edited images in Figure 20, there is enough space to write the word *Sola* with the final *a*.

Detail of Sonnet 321, line n. 8, f. 62v with letter
a transposed from sonnet 196, v. 14, f. 39*r*   Enlargement

Detail of Sonnet 321, line n. 8, f. 62v with letter
a transposed from sonnet 197, v. 12 f. 39*r*   Enlargement

Figure 20. Detail of Sonnet 321, line n. 8 with letter a transposed from sonnet 196 and 197.

The above examples demonstrate that by using Photoshop as a digital editing tool we can manipulate the body of the manuscript from several different points of view: we can overlap folios and compare stains, erasures, and holes that affect the manuscript without the risk of compromising the original. In addition, we can literally disassemble the handwriting—moving letters, comparing them to each other, and highlighting details that would not ever be possible to see with a traditional approach. These digital methodologies, however, are not always successful. The primary limiting factors are poor image quality, extremely heavy deletions or erasures, and manuscript deterioration. Unfortunately, we can rarely control any of these factors.

My final example applies this set of technological tools to the illuminations of the first printed edition of Petrarch's *Canzoniere* made by the poet and painter Antonio Del Grifo.[10] Only one copy of this *editio princeps* (Inc. Queriniano G.V.15), which was printed in Venice by the typographer Vindelino da Spira in 1470,[11] was illustrated by Del Grifo; for this reason it represents an

---

[10] More information about Antonio Grifo can be found on Frasso 1990, Marcozzi 2002 and ID. 2015.

[11] The incunabulum printed by the typographer Vindelino Spira in 1470 is the *editio princeps* of the vernacular work of Petrarch. Nowadays, only twenty-seven of the one hundred copies originally printed survive. Among them, two are made of parchment. The incunabulum Queriniano should be the copy already known by the two bibliophiles Haym and Marsand: owned by the family Gagliardi of Brescia, and then transferred to the Biblioteca dei Filippini in Lodi, and eventually to the Queriniana in Brescia (See Haym 1728; Marsand 1820, 2:310). Additional information can be found

invaluable document for our understanding of readings and interpretations of Petrarch during the Renaissance period (Figure 21). I focus on an analysis of *canzone* 325, "Tacer non posso, e temo non adopre," in which Laura is depicted metaphorically as a house.

Figure 21. Petrarch, *Canzoniere*, Inc. Quer. G.V.15, Opening sonnett, f. 1r.

in Baroncelli 1970, 301, number 717; Sandal 1995; Donati 1952; Cossutta 1998, 419–48; Gibellini 2000; Zaganelli 2000; Zaganelli 2002, 85–129; Cossutta 2004; Zaganelli 2005–06, Zava 2015, Argurio 2019. For more details about the editorial history of some of these incunabula, see Marcozzi Luca, *L'incunabolo vindeliniano di Petrarca e Grifo*, 2003, and Marcozzi Luca, *Comedia di Dante con figure dipinte. L'incunabolo veneziano del 1491 nell'esemplare della casa di dante in Roma con postille manoscritte e figure dipinte. Commentario all'edizione in fac-simile.*, 2015, Maddalo 2019.

This *canzone*, which is placed in the section on the death of Laura, evokes an image of the departed woman through an architectural metaphor: the external building constitutes her physical body, which guards her immortal soul within. We will now analyze the semantics of the Petrarchan text in relation to the interpretation that Grifo provides in his decorations. The roof is gold, to indicate the golden locks of Laura's hair; the door, forged in ivory, represents the perfection of her mouth and teeth; the exterior walls of alabaster replicate the candor of her skin, and the two turquoise windows recall her blue eyes (Figure 22).

Figure 22. Petrarch, *Canzoniere*, Inc. Quer. G.V.15, f. 114v-115r.

The metaphorical house of Laura seems to be set among trees upon a slight promontory that rises a little above a small hill. At the entrance to the house is a detailed laurel tree from whose branches are blossoming green leaves and fruits.[12]

---

[12] The fruits of the laurel are called *drupe*. They are dark in color and contain only one seed.

Figure 23 proposes a digital restoration of this illumination in which areas affected by ink fading and tint aberration are restored using a digital technique that takes advantage of a color range sample tool. By analyzing the results of this digital restoration, we can propose some considerations concerning Grifo's artistic intentions. Grifo interpreted and translated into images the prominent *topos* of the eyes that appears throughout the *Canzoniere*. In the Petrarchan phenomenology of love, which was inspired by the literary trends of the Sicilian School and the Florentine *dolce stil novo* poets, the eyes symbolize an ambivalent vehicle of love that can be understood as an instrument of human passion or as a bridge to God's truth.

Figure 23. Petrarch, *Canzoniere*, Inc. Quer. G.V.15, f. 115r.

The poet's and Laura's eyes are the protagonists of both *canzone* 325 and Grifo's illumination, which directs the reader's gaze towards the windows that symbolize Laura's eyes, allowing him to experience the same ungovernable attraction felt by Petrarch himself. The *canzone* proceeds to praise the spiritual and moral qualities of Laura through metaphors and symbols largely inspired by Christian doctrine and texts:

> D'un bel diamante quadro, et mai non scemo,
> Vi si vedea nel mezzo un seggio altero
> Ove sola sedea la bella donna.
> Dinanzi, una colonna
> Cristallina, et iv'entro ogni pensero
> Scritto, et for tralucea sì` chiaramente,
> Che mi fea lieto, et sospirar sovente. (Petrarch 2008, *RVF* CCCXXV, 24–30)

> Made from cut diamond, never flawed,
> a noble throne was seen within,
> where the lovely lady sat alone:
> in front a crystal
> column, and all her thoughts there
> written, and shining from it so clearly,
> it made me joyful, and often full of sighs.

Grifo illustrated these last lines on folio 115v.

Figure 24. Petrarch, *Canzionere*, Inc. Quer. G.V.15, f. 115v.

The throne and the column are both placed on a squared pedestal. From the seat of the throne emerges a laurel, the personification of Laura. The pedestal symbolizes the strict moral purity of Laura's incorruptible soul, its fullness and greatness.[13] The adjective *scemo* (flawed) was carefully chosen by Petrarch to mark that metaphorical reading; I would argue that Grifo's illumination alludes to Petrarch's Augustinian influence. Carducci, in his commentary on the *Canzoniere*, suggests Augustine's *De civitate Dei* as the primary source:

> Et quod de lignis quadratis fieri iubetur, undique stabilem vitam sanctorum significat; quacumque enim verteris quadratum, stabit; et cetera, quae in eiusdem arcae constructione dicuntur, ecclesiasticarum signa sunt rerum.

> The order of constructing it [the arc of the covenant] with the tables of square form symbolizes the life of saints, stable at every point. In fact from any part a square remains a square, even the other indications on the construction of the arc are symbols regarding the Church.

This passage recounts St. Augustine's metaphor of the square, which symbolizes the incorruptibility of the soul as well as its stability—characteristics that distinguish a saint's virtues and asceticism. Augustine considers the geometry of the square to be not only a symbol of virtue but also the architecture and language of God himself. I would suggest that there is another passage from St. Augustine's *Sermones* 335/E that can be considered another source of the Petrarchan allegory. In this passage, Augustine again focuses on the significance of the square's symbolism as an expression of the incorruptibility of the holy martyrs who—though they were exposed to violence and temptation—remained faithful to the tenets of Christianity and steadfast in God's truth. Augustine intends to emphasize the fact that saints, martyrs, and those who make manifest the will of God do not fear the world because nothing in it is capable of affecting their moral stability ("that which is a square can be tossed but it cannot fall"). He concludes by explaining that men who have led a virtuous life in accordance with Christian doctrine ("squared by truth") will eventually be crowned in heaven:

---

[13] For the multiplicity of possible meanings attributed to the image of the laurel tree by Grifo see also Zava 2015, p. 219.

Nullus martyr fuit qui non fuerit veritate quadratus.

Beatorum martyrum sollemnem diem voluit nos Dominus celebrare vobiscum. Hinc ergo aliquid loquamur, quod donaverit Dominus, qui arcam in qua figuravit Ecclesiam lignis quadratis voluit fabricari. Quadratum enim quacumque in pulverem, stantem invenis. Mira res et quasi impossibilis sed tamen advertite et invenietis; quadratus deici potest, cadere non potest. Deiecti sunt martyres in terra humilitatis sed non ceciderunt, quia in caelo sunt coronati. Nullus martyr fuit qui non fuerit veritate quadratus. (Augustine, *Sermons*, 335/E, 1)

Every martyr is squared by the truth.

It is by the will of God that we should be able to celebrate with you the solemn day of blessed martyrs. Until now, therefore, we wished to say something that the Lord will have inspired, he that willed the Arc, figure of the Church, constructed with square-cut beams. You find in fact that a square object, from every side spun on the ground, it remains in a stable position. It is a strange fact, it seems impossible, but pay close attention and you will note it, that which is square can be tossed but it cannot fall. Against the ground of humility the martyrs were tossed, but they did not fall because they came to be crowned in heaven. There is no martyr that was not squared by the truth.)

By describing Laura's soul as seated on a squared chair, therefore, Petrarch alludes to her sanctity and to her celestial coronation in heaven.

On folio 115v to the right of the column is a marginal note written by Grifo himself: "Coronata" (crowned; see Figure 25) (Frasso et. al. 1990, 131).[14] I argue that the two laurel trees painted by Grifo that appear in front of the palace and on the throne are symbols not only of Love's victory over the Poet but also of the sublimated nature of Laura's soul, which is clearly depicted as that of a saint. With *Coronata* ending in the Italian feminine singular *a*, it can only refer to Laura who is crowned—a link to the Augustinian passage quoted above. I would argue, in fact, that Grifo interpreted the Petrarchan text according to the metaphors and symbols of Augustine's sermon in which squared martyrs are crowned in heaven, and that he wrote *Coronata* above the throne, exactly where Laura should be represented according to the *canzone*.

---

[14] Frasso transcribes only the *incipit* annotation written by Grifo on folio 115r, not the marginalia on folio 115v.

Figure 25. Petrarch, *Canzoniere*, Inc. Quer. G.V.15, f. 115v.

This illumination, therefore, is not a simple illustration that straightforwardly describes an event narrated by Petrarch. Instead, Grifo seems to go beyond the words of the poem with both decoration and annotation to expose subtle poetic meanings hidden in the text. He thus provides visual access to the reading of the poem—access that effectively replaces the role of erudite commentaries printed during the Renaissance.

In order to support this reading, I will demonstrate that the laurel tree to which *Coronata* refers was not decorated in green (like the laurel in front of the palace) but in gold. The area around the laurel *Coronata* is victim to such significant ink fading and discoloration that it is difficult to discern with the human eye whether the laurel tree was indeed intentionally colored gold or whether this impression is merely caused by fading ink. To prove that Grifo intentionally used gold for this laurel, we can analyze the illumination by selecting the area of the image that matches the same color range of the golden beams emitted by the column. The two digitally edited images that result can be seen in Figure 26.

The technique adopted here takes advantage of a specific Photoshop tool that is intended to recognize a given color range within an existing selection or an entire image. Using the "clone tool," it is possible to assign a specific color range sampling to the reference color (in our scenario, the color range used by Grifo to color the golden beam) in the "color range" dialog box. The software will then automatically detect and localize all color clusters that match the sampled color range. This use of image manipulation software is very effective and has wide-ranging potential applications.

Original reproduction   **Selected area with the same color
of golden beams**

Figure 26. Petrarch, *Canzoniere*, Inc. Quer. G.V.15, folio 115v.

The chromatic difference between the green laurel and the golden one that Grifo illuminated distinctly with intention has important hermeneutic implications that, in conjunction with the symbolism of the square, allow us a better understanding of the Christological significance that Grifo attributed to Laura. For Grifo, the golden laurel could represent not only the general concept of the immortality of the soul but also the true sanctity of Laura in particular. It is this Augustinian reading of the Petrarchan lyric that inspired Grifo to include a symbol of Christian resurrection in his illumination without apparently altering the traditional iconography of the laurel—and without, therefore, interrupting the continuity of the codified tradition that identifies the laurel tree with the crowned poet. Grifo's two laurel bushes have chromatic characteristics that differentiate their functions in a decisive way—characteristics that can be difficult if not impossible to distinguish without this image manipulation method. In other words, the adoption of technological tools to perform sophisticated digital techniques can allow us—even without direct contact with original manuscripts and early printed editions—to read and thus to understand them even better, at times, than if we had the physical pages before our very eyes.

WORKS CITED

Augustinus, Aurelius, Domenico Gentili, and Agostino Trapè. 1988. *La città di Dio: testo latino dell'edizione maurina confrontato con il Corpus Christianorum. 2, 2.* Roma: Città Nuova.

Augustinus, Aurelius, Antonio Quacquarelli, and Marcella Recchia. 1986. *Discorsi. su I Santi: testo latino dall'edizione Maurina e delle edizioni postmaurine Parte 5, Parte 5.* Opere Di Sant'Agostino. Roma: Città Nuova.

Barezzani, Rosa Maria Teresa. 2010. "Dalla "pastorella" di Francesco Petrarca al *Cerf Blanc* di Guillaume de Machaut: Alcune brevi annotazioni". In *Civiltà bresciana*, 3–4, pp. 7–61. Brescia: Fondazione Civiltà Bresciana.

Baroncelli, Ugo. 1970. *Gli incunabuli della Biblioteca Queriniana di Brescia (catalogo).* Brescia: Ateneo.

Belloni, Gino, Furio Brugnolo, H. Wayne Storey, and Stefano Zamponi. 2004. *Rerum Vulgarium Fragmenta: Codice Vat. Lat. 3195: Commentario All'edizione in Fac-Simile.* Rome: Antenore.

Bembo, Pietro. 2001. *Prose della volgar lingua: l'editio princeps del 1525 riscontrata con l'autografo Vaticano latino 3210.* Edizione critica a cura di Claudio Vela. Bologna: CLUEB.

Bettarini, Rosanna. 1998. *Lacrime e inchiostro nel Canzoniere di Petrarca.* Bologna: CLUEB.

Cossutta, Fabio. 1998. "Il Maestro Queriniano interprete del Petrarca." *Critica letteraria* 26: 419–48.

———. 2004. "Tra iconologia ed esegesi petrarchesca. Note sulla Laura Queriniana." *Humanitas* 59: 66–82.

Donati, Lamberto. 1952. "Appunti di biblioiconologia (del Petrarca Queriniano, Venezia 1470)." In *Miscellanea di studi di bibliografia e di erudizione in memoria di Luigi Ferrari*, 249–52. Florence: Olschki.

Durling, Robert M. 1976. *Petrarch's Lyric Poems*. Cambridge, MA: Harvard University Press.

Fish, Eugene Stanley. 1976, "Interpreting the 'Variorum.'" *Critical Inquiry* 2.3: 465–85.

Frasso, Giuseppe, Canova G. Mariani, and Ennio Sandal. 1990. *Illustrazione libraria, filologia e esegesi petrarchesca tra Quattrocento e Cinquecento: Antonio Grifo e l'incunabolo Queriniano G V 15*. Padova: Antenore.

Gibellini, Pietro. 2000. "Il Petrarca per immagini del Dilettante Queriniano." *Annali queriniani* 1: 41–62.

Greene, Thomas M. 1982. *The Light in Troy: Imitation and Discovery in Renaissance Poetry*. New Haven, CT: Yale University Press.

Haym, Nicola Francesco. 1728. *Biblioteca italiana o sia notizia de' libri rari nella lingua italiana, divisa in quattro parti principali; cioè Istoria, Poesia, Prose, Arti e Scienze [. . .]*. Venice: Angiolo Geremia in Campo di S. Salvatore.

Lee, Alexander. 2012. *Petrarch and St. Augustine: Classical Scholarship, Christian Theology, and the Origins of the Renaissance in Italy*. Leiden: Brill.

Lollini, Massimo. 2001. *Il vuoto della forma. Scrittura, testimonianza e verità*. Genova: Marietti.

Maddalo, Silvia. 2019. "Commentare in figura la Commedia. Antonio Grifo e i marginalia miniati nell'incunabolo della Casa di Dante", *Dante visualizzato — Carte ridenti III: XV secolo*. Seconda parte, a cura di R. Arqués Corominas e S. Ferrara, Firenze 2019, pp. 193–207.

Marcozzi, Luca. 2003. "L'incunabolo vindeliniano di Petrarca e Grifo." *WUZ*, II(3): 22–27.

———. 2015. *Comedia Di Dante Con Figure Dipinte: L'incunabolo Veneziano Del 1491 Nell'esemplare Della Casa Di Dante in Roma Con Postille Manoscritte E Figure Dipinte: Commentario All'edizione in Fac-Simile*, Roma: Salerno.

Marsand, Antonio. 1820. "Notizia." In *Rime*, by F. Petrarca. Padova: Tip. del Seminario.

Muir, Bernard J. 2002. *Ductus: Digital Latin Paleography.* Parkville, Australia: Bernard J. Muir. Computer file.

Petrarca, Francesco. 1896. *Le rime di Francesco Petrarca restituite nell'ordine e nella lezione del testo originario sugli autografi, col sussidio di altri codici e di stampe e corredate di varianti e note da Giovanni Mestica,* edited with notes by Giovanni Mestica. Florence: G. Barbèra.

———. 1899. *Le Rime Di Francesco Petrarca Di Su Gli Originali,* with notes by Giosuè Carducci and Severino Ferrari. Florence: G. C. Sansoni.

———. 1904a. *Le Rime di Franceso Petrarca: secondo la revisione ultima del poeta,* edited by Cozzo G. Salvo. Florence: G. C. Sansoni.

———. 1904b. *Il canzoniere di Francesco Petrarca riprodotto letteralmente dal cod. vat. Lat. 3195,* edited by Ettore Modigliani. Rome: La Società.

———. 1992. *Canzoniere.* Introduction by Roberto Antonelli, critical essay by Gianfranco Contini, notes by Daniele Ponchiroli. Turin: Einaudi.

———. 2005. *Canzoniere: Rerum Vulgarium Fragmenta,* edited by Rosanna Bettarini. Turin: Einaudi.

———. 2008. *Rerum Vulgarium Fragmenta,* critical edition by Giuseppe Savoca. Firenze: Olschki.

Petrucci, Armando. 1967. *La scrittura di Francesco Petrarca.* Vatican City: Biblioteca Apostolica Vaticana.

Pulsoni, Carlo, and Marco Cursi. 2009. "Sulla tradizione antica dei «Rerum vulgarium fragmenta»: un gemello del Laurenziano XLI 10 (Paris, Bibliothèque Nationale, It. 551)." *Studi di Filologia Italiana* 67: 91–114.

Sandal, Antonio, ed. 1995. *Petrarca, Francesco. Il Canzoniere. I Trionfi, Edizione anastatica dell'incunabolo queriniano G V 15* (Venezia, Vindelino da Spira, 1470), Brescia: Grafo Edizioni.

Savoca, Giuseppe. 2008. *Il Canzoniere di Petrarca tra Codicologia ed Ecdotica.* Florence: Leo S. Olschki.

Savoca, Giuseppe and Calderone, Bartolo. 2011. *Concordanza del Canzoniere di Francesco Petrarca,* Firenze: Olschki.

Schuler, Irmgard. 2009. "La fotografia dei manoscritti nella prospettiva della loro conservazione." The International Federation of Library

Associations and Institutions (IFLA) website 25/03/2020. https://www. ifla.org/files/assets/pac/Satellite_Meeting_Rome_2009/Schuler_ it.pdf.

Simone, Franco. 1970. *Il Petrarca e la cultura francese del suo tempo.* Turin: Società editrice internazionale.

Storey, H. Wayne. 2007. "Doubting Petrarch's Last Words: Erasure in MS Vaticano Latino 3195." In *Petrarch and the Textual Origins of Interpretation,* edited by Teodolinda Barolini and H. Wayne Storey, 67–92. Leiden and Boston: Brill.

Van den Broek, Roelof. 1971. *The Myth of the Phoenix: According to Classical and Early Christian Traditions.* Leiden: Brill.

Zaganelli, Giovanna. 2000. *Dal "Canzoniere" del Petrarca al Canzoniere di Antonio Grifo: percorsi metatestuali.* Perugia: Guerra.

———. 2002. "La storia del Petrarca e la favola del Grifo. Costruzioni narrative." *Annali queriniani* 3: 85–129.

———. 2005–2006. "Narrare per immagini: il caso del Petrarca illustrato da Antonio Grifo." *Atti e memorie dell'Accademia Petrarca di lettere, arti e scienze* 67/68: 275–88.

Zava, Giulia. 2015. "Dilettante nell'illustrazione, Maestro nell'esegesi. Il disegno interpretativo nelle immagini del Petrarca queriniano." *Quaderni Veneti* vol. 4: pp. 201–239.

Translation and Print Networks in Seventeenth-Century Britain: From Catalog Entries to Digital Visualizations

Marie-Alice Belle
Département de linguistique
et traduction,
Université de Montréal

Marie-France Guénette
Département de langues,
linguistique et traduction,
Université Laval

In their introduction to the 2016 NTMRS volume *Early Modern Studies after the "Digital Turn,"* Laura Estill, Diane Jakacki, and Michael Ullyot sum up the critical contribution of digital approaches to early modern studies as a series of challenges to "settled orthodoxies" (Estill, Jakacki, and Ullyot 2016, 2). The new critical narratives enabled by means of digital methods, they argue, call into question linear readings of literary history, revealing instead the multivocal dynamics of early modern textual production and dissemination. They invite us to test the validity of established literary canons and hierarchies, as well as the traditional focus on single authorship and individual "originality." Finally, they contribute to qualifying accounts of literary history merely defined along national boundaries, and help us re-envisage early modern culture in terms of the complex, transnational circulation of texts, ideas, objects, and people.

These critical trends appear to be particularly well represented in recent attempts to approach literary production from a network analysis perspective. The most obvious example for early modern British studies is perhaps the *Six Degrees of Francis Bacon* project, now in its second phase. As made explicit on the project website, its aim is to offer "a digital reconstruction of the early modern social network," as established from the entries in the *Oxford Dictionary of National Biography* (*ODNB*), but also through voluntary scholarly crowdsourcing. Another important initiative, more directly focused on print production, is the University of Iowa's *Shakeosphere* project featuring an interactive interface for network analysis and visualization, based on all titles and imprints recorded in the *English Short Title Catalogue* (*ESTC*). Networks of literary production and circulation for early modern women's writings have been the focus of the University of Galway's *Reception and Circulation of Early Modern Women's Writing 1550–1700* (*RECIRC*) project, an initiative that has yielded new and important insights into women's roles as connectors in

ISBN 978-1-64959-016-9 (paper) ISBN 978-1-64959-017-6 (pdf) ISBN 978-1-64959-037-4 (epub)
New Technologies in Medieval and Renaissance Studies 9 (2022) 195–233

literary circles (Bourke 2017). Transnational perspectives have also been afforded by Ruth and Sebastian Ahnert's *Tudor Networks of Power* project reconstructing diplomatic and intelligence networks from the State Papers (Ahnert and Ahnert 2015, Ahnert 2016a), and by the *Early Modern News Networks*
project focusing on the European circulation of news in the early modern
period (Raymond and Moxham 2016).[1]

Among the many vectors of cultural transmission documented in such initiatives, translation and translators are gradually being acknowledged as significant players. The *Six Degrees of Francis Bacon* project has recently started
to identify translators as a distinct category, or "group." The *RECIRC* database
recognizes translation as a specific mode of reception of early modern wom-
en's writings. Joad Raymond even singles out the conceptual importance of
translation as a *node*, or mode of connection, in networks of early modern
European news circulation (Raymond 2016, 116). Yet so far there has been no
systematic study of the production and circulation of early modern translations from a network analysis perspective. Besides the critical developments
outlined above, we now have at our disposal a rich archive with *The Renaissance Cultural Crossroads Online Catalogue of Translations in Britain 1473-1640* (ed.
Hosington, 2013), and the follow-up *Cultural Crosscurrents Catalogue of Printed
Translations in Stuart and Commonwealth Britain (1641-1660)* (eds. Belle and
Hosington, forthcoming). This essay represents a first attempt to explore
these bibliographical resources from a network analysis perspective.[2] Our
critical outlook is rooted in recent approaches to early modern translation
focusing specifically on material and social aspects of text production and
dissemination (Coldiron 2015, Armstrong 2014 and 2015, Boutcher 2015,

---

[1] See also Stanford University's *Mapping the Republic of Letters* initiative, focusing on
epistolary connections in the eighteenth century.

[2] The analysis presented below has been developed as part of a pilot study at the
Université de Montréal (2017–18), a preliminary step to the broader international
project, *Trajectories of Translation in Early Modern Britain: Routes, Mediations, Networks
(2018–22)*. We wish to acknowledge the financial support of the Université de Montréal
and the Social Sciences and Humanities Research Council of Canada, as well as the
National Endowment for the Humanities and the Folger Shakespeare Library. We are
particularly grateful to the instructors at the Folger 2017 Early Modern Digital Agen-
das summer institute, especially Ruth Ahnert, Sebastian Ahnert, and Jonathan Hope,
and to all participants for their insights and their feedback on earlier versions of the
case studies below. Our thanks also go to William Bowen, Raymond Siemens, Brenda
M. Hosington, and the participants in the New Technologies in Renaissance Studies
panels at RSA 2018 (New Orleans).

Belle and Hosington 2017, 2018). Our analysis of translation networks does not therefore focus on textual or stylistic "shifts" in translation (see Lagresa 2018), nor on patterns of linguistic transfer *per se*. Instead, we approach the early modern printed translation as a material and cultural object enabling us to trace the various actors (both human and non-human) involved in its production, dissemination, and reception. Our aim is to explore the critical potential of network analysis in particular questions raised by the unprecedented flourishing of a market for printed translations in Britain, at a time of intense social, cultural, and ideological polarization. Besides discussing the general critical outlook and methodology developed to that effect, we will present two case studies in which we document, analyze, and visualize various networks underlying the production and circulation of printed translations in early Stuart and Commonwealth Britain. We hope thereby to make a timely contribution to the growing corpus of network-based studies in early modern literary, cultural, and material history.

Theoretical underpinnings: a network-oriented approach to the study of translation and print production in early modern Britain

Defined broadly, network analysis consists in reconstituting the components (*nodes*) in a network and their relationships (*ties*, or *edges*) in order to discern the configuration of the network, the relative importance of its components, as well as the nature, breadth, and intensity of the relationships involved (Hanneman and Riddle 2005). The critical advantages of a network-based historiographical approach can be summed up as follows. First, because of its object-based, "bottom-up" methodology, network analysis has been presented as a relative corrective to canon biases and implicit hierarchies. Indeed, at least in ideal practice, both obvious and less-known actors in the network are included *a priori*, as well as being equally submitted to digital calculation and visualization. This aspect is all the more important for us as translation scholarship and criticism have long tended to ignore or marginalize translations that conform less to modern literary, critical, or even ideological standards, even when they were historically important (see Bassnett 1998, Belle 2007, Goodrich 2015).

Similarly, following Bruno Latour's pioneering studies of the complex "assemblages" of human and non-human vectors in the creation and dissemination of knowledge (Latour 2005), network analysis methodologies pay equal attention to human agents (in our case, translators, printers, patrons, etc.) and non-human actors (such as geographical locations, technologies of text production and transmission, book features, etc.). This proves crucial if one is to document the social and material "cultures" in which translations originate and circulate (see Burke 2007, Newman and Tylus 2015, Demetriou and Tomlinson 2015). A quantitative analysis of the material networks underlying translation production and dissemination seems particularly relevant in the context of the English Civil Wars: not only do the 1640s and 1650s represent pivotal decades for the history of print in Britain (see Kastan 2007, Feather 2007, Peacey 2013), but they also witness an unprecedented surge in the production of printed translations. The *Cultural Crosscurrents Catalogue of Printed Translations in Stuart and Commonwealth Britain (1641-1660)* features almost 1,800 entries, whereas there are 6,000 for the whole period (1473– 1640) covered by *Renaissance Cultural Crossroads*. Of course, we are aware that focusing on early modern printed as opposed to manuscript translations might be considered a way of buttressing dominant narratives on the "book triumphant" (Walsby and Kemp 2011), at a time when manuscript circulation continued to represent a vibrant mode of textual transmission. Unfortunately, the state of the archive is such that we do not currently have access to bibliographical resources that are comprehensive and robust enough to sustain the kind of quantitative study outlined here—although we very much hope to be able to include manuscript translations in our data model at a later stage of the project.

A second important feature of network analysis resides in its macroscopic (Jockers 2013)—also known as "distant" (Moretti 2013), or "telescopic" (McCarty 2012)—perspective, which has proven a useful tool for testing critical hypotheses and generating new research questions. As Raymond notes in the case of European news networks, the project's macro-analytical perspective was key in debunking the Anglocentric narrative about the British origins of modern printed news (Raymond 2016, 102–05). Another recent example, this time in literary history, is Maciej Eder's use of network analysis and visualization tools to tease out stylistic similarities across a corpus of classical and early modern Neo-Latin writings. These, he demonstrates, confirm things we already know, such as the stylistic divide between early modern "Ciceronians" and "anti-Ciceronians," but they also raise new questions about generic marking and the diachronic evolution of stylistic imitation practices (Eder 2016). In book studies, finally, Steve Conway has discussed the historiographical "opportunities" afforded by macroscopic network mapping methods when seeking to reveal the structure and evolution of specific book markets (Conway 2017). While historical network analysis has not yet been systematically applied to a corpus of early modern English translations (see, however, Pym 1998 and Tahir-Gürçaglar 2007 on other historical periods and corpora), the new hypotheses raised by discussions of the social and material contexts of translation are particularly well suited to a macroscopic, network-oriented line of enquiry. For example, recent invitations to pay attention to early modern stationers and to transnational patterns of text-production and dissemination (see Coldiron 2015, Boutcher 2015) naturally call for a "bird's eye" view. Similarly, Coldiron's analyses of printed paratexts (especially prefaces and translators' portraits) have recently questioned Lawrence Venuti's influential thesis about the "invisibility" of translators in early modern English literary culture (see Coldiron 2012 and 2018, and Venuti 1995, respectively). This, again, invites large-scale, quantitative investigation. Finally, it has been established that translators actively participated in the social, ideological, and political polarization of seventeenth-century literary culture, especially in the years surrounding the Civil Wars (see Patterson 1984, Potter 1989, Norbrook 1999). It seems particularly fitting, then, to conduct a study of the various kinds of networks in which they were involved. This first application of network analysis to an early modern corpus of printed translations thus serves as a way of testing, confirming, or potentially enriching current directions in the cultural and material history of translation in the British Isles—and beyond.

Of particular interest to us is the potential of statistical algorithms for identifying significant *nodes* (actors), or *ties* (relations), and assessing the structure and evolution of the networks under study. Recent works by Kelly Stage (2015) and Jenna Townend (2017) have highlighted the relative significance of "strong" vs. "weak" ties with powerful agents as a way of measuring a given actor's status and influence in networks of patronage or literary coteries. In our case, statistical calculations offer useful ways of assessing the connectivity of specific actors (translators, patrons, printers, booksellers, or more accurately stationers, as they were then called, etc.), either in terms of the mere volume of connections they enjoy (*degree*), the brokerage function they may perform (*betweenness*), or their relations to other, particularly well-connected nodes in the network (*eigencentrality*). The modularity algorithm also offers a useful way of identifying close-knit communities, or cliques, within a larger-scale network.[3] Such measurements enable one not only to obtain a general sense of the networks' configuration, but also to identify central actors, or instead, outliers, in the corpus under study. Certain patterns prove particularly noteworthy. Ruth Ahnert has thus remarked that, in

---

[3] For a general discussion of network metrics, their potential significance in terms of social and cultural networks, and the limitations of statistical calculations, see Weingart 2011.

the Tudor intelligence network that emerges from her analysis of the State Papers, a combination of low degree (relatively few connections) and high betweenness (indicating the node's structural importance to the flow of information) was characteristic of "in-between" actors – typically diplomats, double agents, and spies (Ahnert 2016b). The calculation and visualization of network metrics has also helped scholars identify hitherto unrecognized cultural players, as is the case in Evan Bourke's study of women's structural role in the flow of letters across the Hartlib network (Bourke 2017). The potential of such measurements is thus extremely high when dealing with translators, stationers, and their patrons or social connections, whose cultural agency hinges precisely on their capacity to act (if sometimes in an implicit, or "invisible" manner) as textual, cultural, and social "go-betweens" (Burke 2005).

As has often been pointed out, the scholarly benefits of historical network analysis methodologies are maximized when the "distant," quantitative strategies outlined above are combined with fine-grained descriptions of the objects under study, and with more traditional, qualitative, or hermeneutic models that enable one to interpret and contextualize the patterns observed. The dialectics of the quantitative and qualitative (see Jockers 2011, and more recently Townend 2017), which Ingeborg Van Vugt astutely calls "disclose reading" (Van Vugt 2017, 36), lies at the heart of our approach. As detailed in the methodology below, the data we gather for network analysis is the result of close, detailed descriptions of the material features of early modern printed translations.[4] Conversely, once we have established our corpus, or specific sub-corpus, distant methods of network and visualization help us identify zones requiring more intensive (qualitative) scrutiny. Our use of visualization software (see more on this below) is guided by a similar interpretive stance. On the one hand, we are aware of and fully engage with the demonstrative function of network mapping and visualization as an alternative way of constructing an argument (see Conway 2017, 38). On the other, in keeping with the bottom-up logic of network-based approaches, we also recognize the heuristic value of network visualizations and their potential for disclosing patterns that could not be observable through more traditional methods, thus giving rise to new research questions and explanatory hypotheses.

The disclose approach adopted here is all the more important as our analysis of translation networks is not text-based but rather actor-based. As noted above, we are not seeking to establish textual or stylistic patterns across our

---

[4] For the sake of transparency and replicability, the data gathered for both case studies below are available as freely-accessible files on the companion website at Iter Community.

corpus of translations, as is the case for example in Eder's study of imitation (Eder 2016), or more generally, in digitally-oriented translation studies seeking to establish linguistic patterns in translated texts. Instead, we approach the printed, translated book as a historically-situated trace, or a locus of performance, of social and material connections. The implications for a network-oriented study are two-fold. On the one hand, we only record the information about people, languages, locations, print technologies, etc., that is expressed through the medium of the printed, translated book. In this, we differ from the *Six Degrees of Francis Bacon* project, in which social connections are established on a much wider basis (the initial criterion being that two people be mentioned together in the same *ODNB* entry, see Warren et al. 2016). On the other hand, our scope is wider than that of the *Shakeosphere* project, for example, which only documents the connections between writers and printers, as recorded in the *ESTC*. Our data thus includes languages, book formats, and locations, but also, and crucially, the names of translators' dedicatees, and of the various "friends" whose encomiastic pieces (often in verse of varying literary appeal) are found in the liminal pages of the translated book. We are thus dealing with two overlapping kinds of networks: those involved in the material production and circulation of translated books, but also those embedded in the pages of the printed book as a mode of social display. Connections invoked in dedications, for example, may very well be virtual rather than real. Yet we still consider these to be significant, because social and cultural capital, even imagined, represent major components of early modern print culture. Translators and printers were clearly alert to the social potential of their medium, and it is crucial here to acknowledge the performative, symbolic aspects of the early modern network as a means of social identification, cultural self-fashioning, or ideological positioning.

Methodology: from catalog entries to network analysis

As noted in the introduction, we take as our point of departure the bibliographical data in the *Renaissance Cultural Crossroads Online Catalogue of Translations in Britain 1473-1640* (RCC), and the *Cultural Crosscurrents Catalogue of Printed Translations in Stuart and Commonwealth Britain, 1641-1660* (CCC). Both catalogs were compiled with a team of researchers and graduate students, through the process of identifying translations in the British Library's *English Short Title Catalogue* (see Hosington 2011 for a full description of the compiling process). The criterion for inclusion in the RCC catalog was that at least 30% of the printed book consist in translated text—a definition that, for the sake of consistency, was also followed in the *CCC*.[5] While the main bibliographical data have been

---

[5] That being said, we are aware that the mid-seventeenth-century decades were cru-

imported from the *ESTC*, both catalogs include additional material pertaining to the translational nature of the books recorded (source and target languages, names and biographical information about translators), but also to their material features. In the *RCC* catalog, the "Liminary material" field records dedications, notes to the reader, and other discursive paratexts, as found in digital image sets from *Early English Books Online* (*EEBO*) corresponding to each catalog entry (where available, of course). In the *CCC*, we have expanded the description to a full record of both discursive and visual paratextual features (listed under the field "Paratexts"), also based on available *EEBO* digital files.[6]

In order to reconstruct and analyze the material and social networks underlying the production and circulation of printed translations, we have developed a data model structured around four main entities, and drawing from a variety of sources. As noted above, we primarily approach printed translations as books, for which we have adopted the *ESTC*'s main bibliographical data (title, physical description, date of publication) and metadata (reference/citation numbers, and general field structure). We also follow the *ESTC* in terms of geographical data (our second entity). This particularly concerns printing locations for translations: the *ESTC* identifies a number of false imprints, often offering alternative locations: these are reflected in our data. Thirdly, our data about languages is partly derived from the *ESTC*, and partly inferred from the titles of translated books or other general sources where *ESTC* entries are incomplete. This is particularly the case for so-called "second-hand" translations, i.e., translated from an intermediary version of the original text. Finally, our information on human actors is derived from several sources. We generally follow the *ESTC* in terms of identifying authors and stationers. Information on translators has also been partly derived from the *ESTC* files (where translators are sometimes recorded in the "additional name" field, but sometimes also under the "author" category), and partly established through additional biographical and bibliographical research.[7] The examination of paratextual features on *EEBO* has often proven fruitful when seeking to identify

---

cial in the development of printed miscellanies, and we have compiled a parallel corpus of volumes where translated material represents under 30% of the whole text, to be examined at a later stage.

[6] Note that our data is copy-specific and in the *CCC* we duly document the origins of consulted image sets, as recorded in *EEBO* or other sources.

[7] In the case of the *CCC* project, completed under the joint direction of Marie-Alice Belle and Brenda M. Hosington at the Université de Montréal, we wish to acknowledge the work of research assistants, in particular Daniel Lévy but also Faustine Richalet, Olga Stepanova, and Isabelle Aouad (see project website at www.translationandprint.com).

translators. It has also been our main source for establishing the names of dedicatees and "friends" appearing in the paratexts of printed translations.

ESTC Citation:	S107359
STC Citation:	6385
Uniform Title:	**Réplique à la response du sérénissime roy de la Grand Bretagne. English**
Title:	The reply of the most illustrious Cardinall of Perron, to the ansvveare of the most excellent King of Great Britaine the first tome. Translated into English.
Variant Title:	Reply of the most illustrious Cardinall of Perron, to the answeare of the most excellent King of Great Britaine
Publisher/Year:	Imprinted at Douay : By Martin Bogart, vnder the signe of Paris, 1630.
Year:	1630
Physical Description:	[16], 262, 261-295, 294-464 p. ; 2°.
Subject:	PR;
Original Author:	Du Perron, Jacques, 1556-1618
Translator:	Cary, Elizabeth, 1585/6-1639
Original Language:	French
Target Language:	English
Liminary Materials:	1. Dedicatory epistle to Henrietta Maria 2. Note to the reader by translator 3. Commendatory verse to translator (Latin) 4. Commendatory verse to translator (English) 5. Commendatory verse (English) signed F.L.D.S.M. 6. Commendatory verse to translator (English) 7. Admonition to the reader signed F.L.D.S.M. 8. Approbation signed F. Leander de S. Martino, 2 December 1631

Figure 1. Detail of the *Renaissance Cultural Crossroads* catalog entry for Elizabeth Cary's translation of Du Perron's *Réplique* (Douai: M. Bogard, 1630), with mentions of social connections in the "Liminary Material" field.

The first challenge encountered when starting to compile data for network analysis has been the relatively "flat" data model of our source catalogs.

Network analysis can only be conducted on the basis of a structured, relational data model, and a good deal of effort has been devoted to the restructuring of available data. In the case of the *RCC* catalog in particular, while the web interface does feature searchable fields, the results are presented as individual records, which cannot be sorted by date or author, for example, nor downloaded in the form of lists or tables. Similarly, catalog fields sometimes include heterogeneous kinds of data, which need to be extracted and recorded under distinct categories. This is the case, for example, of the "Publisher/Year" (*RCC*) or "Imprint" (*CCC*) fields that include both geographical locations and stationers' names. Similarly, information about dedicatees and other kinds of contributors listed in the "Liminary materials" (*RCC*), or "Paratexts" (*CCC*) fields had to be isolated, restructured, and sometimes completed by additional consultation of the corresponding *EEBO* files.[8] While we are currently working to re-model the *CCC* entries into a relational database in order to facilitate data extraction, the sub-corpora established in this pilot project are in great part the result of minute, time-consuming manual collection and curation.

Another kind of difficulty had to do with the relative degree of incompleteness, or uncertainty, that naturally accompanies early modern historical data.[9] We are aware that our sources are not exhaustive: not all printed translations of the period are extant, nor, for that matter, recorded in the *ESTC*. While we were able to trace some of the unattributed texts in the *ESTC* to their original authors or translators, and to fill out some initials, we still have many orphan texts, so to speak, and a number of uncertain publication dates. This has reverberations in terms of quantitative analysis, since relations between unattributed texts, unidentified actors, and uncertain dates or locations might not be established where they perhaps should. Yet again, anonymous or uncertain publications do not necessarily represent problems to be solved; we may also consider them as data, as such, if we keep in mind the performative aspects of the networks under study. A case in point is the use of false

---

[8] This is particularly the case for *RCC* catalog in which a number of entries marked "still being revised" do not include the liminary materials. One of the first steps of the new Trajectories project will be to complete the missing data.

[9] There are, of course, many cases of orthographic variation (especially when dealing with foreign names). This was important to keep in mind when searching for data in the *RCC* catalog, which does not disambiguate, for example, between "Douai," "Doway," etc. As a result, we had to run separate keyword searches with each variant in order to find all translations printed in that location. A certain amount of harmonization and data cleaning has also been necessary when preparing tables for network analysis, and we have used the open-source OpenRefine software to that effect.

imprints, or pseudonyms, which abound in cases of recusant translations produced for illicit circulation and consumption among early modern English Catholics. Certainly, it is useful to reduce such ambiguities when seeking to assess the output of a certain press, or the total activities and connections of a given agent. In the case of recusant translations, we have actually made good use of Allison and Rogers' annotated catalog of recusant books (Allison and Rogers 1989–94) to that effect. Yet it may also be significant to reconstitute the distinct networks that may develop around the names of, say, Thomas Wilson and Edward Knott—both appearing in printed translations, tracts, and treatises, and referring to the same English Jesuit priest. Similarly, it would certainly be informative to examine, both on a quantitative and a relational basis, the significance of false imprints (i.e., books claiming a Continental printing location when actually clandestinely produced in England) in the corpus of recusant translations circulating in the period.[10]

Tracing the place of women in translation and print networks has also proven tricky at times. Individuals may be represented under various names, titles, or pseudonyms, and additional research has often been necessary in order to establish their historical identities (who is, for example, the "Lady Urania" to whom Thomas Harvey dedicates his 1655 translation of Mantuan's *Bucolica*? Is this a generic, complimentary term, or is there a link to Mary Wroth, or to Anne Clifford?). Women's names may sometimes not appear at all: the title-page for the English version of Manzini's *Discourses* (also 1655) tells us that it has been penned "by an honourable lady." Printed attributions can also be misleading, as in the case of Elizabeth Evelinge's religious translations, all published under the name of Catherine Bentley, another Poor Clare in her convent (see Goodrich 2015, 87). In a way, and perhaps ironically, such difficulties arise from the very relational nature of early modern women's social identities. Women are often recorded in our sources by means of kinship with male relatives: they are daughters, sisters, wives, mothers, widows. This situation, which recalls what Coldiron has recently called the "anonymous visibility" of women in early modern translation and print (Coldiron 2018), is certainly problematic in many ways. Yet it also reflects women's roles as

---

[10] Another instance of apparently inaccurate, yet still relevant data is the case of so-called "pseudo-translations," that is, texts that present themselves as translated from a non-existent, or fictive source. Given their cultural significance in the early modern period (see Bassnett 1998), they have been included in the catalog (see also Toury [1995] on the importance of including them in historical or "descriptive" accounts of translation).

strong connectors in social, cultural, but also political and ideological networks, as will be apparent below.

In this first, pilot exploration of the potential of network analysis and visualization for our corpus of English printed translations, our data collection and structuring strategies have been in part determined by the digital tools at our disposal. In keeping with our goal to make our datasets available to the scholarly community, we have been exclusively using open-source digital resources, so that users may either replicate the analyses outlined below or re-appropriate and manipulate our sub-corpora to their own scholarly ends. One of the standard open-source softwares for network analysis and visualization is Gephi, which we have mainly used in the following case studies to generate visualizations and run statistical measurements. Besides including standard algorithms to calculate factors such as degree, betweenness, eigencentrality, or modularity, Gephi offers many possibilities for graph experimentation and manipulation. The relative importance of nodes and ties can be expressed in terms of size, colours, labels, etc. A system of filters allows one to visualize multi-layered network data (see Figure 5, below, correlating recusant translators, printing locations, and individual printers). Gephi also offers a network projection plugin enabling one to synthesize bipartite networks (linking, e.g., translations and printers) into unipartite networks (only showing connections between translators, see case study below), and a "Timeline" function for dynamic visualizations.

Another useful digital tool has been Stanford University's Palladio platform, which underlies the *Mapping the Republic of Letters* project. Although not including network metrics, and not allowing one to manipulate and save graphs as Gephi does, it offers the advantage of a user-friendly web-based interface, with the possibility of simply "dropping" tables in .csv or .tsv format onto the platform. Visualizations can then be generated in the forms of heat maps and network graphs with minimal additional adjustments.[11] Results can be further refined by a system of filters, or "facets," allowing one to visualize not only connections between, say, translators and printers, or translators and dedicatees, but also correlations between literary genres and source languages, book formats, printing dates, and locations, etc.

Other open-source tools have proven appropriate for the historical study of early modern networks, such as the *nodegoat* platform (Van Vugt 2017), or John Ladd's web-based *Network Navigator*. Our choice of Gephi and Palladio

---

[11] Besides the documentation and guides on the website, see the excellent tutorial by Marten Düring (2017).

was made on the grounds of their exploratory potential for the corpus under study. Equally important for us (particularly in the case of Palladio) was their general availability and accessibility to scholars and students making first inroads (as we do here) into network analysis territory.

Printed translations and the recusant network: Rouen, Douai, and St. Omer, 1617–40

Research on early modern English recusant culture has long highlighted the importance of the English Jesuit colleges established on the Continent. While the network of Jesuit institutions spread across Europe, the main colleges devoted to the education of the English recusant youth were those at St. Omer (founded 1597), then located in the Spanish Netherlands, and at Rouen, in France. Another important center of Catholic education—and, as we will see, translation—was Douai, where the Jesuit college, founded 1608, coexisted with one of the largest English Benedictine colleges on the Continent (Whitehead 2016, 30–31). These hubs of English recusant cultural life are known to have functioned as part of a complex network for the circulation of Catholic priests, students, and books. The colleges were indeed centers of English Catholic print production, especially with the establishment of the Jesuit presses at St. Omer in 1617, although recusant publications also came from a closely-bound network of stationers and printers in all three towns (with further connections to Brussels, Bruges, and other English recusant centers in Europe). Book historians have long recognized the importance of these presses to the early modern English book market (Hoftijzer 2014, 738). They have also noted the coherence of their output as a concerted effort to support and defend the English Catholic cause by making key texts of the European Counter-Reformation available to English readers by having them translated, printed, and circulated (often illicitly) among members of the recusant community (Hoftijzer 2014, 738).

Translation represented a major facet of these activities; in the case of the St. Omer College press, translated texts account for over half the total output for 1617–40.[12] While translations and translators are given their due and listed as such in Allison and Rogers's annotated catalog of recusant literature (1989–94), the place of translation in the program of Catholic print production and dissemination at the English colleges has not been studied in a systematic way. Even in Jordan D. Sly's *Recusant Print Network Project*, proposing to analyze the

---

[12] More precisely, 76 out of the 148 titles printed at the St. Omer English College press from 1617 to 1640 (inclusively), as recorded respectively in the *RCC* catalog and the *ESTC*.

general configuration of early modern recusant print activities from a network analysis perspective, translations are virtually invisible. While Sly uses data from the *EEBO-TCP* initiative to generate a visualization of the recusant print network in the "era of high recusancy (1558–1640)," we will deal here with a more limited corpus. As noted above, our focus is on the three main centers for seventeenth-century recusant education and print production— which actually turn out to also represent the main locations for the printing of recusant translations, as recorded in the *RCC* catalog. Our study also covers a shorter time range. As Conway importantly notes, the way temporal limits are established when sampling data for network analysis is of major importance, since the inclusion of data over extended periods may result in bias (Conway 2017, 33–37). For instance, some human actors (e.g., translators) in a *longue-durée* network may appear, disappear, or seem isolated for purely demographical reasons, which inevitably weakens any hypothesis one may want to formulate about their relative connectivity in the network under study.

Here, it seemed pertinent to focus on data for the years 1617–40. We start with the foundation of the St. Omer press, which gradually becomes the center for translation production and diffusion under the direction of the Jesuit, John Wilson (ca. 1575– ca. 1645). As Joyce Boro has recently noted (Boro 2018), the 1620s see a surge in translation activities from Catholic sources, especially around the time of the so-called "Spanish Match," and in the wake of Charles I's 1625 marriage to the Catholic, Jesuit-friendly, French princess Henrietta Maria. Translation activities remain strong in all three locations through the thirties, but gradually peter out after 1640—this being mainly due to the abolition of the Star Chamber in 1641, which effectively lifts the ban on Catholic books on the English market. The need to print (or appear to print) abroad vanishes, and high-profile Jesuit translations, such as English versions of Nicolas Caussin's various works dedicated to Henrietta Maria, previously printed on the Continent, thus openly appear in London from 1643 onwards.

While our temporal limits thus correspond to a defined chapter in the history of recusant print, the dataset collected for those years is also rather homogeneous demographically. Aside from a small number of reprints of Elizabethan or early Jacobean translations, our sub-corpus represents the work of two overlapping generations of translators, almost all of whom were alive contemporaneously. This confirms the idea of a coherent, coordinated enterprise on the part of recusants on the Continent, and Jesuits in particular, to translate and disseminate works of theology, devotion, hagiography, and religious polemics for an English Catholic readership.

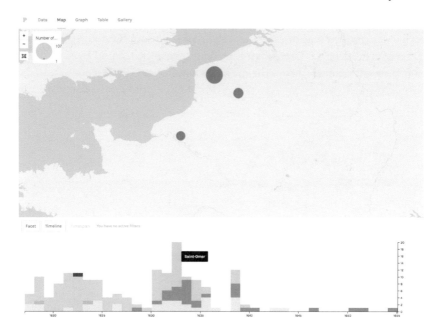

Figure 2. Translations printed in St. Omer (blue), Rouen (dark gray), and Douai (light gray), 1617–60. Palladio, "Map" interface with "Timeline" tool, data from the *RCC* (1617–40) and *CCC* (1641–60).

This collaborative effort of translators and printers is eloquently illustrated in the following bipartite network of translators and printers (Figure 3), here generated as a force-directed graph, with nodes weighted by degree (that is, according to their number of connections).

The major features of the network are easily discernible. John Wilson naturally dominates as the head of the St. Omer College press, but also as a translator, with works printed both at the college press and by the St. Omer-based widow of Charles Boscard; his double role is here represented by a green node. The same is true of John Heigham, who acted as a translator, an editor of translations, and a printer, and collaborated with other printers in Douai (Peter [Pierre] Auroi, Charles Boscard) and St. Omer (Georges Seutin) in the period under study (although he was already active in the 1600s; see Von Habsburg 2011, 190). Other printers stand out as important connectors: Charles Boscard (Douai); his widow, who took the business to St. Omer and John Cousturier (Rouen). The highest-ranking actor in terms of degree is a well-known figure in the recusant network. Thomas Everard (or Everett, sometimes associated with the pseudonym Edward Knott), was a prolific translator, and also shows high connectivity here because he published his works with various stationers. Less well known, although ranking just below Everard, are Edward and William Kinsman, whose translated lives of saints went through several runs of the press both at Rouen and St. Omer.

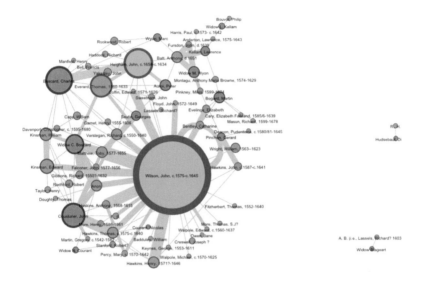

Figure 3. Translators (purple) and printers (green, orange) in the St. Omer-Douai-Rouen network. Gephi, force-directed, nodes and edges weighted by degree.

In order to identify actors who are structurally important to the network, we have generated another visualization of the same data, with nodes weighted this time by betweenness—which measures the frequency of nodes being on the shortest path between two other nodes. Stationers naturally rank high in a network derived from a corpus of printed translations. Looking at translators instead, the Benedictine translator Anthony Batt conspicuously stands out, with links to a variety of interconnected printers in Douai and St. Omer (Lawrence Kellam, Pierre Auroi, the widow of Marc Wyon, and John Heigham).[13]

---

[13] Interestingly, while David M. Rogers had first identified Batt as a "forgotten Bene-dictine translator" (Rogers 1984), Julia Staykova more recently places his translations of (pseudo-)Augustine "at the heart of the recusant book trade" (Staykova 2012, 159), an observation that may here be generalized on the basis of network metrics, at least for our sub-corpus.

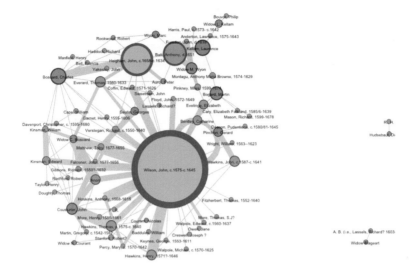

Figure 4. Translators (purple) and printers (green, orange) in the St. Omer-Douai-Rouen network, 1617–40. Gephi, force-directed, nodes weighted by betweenness centrality.

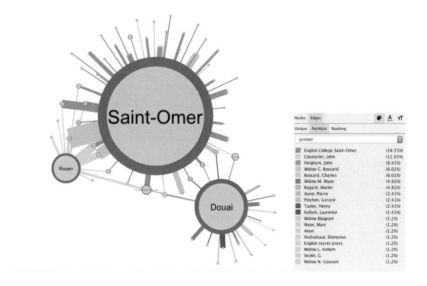

Figure 5. Translators and printing locations, St. Omer-Douai-Rouen network, 1617–40. Gephi, force-directed, weighted by degree; edges colored by printer (see legend).

Collaboration appears in fact to have been a common practice for the production of recusant translations, even in the heyday of the St. Omer College press. The case of Anthony Batt, a Benedictine at Douai connecting with the Jesuit network through John Heigham, is enlightening here. Even if Adrian Johns (1998) is certainly right in identifying the printer's shop as a nexus of social, writerly, and, one may add here, translatorial associations, in our case it appears more relevant to consider the location in itself (Rouen, Douai, St. Omer) as a vector of connection.

Patterns of collaboration may be observed more distinctly through a visualization of the same data in the form of a network relating individual translators to these three interconnected poles (Figure 5). Our goal being to investigate the structure of print production across this specific network, we have here weighted and color-coded the edges, as well as included a breakdown of the main printers involved. The results are quite eloquent. While translations in Rouen are almost exclusively issued by John Cousturier, printing activities in Douai, on the contrary, are spread across a wider network of printers. The St. Omer translations are dominated by the Jesuit press, with a sizeable contribution by Widow C. Boscard (who, for some reason, does not appear at all in Sly's visualization of the recusant print network). Widows clearly play an important role, with Widow C. Boscard (represented by green edges) ranking fourth in terms of degree, and Widow Wyon (red edges) ranking sixth. Other female printers include the widow of Lawrence Kellam, and that of Nicolas Courant. Such findings invite further research on their concerted role and agency, especially in light of recent hypotheses on the reliance of underground networks upon "network sustainers," or "infrastructural figures, as much as powerful leaders" (Ahnert 2016c; see also Smith 2012 on the pivotal role of women in the early modern book trade).

In order to visualize the relations between translators made possible by their joint connection to a common location, we have projected our bipartite network (translators and locations) into a unipartite graph (showing only translators). While there is an obvious loss of information, this synthesized version of the graph allows for some characteristics of the network to stand out more clearly. In terms of betweenness centrality (which, again, measures brokerage in the network), Edward Kinsman and John Heigham continue to rank high, probably for the reasons stated above. Also noteworthy is the high score achieved by Richard Rowlands, alias Verstegan (1550–1640), who has often been placed at the "center" of recusant print activities (Collinson et al. 2014, 47). In a recent study, Hosington calls him "networker extraordinaire" (2018), tracing over 170 contacts across a variety of communities including protestant Dutch exiles, Jesuit book-smugglers, newsbook printers, and members of religious convents. What is remarkable here is that although he was a most prolific writer, editor, correspondent and translator through his trans-European career (Arblaster 2004), he actually has relatively few publications in this specific sub-corpus: one translation of a primer first published in Douai, reprinted four times (twice in Rouen, twice in St. Omer), and two self-translated news tracts published in St. Omer. This is all the more noteworthy in light of Ruth Ahnert's hypothesis about the combination of low degree and high betweenness as a characteristic of diplomats, double agents, and spies (Ahnert 2016b). This description certainly matches Verstegan's profile.

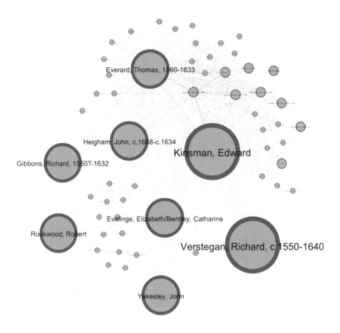

Figure 6. Translators in the St. Omer-Douai-Rouen network, 1617–40. Gephi, projected network, force-directed, nodes weighted by betweenness centrality.

Another notable actor in the network is the one bearing the hybrid label, Evelinge/Bentley. It represents the aforementioned translations overtly attributed to Catherine Bentley, but most probably penned by Elizabeth Evelinge, both women being Poor Clares at the Gravelines convent, not far from St. Omer. As Jaime Goodrich has noted, although for unknown reasons Evelinge is not named in the printed book, her authority was recognized at the time both by her peers at the convent and by the author of one of the translated texts (Goodrich 2015, 87). Her "structural" position in the network here reflects, first, the fact that her translations were published in all three locations, and second, that they appeared in collections also containing the works of other translators (besides the Bentley cover name). The quantitative approach here confirms Goodrich's contention that she was an important player in the concerted effort by English recusants to translate and diffuse devotional material. This is despite the fact that her work has long been obscured, not only by the claims of humility and anonymity perhaps imposed by her religious ethos, but also by modern scholarship's neglect of translators who pursued life paths as remote from ours as that of a seventeenth-century Poor Clare.

The role played by women—and indeed, religious women—in recusant translation and print networks becomes all the more evident when looking at dedication patterns. The significance of dedicatory letters addressed by translators to prominent recusants has been noted frequently, if anecdotally. Julia Staykova remarks, for example, how Anthony Batt used a dedication to Gabriel Gifford, Archbishop of Reims, to raise the profile of his 1621 translation (Staykova 2012, 159). The importance of rich or influent noblewomen as "sustainers" in the recusant network has also long been noted. A famous example is that of Anne Vaux, one of John Wilson's dedicatees, a known "harbourer of priests" whose Jesuit confessor had been involved in the Gunpowder Plot, and who in the 1620s ran a clandestine school for children of the Catholic nobility (Nicholls 2008). From 1625 onwards, a dedication to Queen Henrietta Maria could serve as a powerful marker of Catholic identity, as well as symbolically procuring a special status for forbidden books.

Here again, a more systemic approach yields eloquent results. This is apparent in the visualization below (Figure 7), generated in Palladio, which correlates the translators in our corpus—here narrowed down to the Caroline years of our period (1625–40)—to the dedicatees mentioned in the paratexts of their translations (if any).

Female dedicatees far outnumber men in our corpus, representing thirteen out of twenty named dedicatees, and appearing in twenty-four of the thirty-one printed translations containing a dedication.[14] Henrietta Maria naturally

---

[14] While Hosington (2017, 110) has remarked that female translators in the period tended to dedicate their works to other women, in this particular corpus the practice clearly cuts across the gender divide. Note also the importance of the Hawkinses, a well-known recusant family deeply involved in the Jesuit network: Henry was a prominent Jesuit, Thomas was indicted in 1626 for harboring priests. Their nephew,

dominates, an obvious and emblematic court figure. Another important woman at court is the Duchess of Buckingham, wife to James I's famous favorite and still very influential in the early years of Charles I's reign. Not surprisingly, female dedicatees often belong to old Catholic families, such as the Howards and the Radcliffes. Here, again, abbesses of various orders visibly feature as dedicatees and/or patrons. Their presence is not historically surprising, given that these often were educated daughters of noble recusant families; yet as noted above, nuns are only recently being put forward as objects of scholarly study. Once more, we reap the fruits of a mixed method combining the detailed description of the material features of the printed book (in this case, imprints or dedications) with the quantitative methods of network mapping and analysis. Besides confirming important research directions based, so far, on individual case studies (concerning, e.g., Batt or Evelinge), this dual focus also highlights important, yet still understudied, features and actors of seventeenth-century recusant networks of translation and print production.

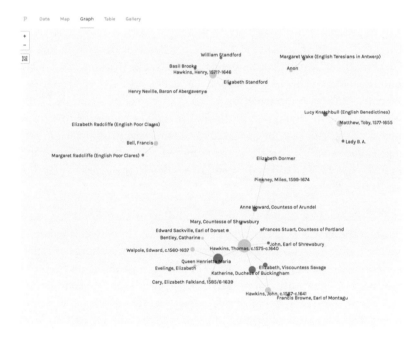

Figure 7. Translators and dedicatees of translations printed at St. Omer, Rouen, and Douai (1625–40). Palladio, force-directed, nodes weighted by degree.

Francis, would also become a Jesuit translator. On the Hawkinses as translators and actors in the recusant network, see Guénette 2016.

Humphrey Moseley, royalist bookseller? Social and political networks in the translations published 1641–60

Our second case study, centered on the London bookseller, Humphrey Moseley, shows how network analysis and visualizations may shed light on the early modern reception of printed translations, as well as on our own critical perceptions of the agents involved in the process.

Humphrey Moseley has already attracted a great deal of critical attention as a major actor in the mid-seventeenth-century English book market. David Scott Kastan has highlighted the impact of his marketing strategies on the "invention of English literature" in the period (Kastan 2007). Recent studies have also noted how Moseley managed to capture an upwardly mobile middle-class readership by branding his books, and particularly, his printed translations, as products of a literary and social elite (Belle 2014, Eardley 2017). His selection of works offered in translation (classics, Continental poetry, historical treatises, French heroic romances) participated in this strategy, as did the systematic branding of authors and translators as "gentlemen"—even if, as Alice Eardley notes, some of the translators were of lower status and mostly commercially motivated (Eardley 2017, 131). A quantitative analysis of the corpus of translations printed by Moseley in the 1640s and 1650s (as established from the *CCC*) also shows that dedications played a key role in giving readers the impression of belonging to a circle of genteel readers. This may be observed in the following visualization, generated in Palladio, which correlates the names of dedicatees appearing in the front material of translations printed by Moseley to the genres of the books in which they feature.

Eardley's observation about the social branding of translated romance as an aristocratic genre, geared towards the ladies, is largely confirmed. The graph certainly shows how Moseley capitalizes on the traditional association of romance with women, here materially embedding it in the margins of the printed book. A quantitative approach further reveals the crucial importance of dedications for that specific genre. Indeed, the following visualization, in which romance features so prominently, only takes into account books that do include dedications, which represent less than half of the total corpus (50 out of 108). If one is to include all books printed by Moseley, the relative importance of the genre significantly diminishes, at 25% of all translations versus 57% of translations containing dedications. This is one more example of how a bird's-eye view, combined with detailed attention to the material features of books, helps at once to corroborate and complete existing analyses of a specific corpus.

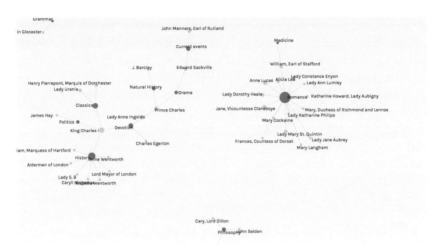

Figure 8. Translated genres and dedicatees in translations published by Moseley, 1641–60 (detail). Palladio, force-directed, weighted by degree.

Another common perception of Moseley's activities concerns his links to the royalist party during the Civil Wars and the Interregnum. These have particularly been highlighted in influential studies on translation, such as the works of Annabel Patterson, Lois Potter, or Lawrence Venuti, as stated above. Yet more recent assessments of his editorial practices have sought to qualify this view. Besides the obvious example of Milton's *Poems*, which Moseley published in 1645, larger-scale examinations of his output paint a more nuanced picture, suggesting "a moderate royalist ethos," one that "accommodated literature, authors and readers of a non-royalist persuasion" (Boutcher 2018). Given the effectiveness of Moseley's editorial branding strategies, we may therefore raise two, interrelated questions: how visibly royalist were the translations he published in the 1640s and 1650s; and how does this shape our critical perception of his political positioning?

First, it is important to note the numerical importance of translations in Moseley's total output; the *ESTC* yields 297 entries identifying him as a bookseller for the years 1641–60, out of which 108 are recorded as translations in the *CCC*. Translated books thus represent over a third of Moseley's publications for the period under study, and the trends we may identify in their political associations are thereby likely to affect general perceptions of his activities.

In order to examine these associations, we have built an *egonetwork* (i.e., a network featuring Moseley as the central node) of his translation- and print-based connections, by extracting from the *CCC* the names, or initials, of the following actors: translators, dedicatees, various "friends" who sign commendatory pieces, and finally, printers collaborating with him, as identified in the *ESTC*. For each recognizable name, we have sought to establish whether the person had royalist affiliations. Research in the *ODNB* (with the occasional cross-check on the *Six Degrees of Francis Bacon* platform) has enabled us to identify a number of confirmed royalists ("CR"), representing, for example, members of Charles I's direct entourage and people involved in the royalist army, or whose positions had been otherwise made clear. A few confirmed parliamentarians ("CP") were also identified through *ODNB* entries. In certain cases, royalist loyalties could not be established with certainty, and we have labeled as "moderate" ("MR" "MP") agents whose affiliations either were described as such in our sources or could be relatively safely derived from known associations—typically, in cases of daughters and wives of known royalists. Others needing more research have been marked as "uncertain" ("U"). Those of wavering loyalties (most famously, Edmund Waller) have also been identified as such ("MR-MP"). These various positions are expressed in the color-coded version of Moseley's egonetwork below (Figure 9). A finer-grained, zoomable online version of this figure is available at Iter Community).

As seen from the dominant blue and green tinge of the network, confirmed (blue) and moderate (green) royalists account for almost 50% of Moseley's total connections, against just over 5% parliamentarians (in pink, orange, and purple), turncoats included. Of course, these results are qualified by the 45% of "uncertain" (pale brown) affiliations, many of which however appear to be linked to known royalists.[15] We wondered if the dominance of royalist-leaning actors in the network was perhaps linked to the inclusion of translations printed in 1659 and 1660, around the time of the restoration of the monarchy, when this kind of political branding was perhaps to be expected. Yet the ratio of royalist-identified connections for these two years is consistent with the rest of the period, thus suggesting a general trend in Moseley's publications.

---

[15] A good part of the missing data concerns here Moseley's printers, whose affiliations are difficult to establish (and perhaps not relevant): more research is needed on this subject.

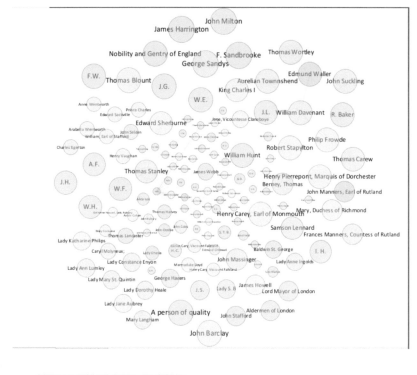

U	(44.93%)
CR	(28.26%)
MR	(21.74%)
MR–MP	(2.17%)
CP	(2.17%)
MP	(0.72%)

Figure 9. Political affiliations of Moseley's translation and print connections, 1641–60. Gephi, force-directed, nodes weighted by modularity class.

One factor, though, that may contribute to the royalist over-crowding of the network, so to speak, is the presence of clusters of royalist-identified names within a single translation, or in a series of interrelated publications. This phenomenon can be measured in Gephi by running the modularity algorithm, which measures frequency of connection between neighboring nodes, thus identifying distinct communities within a given network. In our case, one such community can be plainly identified around Henry Carey, Earl of Monmouth, with connections to a whole coterie of Caroline court poets and translators: Thomas Carew, William Davenant, Aurelian Townshend, John Suckling, Edmund Waller, Robert Stapylton, and, of course, Charles I. Besides the cultural prominence of each individual agent, these associations gather all the more importance as they come clustered (typically, as a series of liminary poems prefacing Monmouth's translations), and en masse. As expressed by the weight (or thickness) of the tie linking him to the central node in the graph, Monmouth is Moseley's most-frequently published translator in the period: eight total publications, with seven separate titles and one reprint.

Figure 10. Cluster of nodes around Henry Carey, Earl of Monmouth in Moseley's translation and print egonetwork, 1641–60. Gephi, force-based, nodes weighted and colored by modularity class, edges weighted by degree.

If we move from the quantitative assessment of the Monmouth network and its royalist associations (despite Waller) to a qualitative examination of their potential impact on the political branding of Moseley's books, the material features of the book come to play a crucial part. First, as noted above, the display of courtly connections, including dedications to Charles I, in the opening pages of the book unequivocally positions the translation as the product of a threatened, and eventually defunct, court culture. Besides, even in translations published without an apparatus of dedications and encomia, visual paratexts are used to great effect. Engraved title-pages, fold-out maps, medallion portraits and other illustrations mark Monmouth's translations as luxury goods, all the more so as they are printed in folio format in all but two cases. The full-page frontispiece portraits of Monmouth posing in a distinctly Cavalier fashion (and thus offering an eloquent counter-example to Venuti's association of the elitist royalist ethos with the "invisibility" of translators) equally participate in the social and political positioning of the translated book.

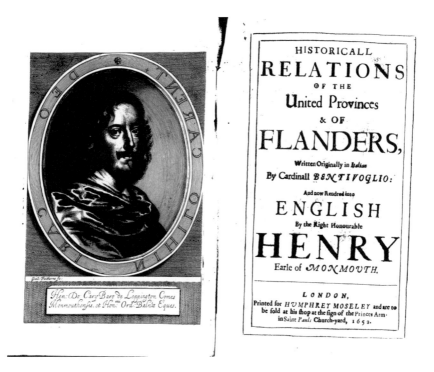

Figure 11. Frontispiece and title-page of Monmouth's *Historical Relations of the Province of Flanders*, translated from the Italian. London: printed for Moseley, 1652. Folio. (Wing B1911, Princeton University Library).

Visual codes played an important role in the political marking of printed translations, if one is to judge from Robert Ashley's *Davide Perseguitato / David Persecuted*, translated from Malvezzi's Italian and published by Moseley in 1650. Although the translation does not bear any tell-tale royalist dedication or liminal poem, the full-page frontispiece illustration gives the "persecuted" King David the recognizable facial features of Charles I, thus clearly displaying the translator's sympathies (Davis 2008, 44). Such strategies of social and political visibility could not but influence readers' perceptions of the bookseller publishing these works.

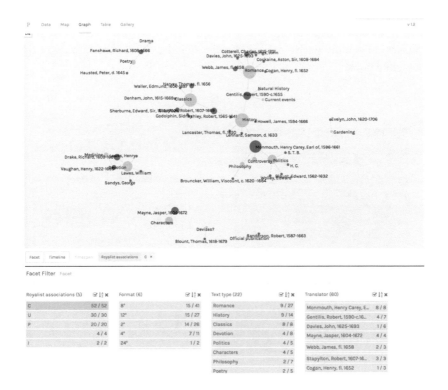

Figure 12. Translations with confirmed royalist associations published by Moseley 1641–60, with translators correlated to literary genres. Palladio, force-directed, weighted by degree, with additional filters indicating political affiliation and book format.

If we finally take format as a potential factor in the visual impact of such books, and we correlate it to the royalist associations displayed in them through the names of translators, dedicatees, or liminary friends, it is significant that fourteen out of twenty-six folios have confirmed royalist associations (see visualization above). This of course illustrates Moseley's savvy marketing of expensive books to a readership that has the means of acquiring them. It also contributes to the high visibility of royalist translators and their friends in his bookshop and beyond. The correlation of translated genre to political branding is also revealing in the cases of the classics (all eight publications carry confirmed royalist associations) and historical treatises (nine out of fourteen). In the first case, this shows Moseley participating in the royalist discourse presenting classical translation as the task of beleaguered nobility keen to preserve high culture from the onslaughts of an iconoclastic multitude (Patterson 1984). In the second, it points to his role in the fashioning of a royalist historiography, with Monmouth's stately translations playing, here again, a key part.

Naturally, these findings should be tested against an analysis of Moseley's complete corpus of publications, but two main points still emerge. First, royalist translators made full use of Moseley's editorial model to display their political loyalties, using printed books as extensions of, and, as it were, substitutes for the social framework of the court after it ceased to gather physically. Second, the common labeling of Moseley as a royalist bookseller, if perhaps not fully justified, can certainly be explained given the prominence of such books in terms of cultural status, material and visual impact, and relative numerical importance. All these factors are integral to the early modern, and, to an extent, contemporary reception of translated books, and can be assessed by the kinds of mixed, or "disclose" methodology we have implemented here.

Conclusion

Our first objective in applying network analysis methods to a corpus of printed translations was to explore their critical potential in the context of a project situated at the interface of translation history, literary history, and book history. Although the two case studies presented here deal with limited sub-corpora (spanning about 170 and 100 catalog entries, respectively), they certainly generate ample matter for observation, hypothesizing, and critical discussion. The first has shed new light on certain aspects of the seventeenth-century recusant print network, highlighting the place of translators, identifying key actors, confirming recent scholarly intuitions, as well as pointing to new research directions. In the second, the reconstruction of Moseley's translation-based social egonetwork has allowed us not only to test common scholarly assessments of the bookseller's political associations, but also to document how such perceptions probably came to be. We expect the exploratory potential of network analysis methods to be maximized in larger corpora, where research questions may be expanded to the overall structure of the market for printed translations in the period, or to the mapping of language flows between Britain and the Continent, or, as suggested above, to a more systematic investigation of the supposed invisibility of translators in early modern English literary culture.

What is clearly confirmed through this pilot study is the fruitfulness of combining quantitative and qualitative analysis, in a back-and-forth movement alternating fine-grained descriptions of specific translated books with a bird's eye perspective on seventeenth-century translation and print practices. More particularly, the application of established network analysis methods to a new corpus of printed translations raising its own set of questions (about cultural transfer, visibility, ideological encoding, etc.) results in a reciprocal enrichment of the fields of enquiry thereby engaged. On the one hand, network-based methodologies yield new insights concerning patterns of production and circulation of translation and print in the period. On the other, the data uncovered by minute attention to the actors inscribed in printed paratexts helps refine our understanding of the place of translation in early modern networks, and of the modes of social, material, and symbolic representation on which they rely. Finally, thanks to the added value, so to speak, represented by the paratextual data in both the *RCC* and *CCC* catalogs, this study has demonstrated the importance of deploying a variety of critical lenses to account for the many-faceted aspects of early modern translation and print production. While such multimodal practices are arguably the norm in the digital humanities, they have also been recently championed by early modern translation scholars attuned to the "multiple semiotic elements" engaged through the medium of print (Armstrong 2015, 81). In our case, they turn out to be particularly well suited to a project specifically aiming to explore the social, material, and cultural languages of the early modern translated book. The approach outlined here should indeed allow us to make the most of the rich, expanding digital archive at our disposal—whether in the form of catalogs, digital image databases, social network databases, or other resources helping us trace the reception of translated works (*RECIRC*, for example, but also the *Private Libraries in Renaissance England* database, and others).

Many challenges still lie ahead. Some have to do with archival gaps: as noted above, significant research will be needed in order to document the place of manuscript production in the translation activities we seek to study. Similarly, a full assessment of the transnational network for recusant translations would have to take into account the actors involved in the smuggling of printed books into England, although they are obviously difficult to trace. We are also working on ways of engaging more fully with the diachronic aspects of our data. We expect our mixed, disclose method to help address the historiographical problem of balancing accounts of *longue-durée* trends with attention to individual actors, outliers, or missing elements in the narrative. Technical aspects will still have to be worked out, as dynamic models for diachronic network visualization are as yet relatively limited in entry-level platforms such as Palladio and Gephi.[16] Such are the directions that we will continue to explore as we work to reconstruct, analyze, and visualize the variegated networks that underlie Britain's "culture of translation" in a most vibrant chapter of its cultural, social, and literary history.

WORKS CITED

Project websites, platforms, and databases

Early English Books Online. Accessed 11 December 2019. http://www.eebo. chadwyck.com/.

English Short Title Catalogue, hosted by the British Library. Accessed 15 August 2019. http://estc.bl.uk.

Mapping the Republic of Letters, directed by Paula Findlen, Dan Edelstein, and Nicole Coleman, hosted by Stanford University. Accessed 15 August 2019. http://republicofletters.stanford.edu/.

Network Navigator, created by John Ladd, hosted and supported by Carnegie Mellon University. Accessed 15 August 2019. http://dh-web.hss.cmu. edu/network_navigator/.

News Networks in Early Modern Europe, directed by Joad Raymond, hosted by Queen Mary University of London. Accessed 15 August 2019. http://newscom.english.qmul.ac.uk/. See also https:// earlymodernnewsnetworks.wordpress.com/. Accessed 11 December 2019.

nodegoat: a web-based data management, network analysis & visualisation environment, created by Pim van Bree and Geert Kessels (2013), developed by LAB1100. Accessed 11 December 2019. http://nodegoat. net.

Oxford Dictionary of National Biography Online, edited by David Cannadine et al. (2014), hosted by the University of Oxford. Accessed 11 December 2019. http://www.oxforddnb.com.

---

[16] See, however, the solution proposed by the *nodegoat* platform.

Palladio, created by Humanities+Design (2014), directed by Dan Edelman and Nicole Colman, hosted by Stanford University. Accessed 11 December 2019. https://hdlab.stanford.edu/palladio/.

Private Libraries in Renaissance England: A Collection and Catalogue of Tudor and Early Stuart Book-Lists, edited by Robert J. Fehrenbach, Joseph L. Black, and Elisabeth S. Leedham-Green, hosted by the Folger Shakespeare Library. Accessed 15 August 2019. http://plre.folger.edu/.

RECIRC–The Reception and Circulation of Early Modern Women's Writings, 1550-1700, directed by Marie-Louise Coolahan, hosted by the University of Ireland at Galway. Accessed 15 August 2019. http://recirc.nuigalway.ie.

The Recusant Print Network Project, created by John Sly, hosted independently. Accessed 15 August 2019. http://www.trpnp.org/.

The Renaissance Cultural Crossroads Online Catalogue of Translations in Britain 1473-1640, edited by Brenda M. Hosington (2013), hosted by the University of Sheffield. Accessed 11 December 2019. http://hrionline.ac.uk/.

Shakeosphere. Mapping Early Modern Social Networks, created by Blaine Greteman and David Eichmann, hosted by the University of Iowa Libraries. Accessed 15 August 2019. https://shakeosphere.lib.uiowa.edu.

Six Degrees of Francis Bacon, edited by Christopher Warren, Daniel Shore, Jessica Otis, Scott Weingart, and John Ladd, hosted by the Carnegie Mellon University Libraries. Accessed 15 August 2019. http://www.sixdegreesoffrancisbacon.com.

Translation and the Making of Early Modern English Print Culture (1473-1660), directed by Marie-Alice Belle and Brenda M. Hosington at the Université de Montréal (2013). Accessed 11 December 2019. www.translationandprint.com.

Tudor Networks of Power, 1509-1603, directed by Ruth Ahnert, hosted by Queen Mary University of London and Cambridge University. Accessed 15 August 2019. http://gtr.rcuk.ac.uk/projects?ref=AH/M004171/1.

Critical studies

Ahnert, Ruth. 2016a. "Maps vs. Networks." In *News Networks in Early Modern Europe*, edited by Joad Raymond and Noah Moxham, 130–57. Leiden: Brill.

————. 2016b. "Tudor Intelligence Networks." Presentation at the Stanford Digital History Seminar, 6 December 2016.

————. 2016c. "Stanford Humanities Center Fellow Q&A: Renaissance Studies scholar Ruth Ahnert." Interview with Tanu Wakefield. Accessed 15 August 2019. http://shc.stanford.edu/news/qa/stanford-humanities-center-fellow-qa-renaissance-studies-scholar-ruth-ahnert.

Ahnert, Ruth, and Sebastian Ahnert. 2015. "Protestant Letter Networks in the Reign of Mary I: A Quantitative Approach." *ELH* 82: 1–33.

Allison, A. F., and D. M. Rogers. 1989–1994. *The Contemporary Printed Literature of the English Counter-Reformation between 1558 and 1640.* 2 vols. Aldershot: Scolar Press / Brookfield, VT: Gower.

Arblaster, Paul. 2004. *Antwerp and the World: Richard Verstegan and the International Culture of Catholic Reformation.* Leuven: Leuven University Press.

Armstrong, Guyda. 2014. "Translation Trajectories in Early Modern European Print Culture." In *Translation and the Book Trade in Early Modern Europe,* edited by José María Pérez-Fernández and Edward Wilson-Lee, 126–44. Cambridge: Cambridge University Press.

————. 2015. "Coding Continental: Information Design in Sixteenth-Century Language Manuals and Transaltions." *Renaissance Studies* 29.1: 78–102.

Bassnett, Susan. 1998. "When Is a Translation Not a Translation?" In *Constructing Cultures: Essays on Literary Translation,* edited by Susan Bassnett and André Lefevere, 25–40. Clevedon: Multilingual Matters.

Belle, Marie-Alice. 2007. "Sur la retraduction de Virgile en Angleterre au XVIIe siècle: enjeux politiques et esthétiques de l'*Énéide* de John Ogilby (1654)." *Études Épistémè* 12: 47–82.

————. 2014. "At the Interface between Translation History and Literary History: A Genealogy of the Theme of 'Progress' in Seventeenth-Century English Translation History and Criticism." *The Translator* 20.1: 44–63.

Belle, Marie-Alice, and Brenda M. Hosington. 2017. "Translation, History, and Print: A Model for the Study of Printed Translations in Early Modern Britain." *Translation Studies* 10.1: 1–21.

————, eds. 2018. *Thresholds of Translation: Paratexts, Print, and Cultural Exchange in Early Modern Britain (1473–1660)*. Basingstoke: Palgrave Macmillan.

Boro, Joyce. 2018. "Spain in Translation: Peritextual Representations of Cultural Difference, 1614–1625." In *Thresholds of Translation: Paratexts, Print, and Cultural Exchange in Early Modern Britain (1473–1660)*, edited by Marie-Alice Belle and Brenda M. Hosington, 101–36. Basingstoke: Palgrave Macmillan.

Bourke, Evan. 2017. "Female Involvement, Membership, and Centrality: A Social Network Analysis of the Hartlib Circle." *Literature Compass* 14.4. Accessed 15 August 2019. https://doi.org/10.1111/lic3.12388.

Boutcher, Warren. 2015. "From Cultural Translation to Cultures of Translation." In *Cultures of Translation in Early Modern England and France, 1500–1660*, edited by Tania Demetriou and Rowan Tomlinson, 22–40. Basingstoke: Palgrave Macmillan.

————. 2018. "Translation and the English Book Trade: The Cases of Humphrey Moseley and William London." In *Thresholds of Translation: Paratexts, Print, and Cultural Exchange in Early Modern Britain (1473–1660)*, edited by Marie-Alice Belle and Brenda M. Hosington, 251–77. Basingstoke: Palgrave Macmillan.

Burke, Peter. 2005. "The Renaissance Translator as Go-Between." In *Renaissance Go-Betweens: Cultural Exchange in Early Modern Europe*, edited by Andreas Höfele and Werner van Kopperfelds, 17–31. Berlin: De Gruyter.

————. 2007. "Cultures of Translation in Early Modern Europe." In *Cultural Translation in Early Modern Europe*, edited by Peter Burke and R. Po-chia Hsia, 7–38. Cambridge: Cambridge University Press.

Coldiron, Anne E. B. 2010. "Translation's Challenge to Critical Categories." In *Critical Readings in Translation Studies*, edited by Mona Baker, 339–58. London: Routledge.

————. 2012. "Visibility Now: Historicizing Foreign Presences in Translation." *Translation Studies* 5.2: 189–200.

————. 2015. *Printers without Borders: Translation and Textuality in the Renaissance*. Cambridge: Cambridge University Press.

————. 2018. "The Translator's Visibility in Early Printed Portrait-Images and the Ambiguous Example of Margaret Roper More." In *Thresholds of Translation: Paratexts, Print, and Cultural Exchange in Early Modern Britain (1473-1660)*, edited by Marie-Alice Belle and Brenda M. Hosington, 51–74. Basingstoke: Palgrave Macmillan.

Collinson, Patrick, Arnold Hunt, and Alexandra Walsham. 2014. "Religious Publishing in England, 1557–1640." In *The Cambridge History of the Book in Britain, Volume IV: 1557-1695*, edited by John Barnard, D. F. McKenzie, and Maureen Bell, 29–66. Cambridge: Cambridge University Press.

Conway, Steve. 2017. "Revealing and Mapping Networks: Potential Opportunities and Pitfalls for Book Trade History." In *Historical Networks in the Book Trade*, edited by John Hinks and Catherine Feely, 29–48. Leiden/Boston: Brill.

Davis, Paul. 2008. *Translation and the Poet's Life: The Ethics of Translating in English Culture, 1646-1726*. Oxford: Oxford University Press.

Demetriou, Tania, and Rowan Tomlinson, eds. 2015. *Cultures of Translation in Early Modern England and France, 1500-1660*. Basingstoke: Palgrave Macmillan.

Düring, Marten. 2017. "From Hermeneutics to Data to Networks: Data Extraction and Network Visualization of Historical Sources." *The Programming Historian*. Accessed 15 August 2019. https://programminghistorian.org/en/lessons/creating-network-diagrams-from-historical-sources.

Eardley, Alice. 2017. "Marketing Aspiration: Fact, Fiction, and the Publication of French Romance in Seventeenth-Century England." In *Gender, Authorship, and Early Modern Women's Collaboration*, edited by Patricia Pender, 130–142. Basingstoke: Palgrave Macmillan.

Eder, Maciej. 2016. "A Bird's-Eye View of Early Modern Latin: Distant Reading, Network Analysis, and Style Variation." In *Early Modern Studies after the "Digital Turn,"* edited by Laura Estill, Diane Jakacki, and Michael Ullyot, 61–88. Toronto: Iter Press; Tempe: ACMRS.

Estill, Laura, Diane Jakacki, and Michael Ullyot, eds. 2016. *Early Modern Studies after the "Digital Turn."* New Technologies in Medieval and Renaissance Studies 6. Toronto: Iter Press; Tempe: ACMRS.

Feather, John. 2007. "The British Book Market 1600–1800." In *A Companion to the History of the Book*, edited by Simon Eliot and Jonathan Rose, 248–64. Malden: Wiley-Blackwell.

Goodrich, Jaime. 2015. "'Ensigne-Bearers of St Clare': Elizabeth Evelinge's Early Translations and the Restoration of English Franciscanism." In *English Women, Religion, and Textual Production, 1500–1625*, edited by Micheline White, 83–100. London/New York: Routledge.

Guénette, Marie-France. 2016. "Agency, Patronage and Power in Early Modern English Translation and Print Cultures: The Case of Thomas Hawkins." *TTR: Traductologie, Terminologie, Rédaction.* 29.2: 155–176.

Hanneman, Robert, and Mark Riddle. 2005. *Introduction to Social Network Analysis Methods.* Riverside: University of California.

Hoftijzer, F. G. 2014. "British Books Abroad: The Continent." In *The Cambridge History of the Book in Britain, Volume IV: 1557–1695*, edited by John Barnard, D. F. McKenzie, and Maureen Bell, 735–743. Cambridge: Cambridge University Press.

Hosington, Brenda M. 2011. "The Renaissance Cultural Crossroads Catalogue: A Witness to the Importance of Translation in Early Modern Britain." In *The Book Triumphant: Print in Transition in the Sixteenth and Seventeenth Centuries*, edited by Malcolm Walsby and Graeme Kemp, 253–69. Leiden/Boston: Brill.

———. 2017. "Collaboration, Authorship, and Gender in the Paratexts Accompanying Translations by Susan Du Verger and Judith Man." In *Gender, Authorship, and Early Modern Women's Collaboration*, edited by Patricia Pender, 92–118. Basingstoke: Palgrave Macmillan.

Hosington, Brenda M., with Marie-Alice Belle. 2018. "Richard Verstegan, Translation, and Print: Visualising a Recusant Network." Paper given at the 64th Annual Meeting of the Renaissance Society of America, New Orleans.

Jockers, Matthew L. 2011. "On Distant Reading and Macroanalysis." Author's blog. http://www.matthewjockers.net/2011/07/01/on-distant-reading-and-macroanalysis/.

———. 2013. *Macroanalysis: Digital Methods and Literary History.* Champaign: University of Illinois Press.

Johns, Adrian. 1998. *The Nature of the Book: Print and Knowledge in the Making.* Chicago: University of Chicago Press.

Kastan, David S. 2007. "Humphrey Moseley and the Invention of English literature." In *Agent of Change: Print Culture Studies after Elizabeth L. Eisenstein*, edited by Sabrina A. Baron, Eric N. Lindquist, and Eleanor F. Shevlin, 105–24. Amherst: University of Massachusetts Press.

Lagresa, Elizabeth S. 2018. "Mapping Translations. Digital Visualization of the *Comedia* in English." Paper given at the 64th Annual Meeting of the Renaissance Society of America, New Orleans.

Latour, Bruno. 2005. *Reassembling the Social.* Oxford: Oxford University Press.

McCarty, Willard. 2012. "A Telescope for the Mind?" In *Debates in the Digital Humanities*, edited by Matthew K. Gold, 113–23. Minneapolis: University of Minnesota Press. http://dhdebates.gc.cuny.edu/debates/text/37.

Moretti, Franco. 2013. *Distant Reading.* London: Verso.

Newman, Karen and Jane Tylus, eds. 2015. *Early Modern Cultures of Translation.* Philadelphia: University of Pennsylvania Press.

Nicholls, Mark. 2008. "Vaux, Anne (bap. 1562, d. in or after 1637)." *Oxford Dictionary of National Biography.* Online edition. Accessed 16 August 2019. https://doi.org/10.1093/ref:odnb/28159.

Norbrook, David. 1999. *Writing the English Republic: Poetry, Rhetoric and Politics 1627-1660.* Cambridge: Cambridge University Press.

Patterson, Annabel. 1984. *Censorship and Interpretation.* Madison: University of Wisconsin Press.

Peacey, Jason. 2013. *Print and Public Politics in the English Revolution.* Cambridge: Cambridge University Press.

Potter, Lois. 1989. *Secret Rites and Secret Writing: Royalist Literature, 1641-1660.* Cambridge: Cambridge University Press.

Pym, Anthony. 1998. *Method in Translation History.* Manchester: St. Jerome.

Raymond, Joad. 2016. "News Networks: Putting the 'News' and 'Networks' Back In." In *News Networks in Early Modern Europe*, edited by Joad Raymond and Noah Moxham, 102–29. Leiden and Boston: Brill.

Raymond, Joad, and Noah Moxham, eds. 2016. *News Networks in Early Modern Europe*. Leiden and Boston: Brill.

Rogers, David M. 1984. "Anthony Batt: A Forgotten Benedictine Translator." *Studies in Seventeenth-Century English Literature, History, and Bibliography: Festschrift for Professor T.A. Birrel*, edited by G. A. M. Jannsens and F. G. A. M. Aarts, 179–93. Amsterdam: Rodopi.

Smith, Helen. 2012. *"Grossly Material Things": Women and Book Production in Early Modern England*. Oxford: Oxford University Press.

Stage, Kelly. 2015. "*Eastward Ho* and the Strength of Weak Ties for Playwrights and Patrons." *Ben Jonson Journal* 22: 208–28.

Staykova, Julia. 2012. "Pseudo-Augustine and Religious Controversy in Early Modern England." In *Augustine beyond the Book: Intermediality, Transmediality, and Reception*, edited by Karla Pollman and Meredith J. Gill, 147–66. Leiden: Brill.

Tahir-Gürçaglar, Sehnaz. 2007. "Chaos before Order: Network Maps and Research Design in DTS." *Meta : Journal Des Traducteurs / Meta: Translators' Journal* 52: 724–43.

Toury, Gideon. 1995. *Descriptive Translation Studies and Beyond*. Amsterdam: John Benjamins.

Townend, Jenna. 2017. "Quantitative and Qualitative Approaches to Early-Modern Networks: The Case of George Herbert (1593–1633) and His Imitators." *Literature Compass* 14.3. Accessed 15 August 2019. http://onlinelibrary.wiley.com/doi/10.1111/lic3.12374.

Van Vugt, Ingeborg. 2017. "Using Multi-Layered Networks to Disclose Books in the Republic of Letters." *Journal of Historical Network Research* 1: 25–51.

Venuti, Lawrence. 1995. *The Translator's Invisibility: A History of Translation*. London: Routledge.

Von Habsburg, Maximilian. 2011. *Catholic and Protestant Translations of the Imitatio Christi, 1425–1650*. Farnham: Ashgate.

Walsby, Malcolm and Graeme Kemp, eds. 2011. *The Book Triumphant: Print in Transition in the Sixteenth and Seventeenth Centuries*. Leiden and Boston: Brill.

Warren, Christopher, Daniel Shore, Jessica Otis, Lawrence Wong, Mike Feingold, and Cosma Shalizi. 2016. "Six Degrees of Francis Bacon: A Statistical Method for Reconstructing Large Historical Social Networks." *Digital Humanities Quarterly* 10.4. Accessed 15 August 2019. http://www.digitalhumanities.org/dhq/vol/10/3/000244/000244.html.

Weingart, Scott. B. 2011. "Demystifying Networks, I and II." *The Journal of Digital Humanities* 1.1. Accessed 15 August 2019. http://journalofdigitalhumanities.org/1-1/demystifying-networks-by-scott-weingart/.

Whitehead, Maurice. 2016. *English Jesuit Education: Expulsion, Suppression, Survival and Restoration, 1762-1803.* London: Routledge.

Collaboration

What's in a Name? *Six Degrees of Francis Bacon* and Named-Entity Recognition

Jessica Marie Otis

Department of History and Art History, George Mason University

Introduction

Six Degrees of Francis Bacon is a digital humanities project that is reconstructing the social network of early modern Britain through a combination of statistical analysis and expert crowdsourcing (*Six Degrees* Team, 2018). Its ambitious aim is to become a vital scholarly source of information about people's relationships in the sixteenth and seventeenth centuries, a social network that includes not just Francis Bacon and the other famous figures of history but also the millions of less famous early modern men and women who lived and died in the British Isles. However, due to practical considerations such as the limited availability of digitized source materials, the initial computationally-generated core of the *Six Degrees* network was derived from a much smaller subset of the early modern population: namely, people mentioned in the *Oxford Dictionary of National Biography* (*ODNB*), whom modern scholars believe to be historically significant in some fashion.

During the first stage of the project, the *Six Degrees* team ran Named-Entity Recognition (NER)—a form of Natural Language Processing that uses machine learning techniques to extract specific pieces of information from unstructured texts—on the full text of the online *ODNB*. NER is commonly used to extract the names of people, organizations, or locations, but can also extract numerical information such as dates and times.[1] In this instance, we focused on people names and generated an initial list of 494,536 possible people to include in the network, which was weeded down to 13,309 people through a combination of computational and manual data cleaning procedures. Names that matched the subject of an early modern *ODNB* biography were automatically included in our social network, while names that only occurred in the full text of ancient, medieval, or modern biographies were automatically excluded as being out of our chronological scope. Names that occurred fewer than five times in the full text of the entire *ODNB* were also eliminated

---

[1] For more on Named-Entity Recognition and its historical development, see Nadeau and Sekine 2007.

ISBN 978-1-64959-016-9 (paper) ISBN 978-1-64959-017-6 (pdf) ISBN 978-1-64959-037-4 (epub)
New Technologies in Medieval and Renaissance Studies 9 (2022) 237–256

at this stage, as they could not provide enough points of reference to give meaningful results during the subsequent statistical analysis that generated the initial network relationships.[2] I then examined and researched the remaining ~1,200 names, identifying their lifespans and other biographical data necessary to determine whether they should be included in or excluded from the network.

This manual cleaning of the NER-generated list of people revealed unexpected patterns of historical association, while also foregrounding historiographical and structural difficulties inherent in mining secondary sources. NER partially mitigated our source material's explicit focus on Britain and historically significant figures from British history by surfacing foreign rulers, intellectuals, and artists as well as highly connected British subjects who did not meet *ODNB*'s criteria for a biography. However, our current inability to automate deduplication and disambiguation of NER-generated names exacerbated known biases in the *ODNB*, particularly the underrepresentation of women. While our NER algorithms were limited by twenty-first-century American cultural biases in naming patterns, which created difficulties in trying to make datasets for early modern studies, employing NER algorithms in conjunction with manual inspection enabled us to leverage both the speed and scalability of NER while still achieving the accuracy necessary for humanistic enquiry.

Project scoping and the illusion of British isolationism

Both *Six Degrees* and the *ODNB* define the scope of their subject material using national boundaries, a common choice in modern scholarship. *Six Degrees* further limits its scope to the early modern period, whose oft-debated chronological boundaries are in this instance set at 1500–1700.[3] Scoping is a necessary part of any historical endeavor and particularly vital in this instance, given the increasingly global character of social networks in and after the early modern period. However, the imposition of nationally-based geographical barriers on historical scholarship has the potential to distort our view of our historical subjects' lived reality. Therefore, one of the most immediately striking results of running NER on the full text of the *ODNB* was

---

[2] For more technical details of the NER process and the subsequent statistical analysis, see Warren, et al. 2016.

[3] People in the *Six Degrees* network must die after 1500 and be born before 1700. The latest death date in the network is currently Jane Lewson, who was reputably born in 1699/1700 and died in 1816. See *ODNB*, "Lewson"; *SDFB*, "Jane Lewson."

the prevalence of foreign popes, monarchs, intellectuals, and other famous historical figures from across Europe and around the world.

The *ODNB* defines the scope for its biographical entries those who "shaped British life between the 4th century BC and the year 2008," and thus allows for the inclusion of some locally influential foreigners (*ODNB*, "For Schools and Teachers"). One example of this can be found in Mary I's husband, Phillip II of Spain, who helped shape almost half a century of English domestic and foreign policies both during and after his wife's reign—most famously by sending the Spanish Armada to invade England in 1588 (*ODNB*, "Phillip II of Spain"). The Winter Queen Elizabeth Stuart's foreign-born sons—Charles Lewis, Rupert, and Maurice—also merit biographies based on their involvement in the British Civil Wars and British navy, while Elizabeth's foreign-born daughter Sophia has an article based on her eventual status as heir to the throne of Great Britain after the 1701 Act of Settlement (*ODNB*, "Charles Lewis"; *ODNB*, "Rupert"; *ODNB*, "Maurice"; *ODNB*, "Sophia"). However Elizabeth's husband Frederick V of the Palatinate has only the stub of a biography inserted into Elizabeth's, despite his role in plunging Europe into the Thirty Years' War (*ODNB*, "Frederick V"). Other foreign husbands of British princesses are excluded entirely, including Louis XII of France, married to Henry VII's daughter Mary Tudor; William II, Prince of Orange, married to Charles I's daughter Mary Stuart and father to the future British king William III; and Philippe, Duke of Orléans, married to Charles I's daughter Henrietta Maria Stuart. Nor was being a British monarch enough to merit an entry for a foreigner with no real influence on local politics: Mary Stewart, Queen of Scots' husband Francis II of France was a king of Scotland before his death at the young age of sixteen, but is also excluded.

While these later historical figures lack their own *ODNB* biographies, they all appear in the full text of other people's biographies—most notably, but not exclusively, their spouses' biographies—and were therefore captured by our NER algorithms. Louis XII of France appears in fifty-nine contemporary biographies and three more from other time periods, while even the short-lived Francis II of France appears in twenty-five biographies. Other European political heavyweights appearing in the full text of the *ODNB* include, but are by no means limited to, Louis XIV of France (305 biographies), Holy Roman Emperor Charles V (101 biographies), Pope Clement VII (62 biographies), Catherine de' Medici (35 biographies), and Pope Gregory XIII (30 biographies). All of these historical figures easily pass the five-mentions test necessary for running the *Six Degrees* statistical analysis; they influenced early modern British politics; and they were an integral part of a European social network that *included* the British Isles, despite not being part of the social network *within* the British Isles.

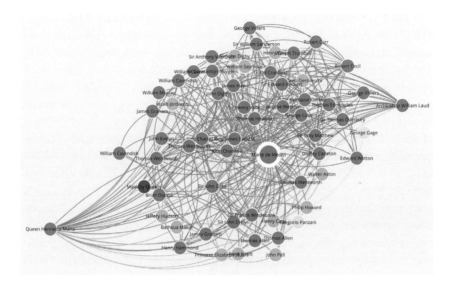

Figure 1. British Social Network of Marie de' Medici.[4]

In order to maintain this sense of connection with the wider European social network, the *Six Degrees* team chose to adopt a different scope than the *ODNB*, using two complementary geographical limitations to delineate between the British and wider social networks. First, the *Six Degrees* social network includes people who were subjects of one of the three British kingdoms—England/Wales, Scotland, and Ireland—regardless of those people's geographical location. British subjects living in the Americas or traveling abroad throughout the world are therefore still considered part of the British social network. Second, it includes anyone who traveled to the British Isles at some point in their life and thus became part of the local social network, albeit on a generally temporary basis. This second criterion allows for the inclusion of foreign historical figures who have *ODNB* biographies but do not otherwise meet the first criterion, such as painters Sir Anthony Van Dyck and Joseph van Aken

---

[4] The nodes in this image have not been repositioned from the force-directed layout that was algorithmically generated based on two degrees' worth of Marie de' Medici's relationships; however, to reduce visual clutter the network has been filtered to only show the first degree relationships. The following link will automatically generate the larger two-degree network: http://sixdegreesoffrancisbacon. com/?ids=10003365&min_confidence=0&type=network.

(*ODNB*, "Dyck, Sir Anthony"; *ODNB*, "Aken, Joseph van"). It also allows for the inclusion of a host of foreign visitors to the British Isles who were captured by our NER algorithms but do not have *ODNB* biographies, such as Marie de' Medici, mother of Charles II's wife Henrietta Maria, who made a three-year visit on the eve of the British Civil Wars; she appears in twenty-one of the *ODNB*'s early modern biographies in contexts ranging from genealogical to political to artistic, and the extent of the influential connections she made at court can be seen in the visualization above (SDFB, "Marie de Medici"). The NER algorithms also yielded a series of Spanish ambassadors to England— Diego Guzmán de Silva, Bernardino de Mendoza, and Guerau de Spes—along with future Constable of France Anne de Montmorency, Italian diarist Lorenzo Magalotti, and Italian astrologer-mathematician Girolamo Cardano.

Socially speaking, no country is an island. However the British Isles' geographical island status makes scholars prone to forgetting that the British Channel and surrounding oceans were more akin to highways than walls in the early modern period. Nationally-based historical narratives and digital resources such as the *ODNB* and *Six Degrees* further reinforce the illusion of political, religious, and cultural isolation. By establishing relationship ties with the rest of the world, the people recovered through the NER algorithms enable us to mar the illusion of British isolationism and remind scholars that social networks do not exist in a geographical vacuum.

Historical significance and weak relationship ties

While the *ODNB*'s selection criteria for biographies allow for the inclusion of some foreigners, the *ODNB* strictly limits itself to people whom modern scholars consider somehow significant to British history and culture. By contrast, the *Six Degrees* social network is intended to include as much as possible of the entire British social network and thus enable scholars to study people who knew and connected people in the network, in addition to people considered notable because of their social status or individual achievements.[5] While the vast majority of the early modern British population is lost to the historical record or can be found only in as-yet-undigitized county archives, NER enabled us to capture a range of people whom the *ODNB* does not consider historically significant in and of themselves, but who nonetheless repeatedly appear in the biographies of the historically significant.

---

[5] For an example of scholarship that closely analyzes network prominence in a smaller early modern network, see Ahnert and Ahnert 2015, 12–20.

One of the most immediately intriguing types of people who appear in the NER results, but who do not have *ODNB* biographies, is the people who were famous for a single incident. In the late sixteenth or seventeenth centuries, such people might have been called a "nine days' wonder" (*OED*, "nine"). This includes men like Thomas Sandys, who connects the biographies of judge George Jeffreys and lawyers Sir Robert Sawyer, Sir George Treby, and Sir William Williams due to an East India Company lawsuit against Sandys for violating its trading privileges. Another example is Edmund Hampden, one of the ship money objectors in the Five Knights' Case, who connects his extended family with a diverse group of politicians and clergymen. But not all the nine days' wonders were associated with legal cases. Robert Nowell appears repeatedly in the *ODNB* due to his deathbed philanthropy, particularly establishing a trust fund for poor scholars at Oxford. These funds, administered by his brother Alexander Nowell, Dean of St. Paul's, connect men such as poet Edmund Spenser, theologian Richard Hooker, geographer Richard Hakluyt, and future bishop Thomas Bilson. Other people briefly surfaced in the *ODNB* in more proactive ways. Captain Robert Gorges sailed to Massachusetts in 1623–24 and established a short-lived government. He figures in the *ODNB* biographies of several presumed shipmates and colonial authorities before returning to England and vanishing from the historical records. These people appear from nowhere in the *ODNB*'s historical biographies, then disappear again with equal speed, leaving behind a snapshot of the social network generated by a single incident or at a single moment in time.

Another group of people to emerge from the NER results are those who, upon the completion of our subsequent statistical analysis, were found to have an unexpectedly high number of relationships compared to the frequency of their mentions in the *ODNB*'s full text. In network analysis parlance, these people have unexpectedly high *degree centrality*, a term which is generally shortened to simply high *degree*.[6] Some of the people in the *Six Degrees* social network have a high degree for obvious reasons. Each of the monarchs, for example, was the center of a web of patronage and every ambitious man or woman in the kingdom wanted to have a relationship with them. Most of these are "weak" relationship ties, which has a specific network meaning that correlates well with a more humanistic reading of the term: acquaintances who do not spend much time with one another or belong to a tightly-knit social group. However, it is precisely these weak relationship ties that enable them

---

[6] Degree centrality—the number of relationships a person has—should not be confused with degree of separation: the number of relationships that separate two people in the network. The project name *Six Degrees of Francis Bacon* refers to degree of separation, not degree centrality.

to act as bridges between more strongly-connected social groups. People with a large number of weak ties are thus useful for navigating large, diverse social networks and it is striking when people who are not, at first glance, "historically significant" nevertheless turn out to have a high number of relationships—especially weak relationships—reflected in the *ODNB* full text.

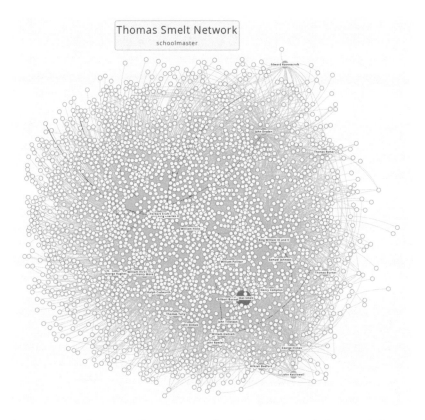

Figure 2. Two degrees of separation from Thomas Smelt (SDFB, "Thomas Smelt").

Several of these unexpectedly high-degree people are schoolmasters, who typically taught a large and ever-changing body of students over time.[7] The NER algorithms captured men like Thomas Smelt, an ardent royalist who taught at the Northallerton Free School in Yorkshire, connecting natural

---

[7] Scholars who have attempted to quantify the reach of teachers in European mathematical schools have estimated that even these highly specialized teachers might reach up to a thousand students, depending on the size of their classrooms and length of their teaching careers. See Van Egmond 1976, 105–06 and Meskins 1996, 140.

philosopher Thomas Burnet, nonjuring clergymen George Hickes and John Kettlewell, Church of Ireland archbishop William Palliser, and literary critic Thomas Rymer. While Hickes and Kettlewell shared an extensive network of mutual acquaintances, Smelt is the only mutual acquaintance of Palliers and Rymer, as well as other pairings of his students, in the *Six Degrees* network. His extensive relationships within the *Six Degrees* network can be seen in the complexity of the image above; the network is so dense that the label of Thomas Smelt's node is actually partially obscured in this visualization. The paler pink nodes, whose labels are also visualized here, represent his first-degree relationships. The unlabeled white nodes are his second-degree relationships, i.e., friends of friends. Edward Sylvester, who ran a grammar school in Oxford, connected a similarly diverse group of students: poet and playwright Sir William Davenant, theologians John Owen and John Wilkins, ejected minister Henry Wilkinson, and physician Thomas Willis. These schoolmasters' relationships with an ever-changing roster of boys particularly enabled them to connect people from different generations as well as those who went on to belong to different political, religious, or social groups.

Another group of high-degree people includes the printers and publishers, whose role in creating the printed historical record also increases their likelihood of appearing in scholarly biographies based on that record. This includes men such as William Barley, a prolific music publisher at the turn of the seventeenth century, and John Kingston, whose diverse publication list included everything from almanacs to a sermon by John Foxe. These printers and publishers would have had only passing relationships with many of their authors, but this is still enough to connect anyone who published with them during the early modern period. While the role of printers and publishers in the *Six Degrees* social network likely parallels their role in the early modern social network, another group of literati likely derive their high degree from the same historical accident that motivated the *ODNB* to grant them biographies: the social networks of diarists like Sir Thomas Aston, Henry Machyn, and Samuel Pepys can be extensively mapped thanks to the writings they left behind.

While most of the people captured by our NER algorithms have not traditionally been studied by scholars and therefore form a seemingly insignificant part of the current narrative consensus around early modern British history, they nonetheless repeatedly appear in the biographies of people deemed historically significant. It is therefore incumbent upon us as scholars to further investigate the roles that they played in early modern British politics, literature, and culture more broadly conceived. Many connect otherwise disparate parts of the *Six Degrees* network, whether through the role they played in incidents that temporarily unified different social groups or through professions that naturally connected large and ever-changing groups of students or authors. As such, they play a vital role in the structure of the early modern social network and have the potential to take on new prominence in studies of the era, more generally, that assign significance to people who knew and connected people, in comparison with traditional measures of significance that focus on personal achievements.

Aliases and gender biases

While running NER on the full text of the *ODNB* is useful for finding people in the British social network who failed to meet the *ODNB*'s criteria for a biography, these algorithms nevertheless have significant limitations when it comes to identifying certain types of people, such as people known by multiple historical aliases. NER is designed to identify and classify names, not to deduplicate them. Some computational intervention is possible with partial name matching, which recognizes that a mention of "Bacon" in the sentence following a mention of "Francis Bacon" probably refers to the same person. Fuzzy matching can also help with the common problems that arise from non-standardized early modern spelling, such as equating Elizabeth, Elisabeth, and Elizabet or Shakespeare, Shakspeare, and Shakspere.[8] However, it is not possible for even the most powerful computer algorithms to equate Catherine Cavenaugh with Christian Davies, Richard Welsh, and Mother Ross unless there is an authority file—a preexisting text or list of people names and the aliases the algorithms should equate those names to.[9] This data is available for people with *ODNB* biographies; however, names that only appear in the full text of the *ODNB* must be cross-referenced manually.[10] Such manual cross-referencing is extremely labor intensive—following the truism that 90% of the effort is done on 10% of the data—and thus can become a low priority for time-strapped scholars. This is a serious concern when using NER on sources like the *ODNB*, because it has the potential to reinforce and exacerbate preexisting gender biases in our source materials.

---

[8] While the text of the *ODNB* employs standardized spelling for major historical figures, spelling is not always consistent between biographies for other names. Working across corpora or with primary sources only exacerbates the issue.

[9] For the complicated case of Catherine Cavanaugh/Christian Davies, see *ODNB*, s.v. "Davies."

[10] While a few people found by NER have associated VIAF or other authority files, the majority do not.

It is patently clear, even at first glance, that there are gender biases in early modern sources and scholarly narratives. The *ODNB* analyzed its own bias by quantifying its biographies and calculating the percentage of male and female biographical subjects over time. The initial version of the *ODNB*—the *Dictionary of National Biography*, begun in 1885—contained only 4.6% women and only 2.1% women in the sixteenth and seventeenth centuries. The new *ODNB*, first published online in 2004, managed to more than double those percentages to a still-unrepresentative 10.2% overall and 5.4% in the sixteenth and seventeenth centuries. Given the extremely skewed ratio of men to women as biographical subjects, it is unsurprising that NER algorithms surface significantly more male names than female names; arguably, women are simply less well represented in texts to begin with (*ODNB*, "Tables"; Weingart and Otis 2016). However, a closer look at the text of the biographies exposes a further structural element that prevents the NER algorithms from identifying the women who did appear: many women are not identified by the "given name + surname" pattern used for men and expected by the NER algorithms, but rather by their given names and a textual description of their relationships to the men in their families.

That there are differences between the modern American identification practices assumed by NER algorithms and the ways that both historical scholars and contemporaries identified each other should not come as a huge surprise. Early modern naming patterns often make it difficult to track people—both men and women—over time, particularly the small number of common given names and the practice of recycling given names from generation to generation within individual families. As of February 2017, the *Six Degrees* social network had eleven men named John Smith and ten more named Archibald Campbell, while it had six each of women named Elizabeth Grey, Elizabeth Howard, and Margaret Neville. For women, this problem is compounded by their systematic surname changes with every marriage, which leaves only their given name as a stable identifier. Of the 3,074 people identified as women in the *Six Degrees* social network, 514 are named Elizabeth, 386 Anne/Ann, 297 Mary, 231 Margaret, 187 Katherine/Catherine, and 153 Jane (*SDFB*, "People"). Except for in the rare cases of unusually named women, such as Mehetabel "Hetty" Wright, given name alone cannot be used with any hope of success to track a woman throughout a multi-surnamed lifespan (*ODNB*, "Wright, Mehetabel").

Scholars have therefore attempted to solve this problem by embedding women's names into the textual equivalent of a social network, linking them to the men in their lives and implicitly capturing all their variant names in a

human-readable format. For example, the woman who today might be identified on her driver's licenses over time as Audrey Boteler, Audrey Anderson,
and lastly Audrey Leigh, Baroness of Chichester, is denoted in the *ODNB* as
"Audrey, widow of Sir Francis Anderson and eldest daughter of John Boteler,
Baron Boteler of Brantfield" (*ODNB*, "Leigh, Francis"). NER algorithms run
on this text capture "Audrey," "Sir Francis Anderson," and "John Boteler" as
three historical people. However, when this list of names is extracted from
the full text of the *ODNB*, in preparation for running the statistical analysis
that generated the *Six Degrees* network relationships, the extraction process
divorces them from the context that gives Audrey's name meaning and
conflates her with the hundreds of other Audreys in the *ODNB*. Audrey—like
all the Elizabeths, Annes, Marys, Margarets, Katherines, and Janes—cannot
be used in constructing the social network and effectively vanishes in the
process. Worse, Sir Francis Anderson and John Boteler remain due to the
NER-friendly construction of their names. John Boteler even passes the five-
mentions threshold because of Audrey and his other daughters—Anne, Mary,
and Olivia or Olive—who are repeatedly mentioned in relation to him in lieu
of being referenced by their various surnames. Human curation was required
to reproduce the network implicit in Audrey's many names and visualize her
familial relationships as seen below; the black edges represent woman-to-
woman and woman-to-man relationships that were added manually, while
the single gray edge between Sir John Boteler and Francis Leigh represents
the man-to-man relationship that was found by our statistical analysis. A
similar pattern appears with Sir Thomas Bellenden of Auchinoul, a justice-
clerk who died in 1546 and passed the *Six Degrees* five-mentions threshold
primarily because of the women in his life. He appears in only one biography
as an active participant—a 1540 meeting with Henry Balnaves and Sir William Evers—but crops up in six more on the strength of his family ties. His
eldest son, John, became a judge and legal writer, meriting his own biography. His sister, Katherine, married a courtier named Oliver Sinclair, while
his daughters Katherine and Margaret had four sons who met the standard
for *ODNB* biographies. The end result of the NER process was thus the unfor-
tunate erasure of women and the substitution of their fathers and husbands,
exacerbating preexisting gender biases in the original sources.

Although the historical underrepresentation of women in sources does not
have a simple technological solution, it is possible to address some of the
structural difficulties in computationally extracting women's names and
other aliases from historical sources such as the *ODNB*. First and foremost,
NER algorithms can be trained to recognize key patterns and phrases such

as "<name>, daughter of <name>," "<name>, wife of <name>," and "<name>, widow of <name>"—along with other variants meant to denote motherhood or sisterhood and combinations of these various phrases—extracting them not as a series of disconnected names but rather as names in and of themselves. NER algorithms can also be trained to recognize patterns around the term *née*, which is often used to link a woman's married name to her maiden name. More generally, computers can be trained to recognize the use of the keyword *alias* to link together variant names. Whether NER algorithms are then used to simply extract relevant data for human curation or combined with computer scripts to generate the relevant collection of names and aliases, it should be possible to modify NER algorithms to better extract and represent women found in historical texts, along with the networks used to precisely identify them.

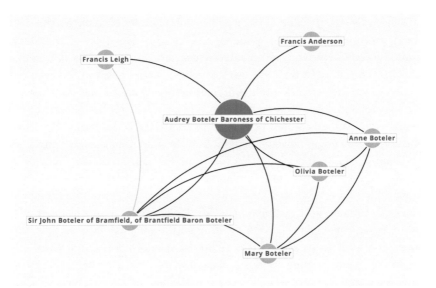

Figure 3. Family network of Audrey Boteler Anderson Leigh, Baroness of Chichester (*SDFB*, "Audrey Boteler").[11]

---

[11] To reduce visual clutter, the nodes in this image have been repositioned from the force-directed layout that was algorithmically generated based on two degrees' worth of Audrey's relationships, and the network has been filtered to only show the first-degree relationships. The following link will automatically generate the larger two-degree network: http://sixdegreesoffrancisbacon.com/?ids=10054874&min_confidence=60&type=network.

Deduplication and disambiguation

As suggested in the previous section, two of the most difficult problems in using NER on historical sources are deduplicating people with multiple aliases as well as disambiguating people who have the same name—whether it be the 514 mononymous Elizabeths, the twenty-two Archbishops of Canterbury, or the ten Archibald Campbells. While it is possible to find some computational solutions to the deduplication and disambiguation problems in the case of women who are referenced in a web of social connections, other instances of these problems are more intractable, leaving scholars to choose between working with messy, imprecise datasets or investing time and money into the painstaking process of manual curation.

Given the time period and location covered by the *Six Degrees* project, one particularly vexing manifestation of both the deduplication and disambiguation problems comes in the form of aristocratic titles, used by both contemporaries and modern scholars. Although titled nobles and religious officeholders constituted less than 1% of the overall population, they are disproportionately prevalent in the ODNB due to modern scholars' focus on political, economic, military, and religious narratives. In one example of the problems associated with identifying people by titles, there were nine different men who possessed the title "Earl of Pembroke" between 1551 and 1700, all of whom can be referred to by the shortened version of their title, "Pembroke." Even texts that also reference the given name and surname of the Pembroke in question do not necessarily resolve the disambiguation issue: three of the earls were William Herberts, three more Philip Herberts, two were Henry Herberts and one was Thomas Herbert. Only the chronological boundaries of the *Six Degrees* project kept the tenth earl of Pembroke—another Henry Herbert—from adding to the duplication of names.

One possible deduplication and disambiguation solution, in the case of noble titles, is to use given names and death dates to separate one holder of a title from another. Associating given names with noble titles can be possible with NER training, in a solution similar to that of deduplicating married names and aliases. Death dates could also provide at least some point of reference for disambiguating title holders, although there will still be instances of chronological overlap when the title passes from one person to another—such as in 1650 when Philip Herbert, Earl of Pembroke, died and was succeeded by Philip Herbert, Earl of Pembroke (*SDFB*, "Philip Herbert"). Unfortunately, using death dates to disambiguate title holders assumes the existence of an authority file that already includes the names and life dates of all noble title holders, including any additional dates on which nobles were granted new titles through deed or inheritance. This method also further assumes that all the in-text *ODNB* references to Pembroke—or other titled members of the aristocracy—are clearly dated, that these dates are captured by NER, and that the results are structured to clearly associate the two.

While aristocrats form a small enough subset of the population that the *Six Degrees* team deemed it more efficient to manually curate them than to attempt a computational solution, removing this special case did not significantly decrease the number of duplicated names in our NER results. Of the 13,309 unique people eventually extracted via NER from the *ODNB* for inclusion in the *Six Degrees* dataset, nearly a thousand have duplicate names. While chronological context is sometimes sufficient to tease apart two men with duplicate names—the lives of Alexander Ross the Church of England clergyman (1591–1643) and Alexander Ross the poet (1699–1784) do not overlap (*ODNB*, "Ross, Alexander"; *ODNB*, "Ross, Alexander, of Lochlee")—other references to people lack any additional biographical data, including birth and death dates. This biographical data is necessary to determine how many different people shared that name, much less which one is being referred to in a specific context. For these instances, the most accurate solution is for a human to manually research—both within the source texts and in outside sources with more genealogical information.

Beyond generating a list of people to populate the *Six Degrees* social network, we also used the NER results as part of the statistical analysis that generated the relationship ties between the people in the network. In simplified terms, we estimated how well the occurrence of a specific name—i.e., Prince Arthur—in the full text of a biography can be used to predict the occurrence of another name—i.e., Henry VII—in that same text. If the occurrence of Person A in a biography always leads to the occurrence of Person B, we assign them a 100% chance of having a relationship. If it leads to the occurrence of Person B 50% of the time, we assign them a 50% chance of having a relationship, and so forth. If Person B shares the same name as Person C, it is crucial for us to be able to distinguish the two in some fashion. As these predictions are done entirely by computers, it requires a computational solution to the disambiguation of repeated names identified within the full text of the *ODNB*, despite the messiness and inaccuracy that could potentially result.

We therefore devised a twofold method to process these duplicate names. First, we employed chronological filters on all our potential relationships. Two people cannot have had a relationship if one died well before the other was born. We do, however, allow a one-year margin of error so that post-humous children may still have relationships with their biological fathers. Second, in the cases where there is chronological overlap in the lifespans of people with duplicate names, we fall back on probabilities to determine which person is mentioned in the text in any given instance. If our duplicates do not have biographical entries, we divide the mentions equally between them; if there is a 50% chance Person A knew either Person B or C, we assign a 25% chance to Person B and 25% chance to Person C. If our duplicates do have biographical entries, we assign each person a probability of being mentioned that is based on the length of their biography. This serves as an approxima-tion of the relative frequency we expect each person to appear in the overall *ODNB*, which we use to weight the mentions accordingly. For example, Fran-cis Walsingham the principal secretary to Queen Elizabeth has a biography that is thirty times the length of Francis Walsingham the Jesuit. Therefore we argue a mention of Francis Walsingham in some other *ODNB* biography is thirty times more likely to refer to the former than to the latter. In theory we should then assign weights of 97% to the principal secretary and 3% to the Jesuit. However, we also "cap" the percentages at a maximum of 75% and a minimum of 25% so that someone with an extremely long biography, like the principal secretary, cannot obscure the Jesuit entirely. Thus, in the period of overlap between their two lifespans, 75% of the instances of this name are attached to the principal secretary and 25% are attached to the Jesuit.

Multiple and duplicate names are a particularly common complication both in NER results and in the early modern world more generally. This forces scholars to make oft-painful trade-offs as they must choose between time-consuming but accurate manual curation or swifter but messier computa-tional data processing. As humanists and their analytical needs increasingly inform the creation or modification of algorithms such as NER algorithms, hopefully the gap between these two modes of data curation will narrow, but they will likely never close entirely.

Conclusion

NER has enormous potential for extracting people from large amounts of unstructured text, although completely automated techniques currently produce messy, imprecise datasets when compared to datasets painstakingly created by hand. The manual cleaning of these datasets is often necessary to acquire the level of precision required for humanities scholarship, and such careful examination of the data has the potential to become scholarly analy-sis in its own right. In the case of *Six Degrees*, this cleaning process enabled the examination of not only our reconstructed version of the early modern British social network, but also modern scholarship about the early modern period and the limitations of the digital tools as employed in this project to produce more such scholarship.

Because NER algorithms do not have a preprogrammed understanding of nationality, historical significance, or network structures, running NER on the full text of the *ODNB* allowed us to capture information about the early modern social network that we would have overlooked if we had focused solely on *ODNB* biography subjects to populate the *Six Degrees* network. In addition to capturing the expected canonical figures of British history, famous for their social status or individual accomplishments, NER surfaced hundreds of people of scholarly interest due to their connections within the British social network. People as diverse as Marie de' Medici, a Catholic flashpoint at Charles I's court on the eve of the British Civil Wars, and modest schoolmasters such as Thomas Smelt, whose students went on to thrive in a variety of different social settings, can now be studied as part of a larger British social network that was never a self-contained association of the "British" or the "historically significant."

In addition to surfacing new facets of the early modern social network to study, our NER results also foregrounded historiographical and structural barriers to this sort of research. The historiographical bias towards men is unsurprising, but it is less obvious that this bias should be exacerbated by the textual networks *ODNB* biographers used to precisely identify historical women through their various surname changes. Scholars need to capture this information about women in lieu of, or at least in addition to, the men in their lives, which currently requires either alteration and training of pre-existing computational tools for NER or human intervention to recover information recorded only in human-readable form.

Issues of deduplicating people with multiple aliases and disambiguating people who share names also highlight the limitations of NER for humanistic research, particularly for time periods when demographic data are so scarce and contested that we do not know the birth date of a queen of England. This lack of authority files to assist in the deduplication and disambiguation process requires scholars to carefully navigate a range of NER options that exist along the spectrum from quick, computational, and messy to slow, manual, and precise. It is this dilemma that inspired the *Six Degrees* team to adopt a combination of computational analysis and human curation in building our social network, using NER and manual examination of the results to ensure the accuracy of the people in our network, then embracing probability to quantify the messiness of our computationally-generated relationship data. While that is, in some sense, achievement enough, we also then turn to crowdsourcing—which is now actively occurring on our website, www. sixdegreesoffrancisbacon.com—in hopes of manually correcting and building upon this messy relationship data, expanding upon our initial network of people and relationships, and eventually becoming the go-to source of scholarly information about the early modern British social network.

WORKS CITED

Ahnert, Ruth, and Sebastian E. Ahnert. 2015. "Protestant Letter Networks in the Reign of Mary I: A Quantitative Approach." *ELH* 82.1 (Spring): 1–33.

Granovetter, Mark S. 1973. "The Strength of Weak Ties." *American Journal of Sociology* 78.6 (May): 1360–80.

Meskins, Ad. 1996. "Mathematics Education in Late Sixteenth-Century Antwerp." *Annals of Science* 53.2: 137–55.

Nadeau, David, and Satoshi Sekine. 2007. "A Survey of Named Entity Recognition and Classification." *Linguisticae Investigationes* 30.1: 3–26.

Oxford Dictionary of National Biography, s.v. "Aken, Joseph van (*c.* 1699–1749), *drapery painter and painter of genre and conversation pieces*," by Susan Sloman. Accessed 28 February 2017. http://www.oxforddnb.com/view/article/28089.

Oxford Dictionary of National Biography, s.v. "Charles Lewis [Karl Ludwig] (1618–1680), elector palatine of the Rhine," by Ronald G. Asch. Accessed 28 February 2017. http://www.oxforddnb.com/view/article/65815.

Oxford Dictionary of National Biography, s.v. "Davies [née Cavenaugh], Christian [Catherine; alias Christopher or Richard Welsh; called Mother Ross] (1667–1739), *female soldier*," by Dianne Dugaw. Accessed 28 February 2017. http://www.oxforddnb.com/view/article/7228.

Oxford Dictionary of National Biography, s.v. "Dyck, Sir Anthony [*formerly* Antoon] Van (1599–1641), *painter and etcher*," by Jeremy Wood. Accessed 28 February 2017. http://www.oxforddnb.com/view/article/28081.

Oxford Dictionary of National Biography. "For Schools and Teachers." http://global. oup.com/oxforddnb/info/library/learning/. Available through the Wayback Machine at https://web.archive.org/web/20171003172503/ http://global.oup.com:80/oxforddnb/info/library/learning/. Accessed 28 February 2017.

Oxford Dictionary of National Biography, s.v. "Frederick V, count palatine of the Rhine and elector of the Holy Roman Empire (1596–1632)," by Ronald G. Asch. Accessed 28 February 2017. http://www.oxforddnb.com/view/ article/88678.

Oxford Dictionary of National Biography, s.v. "Lewson [*née* Vaughan], Jane [*known as* Lady Lewson] (1699/1700?–1816), *eccentric and centenarian*" by Thomas Seccomb, rev. by David Turner. Accessed 28 February 2017. http://www.oxforddnb.com/view/article/16613.

Oxford Dictionary of National Biography, s.v. "Maurice, prince palatine of the Rhine (1621–1652), *royalist army and naval officer*," by Ian Roy. Accessed 28 February 2017. http://www.oxforddnb.com/view/article/18383.

Oxford Dictionary of National Biography, s.v. "Philip [Philip II of Spain, Felipe II] (1527–1598), *king of England and Ireland, consort of Mary I, and king of Spain*," by Glyn Redworth. Accessed 28 February 2017. http://www. oxforddnb.com/view/article/22097.

Oxford Dictionary of National Biography, s.v. "Ross, Alexander (1591–1654), *Church of England clergyman and writer on philosophy*," by David Allan. Accessed 28 February 2017. http://www.oxforddnb.com/view/article/24110.

Oxford Dictionary of National Biography, s.v. "Ross, Alexander, of Lochlee (1699–1784), *poet*," by Roger J. Robinson. Accessed 28 February 2017. http:// www.oxforddnb.com/view/article/24112.

Oxford Dictionary of National Biography, s.v. "Rupert, prince and count palatine of the Rhine and duke of Cumberland (1619–1682), *royalist army and naval officer*," by Ian Roy. Accessed 28 February 2017. http://www. oxforddnb.com/view/article/24281.

Oxford Dictionary of National Biography, s.v. "Sophia, princess palatine of the Rhine (1630–1714), *electress of Hanover, consort of Ernst August*," by Jeremy Black. Accessed 28 February 2017. http://www.oxforddnb. com/view/article/37994.

Oxford Dictionary of National Biography. "Tables." http://global.oup.com/ oxforddnb/info/print/intro/tables/. Available through the Wayback Machine at https://web.archive.org/web/20140323171224/http:// global.oup.com/oxforddnb/info/print/intro/tables. Accessed 28 February 2017.

Oxford Dictionary of National Biography, s.v. "Wright [née Wesley], Mehetabel [Hetty] (1697–1750), *poet,*" by Richard Greene, rev. by William R. Jones. Accessed 28 February 2017. http://www.oxforddnb.com/view/ article/38156.

Oxford English Dictionary Online, s.v. "nine, *adj.* and *n.*" Accessed 28 February 2017. http://www.oed.com/view/Entry/127181?rskey=7IlZBT&result= 1&isAdvanced=false#eid34398413.

Six Degrees Team, *Six Degrees of Francis Bacon: Reassembling the Early Modern Social Network.* Accessed 8 June 2018. http://www.sixdegreesoffrancis bacon.com/about.

Six Degrees of Francis Bacon, s.v. "Audrey Boteler Baroness of Chichester." Accessed 8 June 2018. http://sixdegreesoffrancisbacon.com/?ids= 10054874&min_confidence=60&type=network.

Six Degrees of Francis Bacon, s.v. "Jane Lewson." Accessed 8 June 2018. http:// sixdegreesoffrancisbacon.com/?ids=10007402&min_confidence=60 &type=network.

Six Degrees of Francis Bacon, s.v. "Marie de Medici." Accessed 8 June 2018. http:// sixdegreesoffrancisbacon.com/?ids=10003365&min_confidence=0& type=network.

Six Degrees of Francis Bacon. "People." http://www.sixdegreesoffrancisbacon. com/people. Available through the Wayback Machine at https://web. archive.org/web/20170928192204/http://www.sixdegreesoffrancisbacon. com/people. Accessed 28 February 2017.

Six Degrees of Francis Bacon, s.v. "Philip Herbert." Accessed 8 June 2018. http:// sixdegreesoffrancisbacon.com/?ids=10054821&min_confidence=60 &type=network.

Six Degrees of Francis Bacon, s.v. "Thomas Smelt." Accessed 8 June 2018. http://www.sixdegreesoffrancisbacon.com/?ids=10011186&min_ confidence=0&type=network.

Van Egmond, Warren. 1976. "The Commercial Revolution and the Beginnings of Western Mathematics." PhD dissertation, Indiana University.

Warren, Christopher N., et al. 2016. "Six Degrees of Francis Bacon: A Statistical Method for Reconstructing Large Historical Networks." *Digital Humanities Quarterly* 10.3. http://www.digitalhumanities.org/dhq/vol/10/3/000244/000244.html.

Weingart, Scott, and Jessica Otis. 2016. "Gender Inclusivity in Six Degrees." *Six Degrees of Francis Bacon* (blog) 5 January 2016. http://6dfb.tumblr.com/post/136678327006/gender-inclusivity-in-six-degrees.

Remixing the Canon: Shakespeare, Popular Culture, and the Undergraduate Editor

Andie Silva

York College, City University of New York

A word cloud of student expectations on the first day of any Shakespeare course would likely include, in large font, the words *scary, hard, complicated,* and *old* (whether the language or just the bard himself). Students' fear of Shakespeare has become such a standard at this point that the popular study-guide website, *Sparknotes,* has created a special section of the site called "No Fear Shakespeare." The site purports to address readers' unfamiliarity with early modern English by offering translations in "the kind of English people actually speak today" ("No Fear Shakespeare" 2017). Yet, although the plays' language and syntax can certainly play a role in generating dread, it is perhaps Shakespeare's status in the literary canon that seems most daunting. Undergraduate students in general and students of color and minorities in particular often associate Shakespeare with a rigid, colonialist history, and part of an elitist academic discourse community that is at best alienating and at worst inaccessible. In turn, teaching Shakespeare in undergraduate classrooms demands that instructors deconstruct Western assumptions about canonicity and cultural value.

Digital pedagogy can offer a productive way to address this inherent disconnect by fostering social knowledge production and creativity. Instructors interested in book history and bibliography in particular have a wide range of new digital tools available for developing collaborative, project-driven courses. Open-access, public editing platforms like Scalar facilitate this process by providing spaces where students learn to actively question and respond to literary and historical authority, and to engage with texts and editorial practices on their own terms.[1] Scalar's unique affordances (such as the creation of reading "paths," relatively simple user interface, and multimedia

---

[1] Scalar is a platform developed by the Alliance for Networking Visual Culture, which "seeks to enrich the intellectual potential of our fields to inform understandings of an expanding array of visual practices as they are reshaped within digital culture, while also creating scholarly contexts for the use of digital media in film, media, and visual studies" (Scalar n.d.).

New Technologies in Medieval and Renaissance Studies 9 (2022) 257–278

annotation tools) make it the ideal platform for engaging students in authentic, public-facing academic writing.

Project-based courses are particularly useful for classes that involve digital literacy and scholarship, as students are encouraged not to simply acquire and apply technical skills but to see the outcome of their work take concrete (if digital) form (Helle et al. 2006).[2] This essay outlines one such approach, where students at York College, a liberal arts college in Jamaica (New York State), collaborated on a pop-culture digital edition of Shakespeare's plays. Rather than approach the plays as formal, academic editors, students in ENG 318 ("Shakespeare: The Major Works") were asked to think of specific ways in which Shakespeare resonated in the culture they were already consuming, including television shows, books, music, and art. The course encouraged students to forge close, personal relationships with the plays and to articulate these relationships in ways that might help future learners connect with Shakespeare. In addition to questioning the playwright's position in the Western canon, students pushed back against accepted readings, layering the text with their own interests, critical interpretations, and individual perspectives. With the help of Scalar, we sought to build community within and beyond the classroom, to discuss the value of social knowledge creation, and to produce a version of Shakespeare that was uniquely "ours"—the readings of a largely Black and Brown, cross-national, and cross-generational discourse community.

This essay explores the benefits and challenges of using digital editing as a platform for social knowledge production. First, I discuss the underlying impetus for the project, my choice of Scalar as a digital platform, and a number of specific assignments designed to develop skills toward the final edition. Next, I analyze examples from student work, considering the larger implications of students' annotation choices and the thematic focus each of them chose for their acts. Finally, I outline some of the potential pitfalls of this course. My aim is to privilege students' discovery, negotiation, and ownership of ideas. As a result, I intentionally focus on successful student-writing samples, placing the onus of failure on the instructor. While this essay reflects on the value of teaching with digital tools such as Scalar, I propose new ways of thinking about Shakespeare pedagogy more broadly, focusing on what new insights may be drawn from creating a collaborative, context-specific edition of Shakespeare's plays.

---

2 For more concrete examples of how faculty conceptualize and deal with PBL, see Lee et al. 2014.

Course design

York College is an incredibly diverse institution, where the vast majority of the student population is Black and Brown, many of whom are first-genera-tion students, either immigrants themselves or part of immigrant families.[3] As a result, students at York are often eager to understand and critique he-gemonic structures, particularly with relation to canonic literature. When it comes to Shakespeare, as one student has noted, his centrality in the West-ern canon often obscures the work of people of color writing in and beyond the early modern period outside of Europe, imposing a version of literary history that positions Shakespeare as a unique and inimitable genius.[4] In turn, many students find themselves alienated by his works, and they enter the Shakespeare classroom expecting to passively receive historical, critical, and analytical resources they might memorize but may never quite "own" or contribute to. In ENG 318, I address this by encouraging the practice of social annotation which, as Paul Scharcht argues, "stands in marked opposition to those aspects of higher education pedagogy and scholarship that remain, even in democratic societies, hierarchical, exclusive, proprietary, and com-petitive" (Scharcht 2016, parag. 6). Digital tools help enhance this open and democratic approach by encouraging public forms of discourse: as I explain below, students were challenged to not only seek out individual connections to the plays but also to argue why their annotations could be more broadly relevant to future students taking ENG 318 or similar Shakespeare courses at other schools.[5]

The course, subtitled "Shakespeare in the Digital Age," applied project-based learning strategies to help students produce a digital edition of Shakespeare's plays that tied characters, themes, and motifs to works from contemporary popular culture (see appendix: "Pop Culture Edition"). I first ran the course in fall 2015 with a class of thirty students and again in fall 2016 with nearly

---

[3] As an instructor who herself is Latina-Brazilian and an immigrant, many of the re-search interests and concerns that drive my students resonate with me on a personal level. Indeed, the impetus for this project was a by-product of conversations and de-bates I have had with students in other classes I teach at York.

[4] I am grateful to Alexis Haynie for bringing this very crucial discussion into our "Introduction to Literary Studies" classroom.

[5] The value of the digital humanities within undergraduate pedagogy has been gain-ing more critical attention. See for instance Clement 2012, Murphy and Smith 2017b, and Silva and Schofield (forthcoming).

half the enrollment (sixteen students).[6] The enrollment number allowed for a well-balanced breakdown: groups of five students were each assigned to a play we were scheduled to discuss between weeks four and nine, ensuring that all groups (even those working on one of our last plays in the term) had plenty of time to draft and revise their final project.[7] The course was designed primarily to generate an atmosphere of authenticity wherein "individuals engage in practices of value to themselves and to a community of practice" (Barab et al. 2000, 38).[8] Toward that end, the students and I negotiated definitions of popular culture. Building such a definition helped ground many conversations in class regarding who gets to decide what counts as "high-brow" culture in seeming opposition to popular culture (Lanier 2002, Bristol 1996, Hawkes 1992, Burt 2002, O'Neill 2014). Many students worried that their preferences toward non-Western culture (consuming only *anime* and *manga*, for example) or "throwback" viewing/reading habits (one student brought up *The Jeffersons*) could not be qualified as pop culture. After a number of one-on-one conversations, I followed up with the class and we collaborated on a definition that centralized students' own interests and values: we agreed that any work of fiction in any media (television, print, film, music) that remained culturally and personally relevant to them would fall within our understanding of "pop culture." Although rather broad, this definition takes into consideration what Alastair Pennycook calls "transcultural flows," which in a classroom context calls for "taking student knowledge, identity and desire into account [in order] to engage with multiple ways of speaking, being, and learning, with multilayered modes of identity at global, national and local levels" (Pennycook 2006, 15).[9] Finally, we reserved classroom time to discuss best practices for editing work on Scalar. Working with Scalar 1.0 became particularly challenging, as the marginal references moved arbitrarily across the page whenever the user scrolled down, making it diffi-

---

[6] Although I revised some of the prompts, the overall course design remained relatively stable. Below, I discuss student examples produced in both semesters: one from fall 2015 (Fasanya) and two from fall 2016 (Etienne and Miller). Student work has been reproduced with permission.

[7] I intentionally assigned a completely different selection of plays in the second iteration of the course so that we could build up our collaborative edition (we used the same Scalar book both times). See the course site (http://scalar.usc.edu/works/shakespeare-in-the-digital-age) for the full list of plays.

[8] As Juliette Levy states, this approach requires a "philosophy of teaching in which students are stakeholders of the learning process rather than subjects of it" (Levy n.d.). See also Cook-Sather 2002.

[9] I'm grateful to Matt Garley for pointing me toward this reference.

cult to ascertain what lines corresponded to which references.[10] Nonetheless, Scalar is a convenient and relatively easy-to-use platform, ideal for this kind of project for a number of reasons: 1) it does not require software installations; 2) it allows for multiple author roles; 3) it offers a flexible design; and 4) it includes the option of "paths" to customize readers' experience.

Collectively, students had to work in groups to develop a cohesive edition of their play. Individually, however, each student was allocated to a single act, and instructed to collect references specific to the themes, motifs, and plot elements pertaining to that act. Although we discussed the formal prompt for the final project early on, the only overall direction was that students keep a running list of potential references and ideas using a medium and platform of their choice (e.g., Evernote, Google Drive, or old-fashioned pen and paper). I intentionally did not introduce them to Scalar until much later in the term, when we were able to meet at computer labs and work through step-by-step tutorials.[11] In order to ensure (as much as possible) that each group included some tech-savvy learners as well as more practiced close-readers, I developed a "knowledge survey" that asked students about their experience with Shakespeare, their familiarity with early modern language in particular and literary analysis in general, and their comfort level using new technologies.

All of our work for the course, including five responses, a short formal paper, and in-class writing, was designed to build critical as well as technical skills students would need for creating their edition.[12] Their first response assignment invited students to explore and evaluate existing online sources for Shakespeare's plays, including *Folger Digital Texts*, *Internet Shakespeare*

---

[10] In the second iteration of this course we switched to Scalar 2.0, which provides more static marginalia but still seems to have a problem regarding placement of the images and videos (e.g., some annotations appear ten or twenty lines below the highlighted quotes). Scalar has become a reliable and iterative platform for pedagogical projects: Vimala Pasupathi, Heather Froehlich, and Emily Sherwood for instance recently ran a workshop on editing a digital textbook for instructors and students interested in digital humanities approaches to Shakespeare. I was part of a group of scholars who contributed to the first iteration of this project during a Shakespeare Association of America seminar in spring 2017.

[11] This approach was inspired by Miriam Posner's blog on the use of self-guided tutorials and group work to help students acquire new technology skills. See Posner 2015.

[12] Our completed project, including student work from 2015 and 2016 courses, can be found at http://scalar.usc.edu/works/shakespeare-in-the-digital-age/.

Editions, and *Open Source Shakespeare,* and compare these with their own printed anthology (*The Norton Shakespeare;* see Greenblatt 2008). Together we tried to design criteria for defining a "good" edition, including elements such as number of footnotes, ease of access, navigability, and design. In their responses, students interrogated the ways editorial practices heavily influence readership and reception. Perhaps unsurprisingly, many students preferred digital editions to their printed anthology—not simply because websites do not require lugging around a heavy textbook, but because the hypertext allowed them to navigate non-linearly across plays, scenes, or paratextual materials. Students' familiarity with websites and online reading further contributed to making the works appear less intimidating. And yet, many students noted that they could not properly interact with those digital editions by way of annotating, tagging, or adding sticky notes to mark important places. Some students felt that digital editions were not useful for undergraduate-level scholarship, because they often lacked contextual essays or footnotes.

These reflections helped define our goals for the Scalar edition, which was deliberately aimed at undergraduate students and readers interested in becoming more acquainted with Shakespeare through a less-intimidating format.[13] Additional small-stakes assignments encouraged students to build components for their edition, such as annotated bibliographies with academic sources for their assigned play, and a collaborative "editor's introduction" (drafted in response 3 and revised for response 5) that required them to consider the specific goals, potential audience, and central arguments for their edition.

The "editor's introduction" assignment was the only formal requirement for collaborative work. Since most York students find it difficult to coordinate schedules outside of work and family obligations, I scaffolded the project so as to allow for in-class group meetings and collaborative writing. With several successful examples of editorial introductions in hand (including both our anthology and digital samples from *Open Source Shakespeare* and *Internet Shakespeare Editions*), I asked students to consider the rhetorical goals of critical introductions in general and the specific ways they could also function to assign credit and acknowledge students' labor.[14] Because Scalar does not assign authorship to individual pages, we used the introductions to outline

---

[13] On the pitfalls of public writing within humanities courses, see Josephs 2018 and Jenkins 2009. On the ethics and roles of undergraduate research in digital pedagogy, see Murphy and Smith 2017a.

[14] All student work in the public site is credited in each play's "Editorial Introduction."

each student's contribution to the work. In response to class discussions surrounding the uncertain nature of the term *popular culture*, these introductions further gave students the opportunity to articulate their choices and look for common threads across the group's references as a whole. In addition to asking what Shakespeare meant to them on a personal level, this assignment also introduced students to editorial practices and conventions, encouraging them to reflect first-hand on the influence editors have over the ways we read and study texts.

A multimodal platform by design, Scalar provided space for more formal writing assignments like the essays discussed above as well as our informal interventions like video- and image-centered marginalia. Despite certain structural limitations, Scalar provided a cohesive template where students had control over their own pages but did not have to concern themselves with the visual design of the project.[15] Per the requirements of the assignment, each student was assessed on their ability to:

1. briefly summarize the chosen pop culture reference,
2. explain the critical connection between the source and the action of the play,
3. clarify how drawing this connection enhances our reading of the play itself.

These goals were designed to evaluate students' familiarity with their assigned play as well as their ability to craft persuasive arguments about Shakespeare as a "rhizomatic" object, encompassing "the vast web of adaptations, allusions, and reproductions that comprises the ever-changing phenomenon we call Shakespeare" (Lanier 2014). Indeed, while my initial expectation

---

[15] It should be noted that I did not work with students to select or encode the text of the plays. Although there is much to be gained from introducing students to collation and copy-text selection practices, I wanted them to focus on learning how to use Scalar and on collecting their references. In the first iteration of this course, I preloaded the Scalar page with transcriptions from *Open Source Shakespeare*. In response to issues with format from copying and pasting the text from the website (for example, line numbers all but disappeared), the second edition of the project used the HTML transcriptions provided by the *Folger Digital Texts*. This approach was not without its challenges: for instance, the Folger editions did not always correspond to the text from our printed anthology, making it difficult for students to find the appropriate line numbers for their annotations. In one particular case, the lines a student wanted to use in *Measure for Measure* (1623) were missing entirely, and we had to manually add them using a different copy.

was that students would seek out books, comics, and films that explicitly adapted Shakespeare and his plays, they pushed our understanding of adaptation much farther, inviting comparisons to works that claimed no official ties to or inspiration from Shakespeare, such as Beyoncé and Rhianna lyrics, films like Moulin Rouge and Titanic, and TV shows like Battlestar Galactica and House of Cards.[16] As one student explained, it was as if "culture that I consumed in the past, or was currently consuming, grew tentacles that connected to the themes of Shakespeare once I was made aware of the project."[17]

Our use of Scalar also invited unplanned conversations about copyright and fair use, as we considered the broader demands of an increasingly-dynamic visual culture. For example, many links that were active at the time students added them were later taken down from YouTube due to copyright violations, while others could never be uploaded in the first place because they belonged to proprietary streaming services such as Netflix and Hulu. Students who did not or could not provide a visual illustration for their work felt as if their project was somehow lacking, even though the use of images was never a feature they had identified as a requirement for successful scholarly editions. Yet, these setbacks also allowed many students to more carefully consider the role of the textual notations that were required to accompany the text; because some annotations lacked videos or images, students understood that their editorial notes needed to be particularly detailed and carefully edited to ensure clarity.

Nevertheless, the course succeeded in getting students to produce original and thought-provoking work. Over the course of the term, we discussed the role of editorial practices in shaping the reception history of Shakespeare's plays and the emergence of Bardolatry, and considered the impact of popular culture on the production and reproduction of cultural norms. By combining digital technologies with traditional close-reading practices, this project effectively immersed students in the process of conceptualizing, curating, and publishing a digital edition. Digital projects require careful descriptions about methodology, audience, and data collection. As such, they provide an

---

[16] The next section of this essay discusses some examples in more detail.

[17] Afolami Fasanya composed this as part of a short reflection for our collaborative presentation at the CUNY Digital Humanities Initiatives (DHI) lightning talks, 2015. As I discuss below, Afolami applied a social justice lens to their interpretations, thinking through how contemporary culture, from *Harry Potter* to world renowned artist Kahinde Wiley can be read in relation to Shakespeare's own efforts toward representation of people of color.

ideal platform for conversations about discourse communities, encouraging students to find authentic ways to engage with early modern literature.

As they compiled a list of potential references for their assigned play, students were faced with broader questions regarding project management and editorial choices, as well as technological obsolescence. This hands-on process ensured that students did not simply use digital tools but rather engaged critically with the ways such tools have the power to shape their learning. Student feedback confirmed that students found themselves deeply and personally connected to their assigned play. Their annotations required them to showcase a much deeper understanding of the themes and motifs in their play than can typically be accomplished in a survey course (particularly in a course capped at thirty students). Scalar provided students with a platform on which to develop public-facing scholarship, helping them push the boundaries of traditional academic research and literary analysis. These goals are arguably crucial to any twenty-first-century classroom since, as J. Elizabeth Clark claims, "the future of writing—based on a global, collaborative text, where all writing has the potential to become public—informs our classrooms and forms a new, 'digital' imperative, one that asks how we can reshape our pedagogy with new uses of the technologies that are changing our personal and professional lives" (Clark 2010, 28).[18]

Digital editing and feminist critique: three student samples

The most successful contributions to the project came about as a combination of independent research and collaborative work.[19] Those students who were able to meet and discuss ideas outside of class managed to compose cohesive introductions and rationales, which in the end helped guide the central arguments within their individual acts. Students who considered the project as an extension of and complement to in-class lectures saw in their annotations the opportunity to undertake analyses of minor characters and, more broadly, to reflect on how gender, race, and ethnicity feature across Shakespeare's works in fascinating yet problematic ways. Afolami Fasanya, for instance, found themselves surprised to discover that Shakespeare's plays included minorities as protagonists. This realization propelled them to think about the cultural constructs of race both in the early modern period as well

[18] On public- and open learning, see the entire special issue of the *Journal of Interactive Technology and Pedagogy* (JITP) 2014.

[19] All writing quoted below is presented with permission from the students. I would like to thank Afolami Fasanya, Claudia Etienne, and Kirsten Miller for their thought-provoking interventions and excellent contributions to the project.

as in the contemporary Western world. In their annotation for act 2 of *The Merchant of Venice* (1600), for instance, they observe that Dobby, the house elf from the film series *Harry Potter*, and Launcelot were both constrained within the limitations of their social status in ways that denied them agency. They both relied on their socially- and economically-superior allies to "provide" them with their freedom (Figure 1).

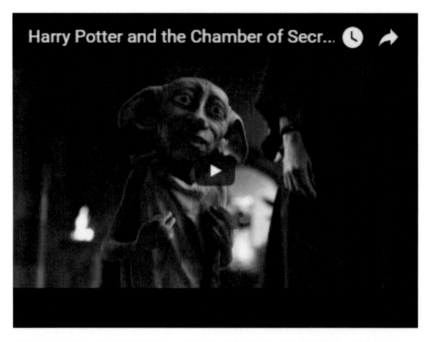

This clip shows Dobby the house elf being set free by his master Lucius Malfoy, or Harry Potter.However you want to see it.Dobby is a character that grapples with loyalty to his master versus his own agency.He does things that strongly demonstrate his desire to be free from the Malfoy's. Ultimately, due to structure, he can't be the one to set himself free.It belongs to someone else.This is the case with Launcelot, who wants to maintain loyalty but also wants nothing to do with his master, Shylock.It is his father who has the power to set him free from Shylock,no matter how strong his own desire burns

Figure 1. Afolami Fasanya's annotation for 2.2.102–12.

Fasanya's argument raised deeper issues regarding power and class in *The Merchant of Venice*, focusing on a character we did not have much time to analyze in class. Even when Launcelot was the subject of conversation, we often focused on the ways the character helped contextualize Jessica's conversion and her treatment of Shylock. Yet this character can be crucial to deconstructing some of the play's problematic binaries. Laura E. Donaldson argues that although Launcelot's character is often reduced to the role of clown, he can in fact be "a figure so threatening that readers privileging homogeneity and segregation must necessarily remain blind to the way he generates other constellations of meaning within the play" (Donaldson 1995, 199). Calling for a perspective that blends post-structuralism with Gloria Anzaldúa's New Mestiza theory, Donaldson looks at Launcelot's place outside the Christian/ Jew binary, positioning him as a case-point for "the mestiza's capacity . . . not only to destabilize but also to transform the agonizing opposition of the Christian and Jew" (Donaldson 1995, 195). Fasanya's annotations reflect a similar call for disruptive readings, focusing on the Other as central, rather than incidental, point of analysis.

The same critical impulse is evident when Fasanya draws a connection between the play and the work of Kehinde Wiley, an African-American painter known for recasting European, heroic, and iconographic paintings with Black and Brown models (Figure 2). Rather than locate Shakespeare at the center of their analysis, Fasanya themselves become the critical interpreter of the racialized bodies in *Merchant of Venice*. Instead of focusing on Shakespeare's choices for characterizing Shylock, Fasanya considers another displaced Other, the Prince of Morocco, as a "foreigner trying to fit into European customs." Significantly, Fasanya's connection here bypasses a discussion of Shakespeare's choices in representing a Black figure, but instead makes this a point to reflect on the broader significance and potential disruption of the Black body in a European context.

As may be evident from the examples above, students enrolled in the second iteration of this course benefited from having strong models to inspire their own editions.[20] In their final drafts, a number of students chose to address the corruptive nature of hegemonic power and its inevitable ties to toxic masculinity. In her annotations for act 2 of *Measure for Measure* (1623), for example, Claudia Etienne focused on the incongruous association between law, mercy, and social class using examples from films and television shows such as *300*, *Titanic*, and *The Flash*. Etienne began by exploring how Christian values

---

[20] In this way, our first edition became what Trevor Owens called "the required reading that we write ourselves"—it became a platform for students to produce material for future students, therefore disrupting the top-down delivery of content from instructor to student. See Owens 2012.

often become convenient facades that conceal prejudice and discrimination. In particular, she reflected on the power structures that allowed for Angelo's unrestrained behavior and trapped Isabella into an impossible decision. As she observed, Angelo's position as interim duke and his reputation as a man of honor both play a role in his choice to proposition Isabella. Connecting *Lord of the Rings'* protagonist Frodo to Angelo, Etienne concluded that "temptation" was a running motif in Shakespeare that allowed the playwright to critique the unchecked power structures of early modern England (Figure 3). Rather than judge Angelo's decision, Etienne chose to reflect on the ways the play's cultural imperatives ultimately set the characters up for failure.

DESCRIPTION   DETAILS   CITATIONS   SOURCE

Besides complexion, there's the larger issue of the Prince being a foreigner trying to fit into European customs.This exhibit by artist Kehinde Wiley takes masculine black urban males and places them into European styled potraits generally reserved for the aristocracy .The aspect of the black male and European context speaks specifically to the Prince in this act.But the fact that many of the portraits have a feminine aura speak to the general gender fluidity in a lot of Shakespeare's work such as Twelfth night and Venus and Adonis.

Figure 2. Afolami Fasanya's annotation for 2.7.16.

As a whole, Etienne's annotations are evidence of her semester-long interest in the intersections of gender, class, and politics. Looking back on her knowledge of the plays as a whole, Etienne concludes that "duplicity is one of Shakespeare's more enduring themes"—in comedies, feigning and disguise become a strategy employed by lower-class and women characters in order to bypass restrictive or excluding power dynamics. Yet, as Etienne notes, Angelo's disguise is more complex, since "the disguise was [in fact] Angelo's reputation and the outward persona he shows the world." Although we did not cover notions of interiority too deeply in class, students like Claudia Etienne and her group mate Kerstin Miller produced thought-provoking reflections on the centrality of identity as performance in Shakespeare. Looking beyond the theatrical conventions of asides and soliloquies, they found in Shakespeare's plays a constant tension between outward and inward expressions of the self. As Miller so poignantly asks, "are we wearing a mask, or are we the mask?" (annotation for 3.1.5).

M4M the lord of the rings
Theme - Temptation. In the movie, the Lord of the Rings: the Return of the King, Frodo Baggins faces the temptation of using a ring of power. Although using the ring could have disastrous effects, Frodo still succumbs to temptation. In Measure for Measure Angelo faces temptation as well when faced with the righteous Isabella (2.2.218-220). Modern day audiences can better understand Shakespeare's theme of temptation by the observing the ease which someone succumbs to temptation. That observation can act as tool to measure one's character. For example, Angelo quickly easily succumbs to temptation when he propositioned Isabella; however, Frodo fought and struggled with temptation for a long time before finally giving in. In Frodo, you see strength and goodness in his battle with temptation; however, Angelo's hasty fall from temptation is a good example of Shakespeare's penchant for portraying people in power negatively.

Figure 3. Etienne's annotation for 2.2.218–20.

Miller's question and indeed her pop culture reference (the film *The Mask*) exemplify one of the most unexpected results of this project: students' ability to draw critical connections between the most seemingly disparate genres and cultural elements. Students like Miller were quick to understand that, as Marjorie Garber so aptly observes, "Shakespeare makes modern culture and modern culture makes Shakespeare" (Garber 2008, xiii). The project additionally encouraged students to discuss deeply endemic problems with relation to the treatment and representation of women. Identifying misogyny in popular culture was arguably too easy: as Etienne notes, films like *300* continue to feature plots where women's bodies and sexuality are exploited for the sake of drama. These films, and the realities they illustrate, shed light on the larger problem, "which is that women are subject to laws created in a male dominated world" (Miller, annotation for 3.1.106–10). By drawing a connection between *Measure for Measure* and a *Battlestar Galactica* episode depicting a ban against abortion, Miller further reflected on how little power women had and continue to have over their own bodies. Conversely, whenever women do assert their power (in Shakespeare and beyond), they are often, like Isabella, "labelled as misandrists and carry over unpleasant [i.e., derogatory] titles" (Miller, annotation for 3.1.153–57).

These three examples showcase the range of critical issues students chose to address in their Pop Culture Edition project. While none of the abovementioned students focused solely on a single topic, their annotations revealed how much passion they developed toward their "adopted" plays. Indeed, the most successful annotations were ones where students looked for references in films and shows they already knew and loved, and where their research was undertaken consistently throughout the semester. The students who fully embraced the project saw their research change over time—some annotations were abandoned along the way while new ideas were identified in conversations during group meetings. Although some students struggled at first to find sources, our broader definition of popular culture was flexible enough to inspire even those students who did not watch television or who were not familiar with many American or otherwise Western-produced films. My own assessment also changed as I learned more about students' individual projects and goals. The prompt for the project implied a cultural-studies focus, but many annotations excelled in traditional close-reading. A number of successful annotations eschewed comparisons to contemporary issues altogether, reflecting instead on how modern shows and films could help other Shakespeare learners better analyze character motivation, themes, or recurring motifs.

Digital pedagogy: challenges and reflections

Through the process of conceptualizing, collecting, curating, and writing their pop culture references, students created their own discourse community and definitions of cultural criticism. Further, they resisted forms of passive learning in favor of questioning and remixing canonic texts, holding both academic critics and their own contemporary culture accountable for reproducing problematic representations of class, gender, race, and ethnicity. Yet the course was not without its challenges. In both sections (fall 2015 and fall 2016), we did not work with Scalar until later in the term, by which time students were expected to have a complete list of references including links, images, and any relevant notes. This choice affected some students negatively, as it did not provide them with much motivation to work on drafting sections of the project earlier in the semester. Even by the time we began peer- and instructor review, I found that a number of students had not managed to post their references to their assigned act. Because Scalar stores pages on the back end, student editors had to deliberately select lines in their acts where they wanted to attach their annotations, which would otherwise remain invisible to anyone visiting the site. For those students working at the last minute, much of the page creation was completed during computer lab hours, and many of those students did not finish their work in time to receive feedback.

As I mention above, image and video selection provided another unexpected challenge. Even when students chose to use open-access platforms like YouTube, many of their videos eventually disappeared from the site due to copyright infringement issues. As this project thrives on the use of visuals, the loss of video segments had an immediate impact on the longevity of the project. Instructors considering a similar project should think carefully about their goals for the project. If their goal is to create a stable, reliable resource for future Shakespeare students, some class time should be devoted to discussing fair use in detail, pointing students to Creative Commons image repositories such as Flickr, and discouraging the use of proprietary material. Such restrictions are, of course, particularly difficult when it comes to a project focused exclusively on analyzing popular culture. Instructors may decide that the immediate project outcomes (including individual benefits with regards to student learning and knowledge creation) supersede any outside audience beyond the classroom. In my course, my goals were to centralize students' knowledge creation first, and to build a fully-functional resource second. As I continue to think through the purposes and goals of this course, I find that the process of building the edition, and understanding as well as questioning the roles of publishers in how and why we read the canon, are the most valuable takeaways of the course.

Additionally, because students were only collecting (but not writing about) their sources throughout the term, overall final annotations displayed varying levels of critical analysis. To address this, the second iteration of the course included more writing and revision opportunities. Even so, a response assignment requesting annotation drafts may help with early- or mid-term assessment. Another major hurdle, particularly for small liberal arts colleges such as York College, is the issue of access to technology, both individually for students who do not own computers or laptops, and at the institutional level, where computer labs are in high demand and thus difficult to schedule. Students without access to the technology may feel at a disadvantage, and may thus require additional support in the form of office hours and in-class time to work on their projects.

Writing for a public audience can encourage students to think more carefully about self-presentation, tone, and style, but such an audience may indeed never come to fruition without intensive marketing and publicity. Instructors engaged in digital pedagogy must consider how to manage expectations for small-scale digital projects and design their learning objectives accordingly. In light of the learning objectives for our course, the potential disappearance of YouTube videos did not affect students' performance or indeed my assessment of their work. Although the addition of images and videos made the edition more attractive and took advantage of Scalar's versatile affordances, our primary goal was always to produce the kinds of in-depth written analyses English majors are expected to master. This perspective reinforces the fact that digital tools need not necessarily reconfigure pedagogical practices, but instead offer new avenues for student-centered learning, particularly in the ways students take ownership of the production of knowledge.

Carefully scaffolded digital pedagogy projects can encourage students to interrogate who controls and who has access to the academic production of knowledge. Platforms like Scalar invite the disruption of temporal and physical learning spaces by providing several different layers of content creation and user experience. By focusing on popular culture as their driving inspiration, students were encouraged to collapse time and periodization, looking instead at the (often ahistorical) ways in which hegemonic powers impact social norms and individual behavior. Although this approach may be particularly suited for courses that center on more canonical authors, many of the practices discussed here are likely useful for other literature surveys, and particularly for courses that cater to non-English majors. By centering on process and creativity (foregoing in particular a formal, end-of-term essay), this assignment provides a platform for students to showcase their critical thinking and close-reading skills. Students who may be intimidated by formal academic essays but nonetheless are thoughtful critics will especially benefit from such work; I believe a number of my students might have slipped between the cracks otherwise, and I would have lost an opportunity to talk to them about how to effectively apply their ideas to essay writing and help them overcome any potential barriers in terms of their self-confidence as authors. While digital tools can arguably complicate the learning process by requiring the teaching of technical skills in addition to the teaching of literature, overcoming the challenges involved in building an online edition provides a form of tacit knowledge that is otherwise difficult to acquire. Provided that instructors are open to identifying, addressing, and discussing problems as they surface, such challenges can be productive for developing and supporting authentic learning environments. After all, identifying errors and learning from failure is often the only way digital and analog projects—especially in undergraduate classrooms—move forward.

Appendix: "Pop Culture Edition": prompt from Shakespeare in the Digital Age course

As we always discuss in class, editors and publishers play a big role in how and where we read texts. The plays we experience today have come to us from mediator upon mediator: not just Shakespeare himself, but his actors, first editors, eighteenth-century editors, and contemporary critics and scholars, all whom have had a hand on explaining to us what these works mean. As such, it's important that we question and deconstruct some of these editorial practices, trying to see the plays within and beyond pre-imposed interpretations in order to find our own way.

But editions are important: Shakespeare exists within a rich culture that extends before, during, and much after his own time. Without contexts, we miss out on the things that have made and continue to make Shakespeare relevant to readers, writers, and artists alike. As such, our goal in this class is not simply to understand what makes a strong critical edition, but to actually produce our own. I have started a book on the platform Scalar with full-texts of the plays we will study. Early in the semester, everyone will be assigned a play and a single act. As a group, as well as independently, you will work throughout the semester to produce an annotated edition that focuses solely on Shakespeare and popular culture.

Much of your work throughout the semester will be part of that edition. In addition, you will also have an important, semester-long task: to keep track of references to and about your assigned play (and potentially specific elements regarding your assigned act) which will later in the term be used as annotations (like footnotes, but more interactive, because they'll be online and can include media files, images, and links) to our critical edition. I encourage you to go outside the box: look not only for films and television, but other ways in which artists have created new things after being inspired by the bard: comics, games, Twitter characters, blogs, Tumblrs, Memes, even dolls and household objects. Anything goes! Ok, there are a few rules:

1. By the time you meet with your group to compose Response 3, you should have *at least four (4) references* to share. Those do not need to all appear in the final edition, but they will be a start as you collaborate with your group to find a guiding rationale.
2. By Week 13, you should come to class ready with a list of selections you wish to include in the Critical Edition. You will learn how to post them on Scalar, so you'll need to keep track of links and make sure everything is appropriate for public consumption (no copyright violations).
3. Your goal for the end of the semester is to have at least ten (10) references annotated in your act. *At least five (5) of those should be directly in reference to the play you're working with*, not just references to Shakespeare.
4. At the last class meeting of each month (Weeks 5, 9 and 13) you should be prepared to print or email me a list of the links, images, videos, etc you have collected. This will ensure that you're continuously looking for ideas and new things to add and that you have plenty of items to choose from once your group decides on a rationale. Your list will of course grow as we move through the semester, but I expect *at least two to three new items at every check-in date.*

Here are some things you can start doing now to help you find and maintain this list:

*   Sign up for a Google Notification for new publications about Shakespeare (requires Google account)
*   Follow Shakespeareans on Twitter (some to get you started: @MichaelWitmore; @wtfRenaissance, @folgerlibrary, @paulbudra, @internetshakes, @goodticklebrain)

- Consider using a tool like Evernote, Pocket, or Zotero to keep track of your findings

WORKS CITED

300. 2007. Directed by Zach Snyder. Performed by Gerard Butler, Lena Headey, and David Wenham. Warner Bros.

Barab, Sasha, Kurt D. Squire, and William Dueber. 2000. "A Co-Evolutionary Model for Supporting the Emergence of Authenticity." *Educational Technology Research and Development* 48.2: 37–62.

Berlanti, Greg, Geoff Johns, and Andrew Kreisberg, creators. 2014. *The Flash.* Berlanti Productions, DC Entertainment, and Warner Bros.

Bristol, Michael D. 1996. *Big-Time Shakespeare.* London: Routledge.

Burt, Richard, ed. 2002. *Shakespeare after Mass Media.* New York: Palgrave.

Clark, J. Elizabeth. 2010. "The Digital Imperative: Making the Case for a 21st-Century Pedagogy." *Computers and Composition.* 27.1: 27–35.

Clement, Tanya. 2012. "Multiliteracies in the Undergraduate Digital Humanities Curriculum: Skills, Principles, and Habits of Mind." In *Digital Humanities Pedagogy: Practices, Principles and Politics*, edited by Brett D. Hirsch, 365–88. Digital Humanities Series. Cambridge: Open Book Publishers. http://www.jstor.org/stable/j.ctt5vjtt3.20.

Cook-Sather, Alison. 2001. "Unrolling Roles in Techno-Pedagogy: Toward New Forms of Collaboration in Traditional College Settings." *Innovative Higher Education.* 26.2: 121–39.

Donaldson, Laura E. 1995. "Teaching Poststructuralism and the New Mestiza." In *Order and Partialities: Theory, Pedagogy, and the "Postcolonial,"* edited by Kostas Myrsiades and Jerry McGuire, 189–203. New York: State University of New York Press.

Donovan Gregory T. and Suzanne Tamang, eds. *Journal of Interactive Technology and Pedagogy* (JITP) 5. 2014.

Folger Shakespeare Library. 2017. *Shakespeare's Plays* from Folger Digital Texts, edited by Barbara Mowat, Paul Werstine, Michael Poston, and Rebecca Niles. Accessed 1 March 2017. www.folgerdigitaltexts.org.

Garber, Marjorie. 2008. *Shakespeare and Modern Culture*. New York: Pantheon Books.

Greenblatt, Stephen, Walter Cohen, Jean E. Howard, Katherine Eisaman Maus, Gordon McMullan, and Suzanne Gossett, eds. 2008. *The Norton Shakespeare*. Second edition. New York: W.W. Norton.

Harry Potter and the Chamber of Secrets. 2002. Directed by Chris Columbus. Performed by Daniel Radcliffe, Rupert Grint, and Emma Watson. Warner Bros.

Hawkes, Terrance. 1992. *Meaning by Shakespeare*. London: Routledge.

Helle, Laura, Päivi Tynjälä, and Erkki Olkinuora. 2006. "Project-Based Learning in Post-Secondary Education: Theory, Practice and Rubber Sling Shots." *Higher Education* 51.2: 287–314.

Internet Shakespeare Editions. 1996. University of Victoria. Accessed 1 March 2017. https://internetshakespeare.uvic.ca/m/index.html.

Jenkins, Henry, et al. 2009. *Confronting the Challenges of Participatory Culture: Media Education for the 21st Century*. London: MIT Press.

Josephs, Kelly Baker. 2018. "Teaching the Digital Caribbean: The Ethics of a Public Pedagogical Experiment." *Journal of Interactive Technology and Pedagogy* 13. Accessed 1 March 2017. https://jitp.commons.gc.cuny.edu/teaching-the-digital-caribbean-the-ethics-of-a-public-pedagogical-experiment/.

Lanier, Douglas. 2002. *Shakespeare and Modern Popular Culture*. Oxford: Oxford University Press.

———. 2014. "Shakespearean Rhizomatics: Adaptations, Ethics, Value." In *Shakespeare and the Ethics of Appropriation*, edited by Alexa Huang and Elizabeth Rivlin, 21–40. New York: Palgrave.

Lee, Jean. S. Sue Blackwell, Jennifer Drake, and Kathryn A. Moran. 2014. "Taking a Leap of Faith: Redefining Teaching and Learning in Higher Education Through Project-Based Learning." *Interdisciplinary Journal of Problem-Based Learning* 8.2: 19–34.

Levy, Juliette. n.d. "'Digital Zombies'—A Learner-Centered Game: Social Knowledge Creation at the Intersection of Digital Humanities and Digital Pedagogy." *Social Knowledge Creation in the Humanities*. Accessed 1 March

2017. https://ntmrs-skc.itercommunity.org/tracing-movement-ideas/digital-zombies-learner-centered-game-social-knowledge-creation-intersection-digital-humanities-digital-pedagogy-juliette-levy/.

Moore, Ronald D., and Glen A. Larson, creators. 2004. *Battlestar Galactica.* British Sky Broadcasting.

Murphy, Emily Christina, and Shannon R Smith. 2017a. "Undergraduate Students and Digital Humanities Belonging: Metaphors and Methods for Including Undergraduate Research in DH Communities." *Digital Humanities Quarterly.* 11.3.

———. eds. 2017b. "Imagining the DH Undergraduate: Special Issue in Undergraduate Education in Digital Humanities." 2017. *Digital Humanities Quarterly* 11.3.

"No Fear Shakespeare." *SparkNotes* website. Accessed 1 March 2017. http://nfs.sparknotes.com.

O'Neill, Stephen. 2014. *Shakespeare and YouTube: New Media Forms of the Bard.* New York: Bloomsbury Publishing.

Open Source Shakespeare. 2003. Edited by Eric M. Johnson. Accessed 1 March 2017. http://www.opensourceshakespeare.org/.

Owens, Trevor. 2012. "The Public Course Blog: The Required Reading We Write Ourselves for the Course That Never Ends." In *Debates in Digital Humanities*, edited by Matt Gold. Accessed 1 November 2018. http://dhdebates.gc.cuny.edu/debates/text/6.

Pennycook, Alistair. 2006. *Global Englishes and Transcultural Flows.* Abingdon, UK: Routledge.

Posner, Miriam. 2015. "A Better Way to Teach Technical Skills to a Group." Author's blog, 9 December 2015. Accessed 1 March 2017. http://miriamposner.com/blog/a-better-way-to-teach-technical-skills-to-a-group/.

Scalar. n.d. Authoring and Publishing Platform on the *Alliance for Networking Visual Culture* website. Accessed 1 March 2017. http://scalar.usc.edu.

Scharcht, Paul. 2016. "Annotation." *Digital Pedagogy in the Humanities: Concepts, Models, and Experiments*, edited by Rebecca Frost Davis, Matthew K. Gold, Katherine D. Harris, and Jentery Sayers. MLA Commons. 66 paragraphs.

Accessed 1 March 2017. https://digitalpedagogy.mla.hcommons.org/keywords/annotation/.

Shakespeare, William. 1600. *The Most Excellent History of the Merchant of Venice*. London: I.R. for Thomas Hayes.

————. 1623. *Measure for Measure: Mr. William Shakespeares Comedies, Histories, and Tragedies*. London: Isaac Jaggard and Ed. Blount.

The Lord of the Rings. 2001. Directed by Peter Jackson. Performed by Elijah Wood, Ian McKellen, and Orlando Bloom. New Line Cinema.

The Mask. 1994. Directed by Chuck Russel. Performed by Jim Carey and Cameron Diaz. New Line Cinema.

Titanic. 1997. Directed by James Cameron. Performed by Leonardo DiCaprio and Kate Winslet. Twentieth Century Fox Film Corporation.

Digital Interventions: Towards the Study of Women Artists in the Early Modern Courts*

Tanja L. Jones

Department of Art and Art History, University of Alabama

Inspired by the groundbreaking work of art historians in the 1970s, the past four decades have witnessed a sustained effort to address the roles of women in early modern art—as artists, patrons, and subjects—a topic rarely considered previously.[1] Linda Nochlin and Anne Sutherland Harris's catalog, *Women Artists 1550-1950*, accompanying the eponymous exhibition that opened at the Los Angeles County Museum of Art in 1976, played a foundational role within this evolving field. The text offered, for the first time, a chronologically arranged survey of women artists comparable to those dedicated to men that had defined the discipline (Harris and Nochlin 1976). The exhibition was presaged by Nochlin's article "Why Have There Been No Great Women Artists?", exposing the societal and institutional barriers that women artists historically confronted (Nochlin 1971). A handful of women painters of the sixteenth and seventeenth centuries are now regularly included in introductory art history survey texts—the Flemish-born Catharina van Hemessen (c. 1528?–aft. 1587; Figure 1) and two Italians, Sofonisba Anguissola (c. 1532–1625; Figure 2) and Artemisia Gentileschi (1593–aft. 1654), prominent among them. Extraordinary contributions have been made to our knowledge of these artists via focused studies, and each has been the subject of monographs, articles, or retrospective exhibitions in the last three decades.[2] But,

---

* A portion of this essay appeared as Jones 2017. I would like to thank the editors of this volume for the opportunity to expand that work with an emphasis on the significance of the project to the digital humanities.

[1] Recent surveys of the state of research in these fields include ffolliott 2013 and, in the same volume, Reiss 2013.

[2] Monographs dedicated to van Hemessen are De Clippel 2004 and Droz-Emmert 2004. For a bibliography of prior Anguissola literature, see Garrard 1994. On Gentileschi literature, see Spear 2000. Subsequent studies include Bal 2005; Mann 2005; and Locker 2015. Allied exhibitions dedicated to Anguissola in Cremona, Vienna, and Washington, DC in 1994/95 were accompanied by Buffa 1994; Ferino-Pagden 1995; and Ferino-Pagden and Kusche 1995. These were followed by the joint exhibition catalog, Christiansen and Mann 2001. Most recently, the Museo del Prado opened an

ISBN 978-1-64959-016-9 (paper) ISBN 978-1-64959-017-6 (pdf) ISBN 978-1-64959-037-4 (epub)

New Technologies in Medieval and Renaissance Studies 9 (2022) 279–304

as Sheila ffolliott noted in a recent analysis of scholarship dedicated to early modern women artists, significant areas of need remain (ffolliott 2013, 432).

Figure 1. Catharina van Hemessen, Self Portrait at an Easel, 1548, oil on panel, 32.2 x 25.2 cm, Basel, Kunstmuseum Basel, Inv. Nr. 1361. Credit: Kunstmuseum Basel; Photo Credit: Martin P. Bühler.

---

exhibition dedicated to Anguissola and Lavinia Fontana (2019–20).

Figure 2. Sofonisba Anguissola, Self Portrait, c. 1556, varnished watercolor on parchment, 8.3 x 6.4 cm, Boston, Museum of Fine Arts, Boston, Emma F. Munroe Fund, 60.155. Credit: Photograph © 2017 Museum of Fine Arts, Boston.

The allied goals of this essay are, first, to provide an overview of existing art-historical literature in one such area of need, the study of women artists in the early modern courts of Europe; and second, to propose a series of

methodological approaches of particular value to advancing scholarly discourse and inquiry in the field, with an emphasis on those grounded in the
digital humanities. Even as understanding of women as patrons and subjects
of works of art produced in the European courts has advanced, the analysis
that follows reveals that studies dedicated to the activities of female artists in that sphere are markedly few. Digitally-based methods of scholarly
collaboration and social network analysis offer the opportunity to extend
consideration and expand knowledge of women's contributions as hands-on
producers or makers of visual culture within the courts. The essay concludes
with an introduction to the project *Global Makers: Women Artists in the Early
Modern Courts*, a web-based platform (http://globalmakers.ua.edu) conceived
as a means of addressing the needs outlined.

As an art historian whose research focuses primarily on the courts of Italy,
my own interest in the activities of women artists in the courts was prompt-
ed, in no small part, by classroom experiences. Teaching a graduate seminar
dedicated to court culture several years ago, I assigned a series of readings
addressing the career of the Cremona-born painter Sofonisba Anguissola,
who received an appointment at the Spanish court in 1559 (Garrard 1994,
Jacobs 1994, King 1995, Ruiz Gòmez 2019, Cole 2020). Students were intrigued
by Anguissola, both as a woman artist and one who left her homeland for
a foreign court. Their requests for additional readings led to discussion of
an issue I encountered in preparing an initial bibliography for the course:
the absence of a synthetic consideration of the contributions of women artists to the visual culture of the early modern courts. A notable exception is
Valerie Mainz's entry dedicated to the topic in the *Dictionary of Women Artists*
(Mainz 1997). This offers a welcome introduction, but discussion is limited
by the constraints of the publication format. Martin Warnke's monumental
The Court Artist: On the Ancestry of the Modern Artist (Warnke 1993) omits sub-
stantive discussion of women, briefly referencing Anguissola—and then as
an aside.[3] Recognizing this lacuna, a series of lively classroom discussions
followed as did, ultimately, another graduate seminar with extended consideration of the archival, semantic, epistemological, and methodological
concerns that might inform emerging studies in this field.[4]

---

[3] Somewhat surprisingly, critiques of Warnke's text were largely silent on that point.
It was noted in Baldwin 1995, 55–56; and Freisen 1995, 76–78.

[4] My thanks to the student participants in those seminars, especially my teaching
assistants, Emee Barrow Hendrickson and Sara Bernard, for their enthusiasm and
support.

Figure 3. Levine Teerlinc (?) or Nicholas Hilliard, Queen Elizabeth I, 1572, watercolor on vellum, 5.1 cm x 4.8 cm, London, National Portrait Gallery, London, NPG 108. Credit: © National Portrait Gallery, London.

The availability and interpretation of archival data are often cited as impediments to analyses of the roles and contributions made by women artists in the courts. This assumption is belied, in part, by the numerous studies, some published and others not, dedicated to individual women artists in recent decades that are grounded in significant archival material. These include the work of Maria Kusche, Pamela Baldwin, Jorge Sebastián Lozano, and Cecilia

Gamberini dedicated to Anguissola (Kusche 1989, 1992a, 1992b, and 1994; Baldwin 1995, and Gamberini 2016); Susan James's treatment of Susanna Horenboult (c. 1503/04–c. 1553) and Lievene Teerlinc (c. 1510/20–1576), two Flemish miniaturists at the Tudor courts (James 2009); and Cathleen Hall-Van den Elsen's extensive studies of the Spanish sculptor Luisa Roldán (1650–1704), her career, and appointment as *escultora de cámara* by the Spanish king Charles II (Hall-Van den Elsen 1992, 1997, and 2018). Without doubt, attempts to trace the court careers of early modern women are met with significant challenges, not the least of which is establishing an artist's oeuvre based upon a few or even no securely attributed surviving works. This is the case, for example, with Teerlinc, to whom numerous works have been assigned including, most recently, the so-called Roses miniature portrait of Queen Elizabeth I of England (Figure 3), a painting traditionally identified with the Tudor court miniaturist Nicholas Hilliard (James 2009, Harris and Nochlin 1976, Tittler 2016).

Such focused monographic studies dedicated to individuals are invaluable in advancing understanding of the oeuvres and achievements of specific artists. They are, as well, foundational to study of the broader topic of the woman artist at court. But, as ffolliott notes, feminist scholars must "still wrestle" with the fact that treatment of the singular exemplar may, simultaneously, perpetuate the isolation of their subject from the broader field of art history (ffolliott 2013, 425). That observation suggests the importance of avoiding isolating or "siloing" information, a distinct impediment to integrating an under-studied field into a broader, critical discourse.[5]

The researcher is, as well, confronted with semantic issues including consideration of precisely what is meant by the terms *court* and *artist*. References to a court in existing literature are often intended to designate a distinct geographic location or building, the space inhabited by the ruler/patron. Yet the term might also be employed to designate the shifting network of individuals not bound by geography but tied to the ruler/patron through a variety of relationships, be they political, familial, or social, and which may or may not be documented via the award of specific payments or titles.[6] Recent critiques have pointed out that the term *court artist* is frequently applied to both

---

[5] For a recent, broad-based analysis of existing information regarding the training, production, and positions of women artists in the early modern courts, a much-needed advancement towards establishing an ontology upon which future considerations of the topic might be based, see Strunck 2017.

[6] On this issue, see Fantoni 2012; Campbell 2004, 16; and Welch 2004, 19–20.

those who attained official appointments and those who carried out tasks or commissions for patrons identified with a court. Studies strictly defining the artist at court as one who received an official appointment or a regular salary, signified by inclusion on payment rolls, have followed (Fumagalli and Morselli 2014).[7] While such objectivist approaches yield significant prosopographic insights, we should, as well, recognize their limitations.

Of particular concern here is that to circumscribe the definition of the court artist as one whose role is defined solely via the award of a specific title as such or receipt of distinct payments for works produced would exclude the nuances of women's experiences and contributions to the broad range of visual culture that characterized the sphere. That approach would, for example, overlook Anne Gulliver and Alice Herne, both painters who were married, respectively, to John Brown (d. 1532) and William Herne (or Heron) (d. 1580), two Sergeant Painters at the Tudor court. The wills of both men suggest the active role their wives played in their workshops, but much work remains to be done to better understand those women's professional activities in relation to the court, both before and after their husbands' deaths.[8] Further, to limit consideration of artists at court to those who received official notice or payments as such would eliminate women (and men for that matter) who we are certain produced works of art but did so, on the basis of that definition, in archival anonymity.[9]

The experiences of Sofonisba Anguissola in Spain serve as a case in point. The terms of Anguissola's appointment, absence from payment rolls for specific commissions, and lack of signed works have, historically, posed challenges to establishing the oeuvre of an artist who we know to have been a productive and valued presence at the court. Phillip II appointed the young noblewoman from Cremona as a *dama de la reina*, a lady in waiting to his third wife, Isabel de Valois. The appointment remained unchanged even as Anguissola attended to the creation of multiple portraits of the royal family, including those of queen, king, and the *infantas*.[10] That Alonso Sánchez Coello, appointed *pintor*

---

[7] For a thorough introduction to the methodological approach there employed, and its value to court study more broadly, see Guerzoni and Alfani 2007.

[8] For an introduction to this topic, see James 2009, 236–42. For a critique of James's work and a thorough discussion, see Tittler 2016.

[9] Although argued within a different context, this issue is also addressed by Welch 2004, 19–20.

[10] The existence of these works is confirmed archivally only via correspondence—not via commission documents or payments. On this, see Baldwin 1995, 32, 170–76,

de cámara by Philip II c. 1560, a year after Anguissola's arrival at the court, made numerous copies after her original compositions, including one of Philip's son and heir Don Carlos, suggests the high esteem in which Anguissola's paintings were held.[11] While numerous contracts, official requests, and payment records survive to document works produced by Sánchez Coello, as his official appointment and the mechanisms of court administration dictated, no such documents survive for Anguissola.

The strictures of court decorum appear to have prohibited the young Italian woman from receiving the sort of direct, and therefore documented, commissions that characterized Sánchez Coello's career. This is hardly surprising at a court that, until 1677, designated artists who received payment for work as craftsmen.[12] While Anguissola did not receive remuneration for her paintings *per se*, she received a regular salary as a *dama de la reina* (100 ducats per year). She was also compensated with gifts within the traditional system of *clientage*, an economy of reciprocity, exchange, and obligation, that both insulated and excluded her from the professional world.[13] Further, Anguissola, who consistently signed and frequently dated paintings prior to arrival in Spain, ceased to do so following her appointment as *dama de la reina*. Such signatory abstinence suggests the liminal position the young noblewoman occupied at the court.[14] Thus, even as Anguissola's work as an artist at court is confirmed by both her extant paintings and related correspondence, it escapes notice via official appointments or documented commissions.

Recognizing both the potential benefits and distinct challenges posed by the objectivist view and methodology outlined above, it seems that to both establish and maintain a constructivist approach to the study of the woman artist at court is essential to advancing not only gender-based considerations but also a robust vision of artistic practices in the early modern period. As Marcello Fantoni notes,

---

202–203.

[11] As in, for example, copies made after Anguissola's portrait of Don Carlos; see Baldwin 1995, 53–62.

[12] Ferino-Pagden and Kusche 1995, 60. For the changing status of artists in Renaissance Spain, see Francchia 2011, 132–33.

[13] For the compensation of Sánchez Coello vs. that of Anguissola, see Baldwin 1995, 61–62. On Anguissola's salary see Ferino-Pagden and Kusche 1995, 60.

[14] On this, Kusche 1989, 393; Ferino-Pagden and Kusche 1995, 60; and Woods-Marsden 1998, 195.

In general, we should not be afraid of a too generous use of the notion
of court or overly broad temporal and geographic frameworks. The
time is ripe for broadening our horizons ... for this it is necessary
to foster international dialogue, with full awareness of the language
and ideological barriers, but also motivated by more ambitious
objectives, in the effort of renewing topics and methods (Fantoni
2012, 12).

An inclusive ontology would, it is to be hoped, avoid the historical privileging of artists practicing in the traditionally canonical genres, i.e., large-scale
painting and sculpture, which early modern women accessed only rarely in
a professional sense. This would include continued and expanded consideration of individual makers of works in a variety of media—embroidery and
printmaking, for example—at courts across Europe.[15]

One of the significant contributions of Warnke's richly documented study
was to illuminate, via the assemblage of a staggering amount of data regarding diverse individuals, the wide variety of circumstances male artists at
court encountered including duties assigned, titles awarded, and financial
rewards received. Even brief reference to the careers of two relatively well-
documented female painters—Sofonisba Anguissola in Spain and Lievene
Teerlinc in England—suggests that there is, likewise, much to be gained from
comparing the experiences of near-contemporary women working at different courts.

Anguissola, as we have seen, entered the Spanish court as a member of the
queen's household, a position she retained even following Isabel's death in
1568.[16] By contrast, the appointments awarded to Lievene Teerlinc at the
Tudor court shifted over time. Teerlinc arrived in London in 1545, having
trained in the Bruges workshop of her father, the miniaturist Simon Binnick

---

[15] That is not to say that substantial literature has not been dedicated to individual
women artists working in diverse media. To confirm this, we need only look to the
numerous monographs and articles dedicated to the needlework of royal and aristocratic women, such as Mary, Queen of Scots, Bess of Hardwick and Elizabeth Tudor.
The substantial literature includes, most recently, Levey 2007, Bath 2008, and Mason
2015. On Elizabeth Tudor's embroidery, see Klein 1997, Frye 1999, and Quilligan 2001.
But those contributions remain too few and far between and are—still too often—
excluded from the art historical mainstream, marginalized as studies of the "minor
arts" practiced by "dilettantes." For a discussion of the tendency to marginalize the
study of aristocratic vs. "professional" women, see Honig 2001/02.

[16] Baldwin 1995, 35–36; Ferino-Pagden and Kusche 1995, 69–74.

(alt. Bening, c. 1483–1561).[17] She was appointed lady-in-waiting in the house-hold of Catherine Parr (1512–48), sixth wife of King Henry VIII (James 2009). Teerlinc was not the first female artist to be so honored. Susanna Horenboult, also from Flanders, served as a gentlewoman in the household of the English queens from c. 1522.[18] But, in a departure from both Horenboult's experiences in England and those of Anguissola in Spain, Teerlinc was officially appointed *paintrix* to the king shortly after her arrival at court, in the spring of 1546. Following Henry VIII's death in 1547, she served each of his children in turn: Edward VI, Mary Tudor, and Elizabeth I, who designated the artist *pictrix domine regine*.[19] Like Anguissola, Teerlinc was apparently not paid for specific works of art produced.[20] Rather, in a pattern typical for the court artist, she too was compensated via an annual stipend attached to her appointment, likely supplemented by gifts of material goods.[21] Of particular interest is the fact that, during her first years at the Tudor court, Teerlinc moved from the queen's household to that of the king and, for a time, was part of both. This dual appointment compounded Teerlinc's fiduciary rewards. As *paintrix* to the king, she was allotted £40 per annum, twice the amount paid to Hans Holbein. Further, as she remained a member of Catherine Parr's household, she retained a stipend from the queen.[22]

The similarities and differences between Anguissola and Teerlinc's experi-ences might be attributed to a range of factors including social and mari-tal status and, more broadly, the relative status accorded to painters at the two courts. The most striking variance, Teerlinc's movement from the queen's household to that of the king and receipt of an official appointment as painter, was likely due to a combination of these. Teerlinc was part of a family of professional artists and was married prior to arrival at court, factors that likely informed the social acceptability of her appointment as painter to the monarch. There was also a tradition of women painters sur-rounding the Tudor court in various capacities. In addition to the example of Horenboult, there were the wives of Sergeant Painters to the court about whom one would like to know much more. Teerlinc and her husband, much

---

[17] Harris and Nochlin 1976, 102; Edmond 2003; and James 2009, 287–90.

[18] For the assertion that Horenboult was "hired" as a painter by Henry VIII, but placed in the queens' households, see James 2009, 244–46. See also, Campbell and Foister 1986, 725–27.

[19] On Teerlinc's appointments, see James 2009, 291–92, 305.

[20] James 2009, 293.

[21] On this practice more widely, see Warnke 1993, 132–55; and Campbell 2004, 11.

[22] On Teerlinc's pay, see James 2009, 291.

like Susanna Horenboult and her spouse, maintained residence outside the court in London. As James has discovered, the Teerlincs lived near St. Bride's Church, an area in which other painters to the king resided (James 2009, 247–48, 293).

By contrast, the unmarried Anguissola was a member of a minor noble family and, entering the queen's household in Spain, became part of a group of women traditionally drawn from the highest ranks of nobility, families of greater prominence than her own. Anguissola, like the other *damas*, was officially under the protection of the king while at court, a fact her father alluded to in a letter to Phillip prior to her arrival there. Amilcare Anguissola wrote, "I take comfort in knowing that I have given [Sofonisba] into the service of the greatest and best king, Catholic and Christian above all others, and knowing also that Your Majesties [sic] house is by reputation and in actuality run like a convent".[23] Indeed, the Spanish court was particularly noted for the strict moral codes imposed upon the *damas de la reina*, whose activities, movements, and residence within the physical spaces and social sphere of the court were closely governed.[24] The young painter left her father's household for that of the queen where she, like the other unmarried residents, was secured within a patrimonial system that placed her in the care of the monarch. The king was customarily obligated to, eventually, arrange for both Anguissola's marriage and dowry.[25] Following the death of Isabel of Valois in 1568, Anguissola remained in service to her daughters, the *infantas*, and ultimately to Phillip's fourth wife, Anne of Austria. Meanwhile, and reportedly upon the artist's request, the king sought a match for her with an Italian. Anguissola married Don Fabrizio de Moncado by proxy in May 1573 and departed Spain to join her husband in Palermo.[26]

Social network analysis, the study of the relations between individuals and groups, represents a valuable method for exploring the multivalent roles and contributions of women artists, such as Anguissola and Teerlinc, both within a single court and across multiple courts with which they held connections. While literary and social historians have embraced digital modes of network analysis and data visualization for a variety of functions (textual analysis, mapping social networks, and considering the history of ideas), art history

---

[23] The document is Archivo General de Simancas, Papeles Estado Milano, Legajo 120, fol. 190, quoted in Baldwin 1995, 30; and Ferino-Pagden and Kusche 1995, 49.

[24] See Baldwin 1995, 37–42; and Ferino-Pagden and Kusche 1995, 57.

[25] For the *damas de la reina* as "wards of the king," see Baldwin 1995, 28–30.

[26] Baldwin 1995, 49–50; and Ferino-Pagden and Kusche 1995, 68–74.

as a discipline has often been deemed slow to employ such methodologies (Drucker 2013, Zweig 2015). It might, though, be more accurate to state that the discipline has been, paradoxically, both an early and late adopter. Art historians have traditionally analyzed networks of influence or contact—between artists, patrons, objects, or consumers—and, for pedagogical purposes, these ideas and connections have long been expressed via charts, maps, and graphs. One of the best-known, and frequently debated, examples of this is the chart created by Alfred H. Barr, Jr., director of MOMA, to illustrate the development of modern art from 1890 to 1935 (Figure 4) which appeared on the dust jacket of the exhibition catalog *Cubism and Modern Art* (1936).[27] Despite this lineage, art historians have only recently begun to adopt digital methods of both generating network information and visualizing the same.

Digital projects in art history during the past three decades have focused largely upon discrete considerations such as digitizing documents and archives, creating—often revelatory—object scans or conducting spatial analyses of specific sites (Zweig 2015 and Drucker et al. 2015). Such projects align with what Johanna Drucker has termed "digitized" art history—that which propels traditional practices via technological advances (Drucker 2013, 7).[28] By contrast, "digital" art history, according to Drucker, is that which utilizes emergent technologies and techniques to expand the traditional methods employed by art historians—this would include network analysis.[29] The value of projects utilizing network mapping models (social or spatio-temporal) to advance understanding of complex relations between objects, sites, individuals, and groups was suggested in a 2014 review of the Kress Foundation Summer Institute on Digital Mapping and Art History, which notes that "the potential for digital mapping and other forms of spatiotemporal visualization in art history is profound . . . as digital methods offer one way of productively bringing together heretofore disparate points of evidence into dialogue with one another" (Whiteman 2014). The institute focused on the creation of tools that would move beyond gathering and organizing data, to creating new pathways of thought and approach.

---

[27] On this and for a history of information visualization, see Bailey and Pregill 2014, esp. 168–70.

[28] This distinction was observed as well by Pamela Fletcher, when she divided her remarks between "digitizing art history" and "computation" projects; see Fletcher 2015.

[29] A short historiographic consideration of the field of digital and digitized art history is given by Zweig 2015, 40–45.

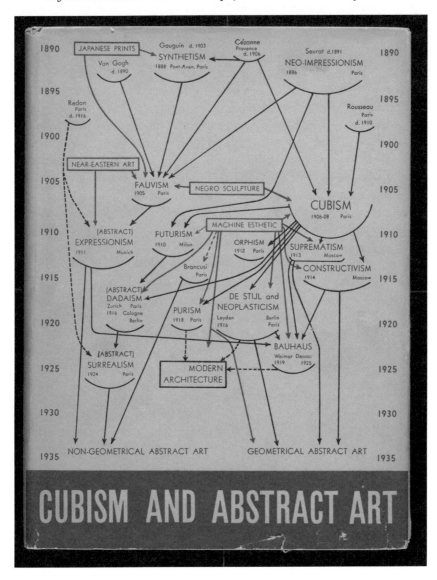

Figure 4. Alfred H. Barr, Jr., Dust jacket with chart prepared by Alfred H. Barr, Jr., of the exhibition catalog *Cubism and Abstract Art*, 1936, offset printed in color, 25.7 cm x 19.7 cm, New York, The Museum of Modern Art Library. Credit: © The Museum of Modern Art / Licensed by SCALA / Art Resource, NY.

The charge to integrate network analysis into the research process—rather than as a means to illustrate an argument articulated through text—answers the call by Paul B. Jaskot et al., organizers of the aforementioned Summer Institute. They note, "most digital mapping in art history today divides the research and visualization aspects of the project and does not consider the visualization to be part of the research project" (Jaskot et al. 2015, 66). An allied concern, expressed by Matthew Lincoln and others, is the need for projects that utilize computational tools to lead towards "fundamentally new research questions and interpretations" (Lincoln 2014). Lincoln's own recent analysis of network centralization in the printmaking industry of the early modern Low Countries provides an excellent model for this (Lincoln 2016). Without question, integrating models of network analysis into the research process can feel daunting to the art historian not trained in digital methods. Cost is of concern as well, both in terms of time and technology access.[30] Importantly, the tools required for generating a simple network visualization need not be complex and might be accessed without significant technical or computational skill. As Pamela Fletcher notes, "Many comparatively simple tools for mapping or network analysis can yield insights that transform a scholar's understanding of a subject, organizing and visualizing even relatively small amounts of data in ways that make patterns and relationships more visible" (Fletcher 2015).

For an area of study, such as women artists in the courts, in which the subjects—either artists or works of art—have traditionally been studied in isolation, network visualization and analysis offer an array of opportunities to advancing discourse. Here, again, reference to the careers of Lievene Teerlinc and Sofonisba Anguissola is instructive. It has often been suggested that, as a young artist in Cremona, Anguissola was aware of and inspired by Teerlinc's success at the English court (Baldwin 1995, 118).[31] This supposition is based in large part upon the women's apparent mutual acquaintance with the miniaturist and collector Giulio Clovio (1498–1578). A portrait (Figure 5) attributed to Anguissola is often cited as visual support for this theory (Buffa 1994, 194; Baldwin 1995, 117–19, 194; and Ferino-Pagden and Kusche 1995, 46, pl. 9).

---

[30] On the leadership role that the College Art Association (CAA) has taken in addressing these concerns, including the "problem of research evaluation criteria," see Drucker et. al. 2015, 2.

[31] The occasional supposition that Teerlinc studied with Clovio is disputed by Garrard 1994, 575, fn. 40.

Figure 5. Sofonisba Anguissola, Portrait of Giulio Clovio, c. 1556, oil on canvas, 100 cm x 79.5 cm, Mentana, Fondazione F. Zeri. Credit: This photographic reproduction was provided by the Photo Library of the Federico Zeri Foundation. The property rights of the author have been met.

In it, Clovio holds what is purported to be a portrait of Teerlinc. Archival evidence confirms that Clovio, resident in Parma, corresponded with the Flemish artist in England, requested a miniature portrait from her hand, and identified the now-lost painting as "the dearest thing that I could have"

(King 1995, 396–97; James 2009, 306–8). That Clovio received the miniature is suggested by a 1578 inventory that identifies among his possessions "a portrait of Livinia miniaturist to the Queen of England" (King 1995, 395–96; James 2009, 306–08). Whether that miniature is, indeed, the one that Clovio holds in the Anguissola portrait is uncertain, but the oft-cited triangulation of acquaintance and esteem suggested by Clovio's correspondence, Teerlinc's now-lost self-portrait miniature, and Anguissola's portrait of Clovio offers an opportunity to consider the epistemological insights that might be gained from visualizations of such relationships.[32]

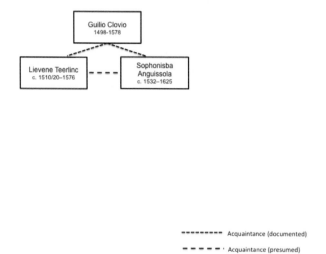

Figure 6. Network visualization: Contact between Giulio Clovio, Sofonisba Anguissola, and Levine Teerlinc. Credit: Author.

The connections between the three artists are expressed by an ego network (Figure 6) in which Clovio is the focal actor (ego) and Anguissola and Teerlinc appear as alters.[33] Variances in the lines that connect the three artists signal the type and strength of their associations. Dashed lines indicate relationships with a basis in archival or object-based evidence; these join both Anguissola and Teerlinc with Clovio. The more widely-spaced dashed line indicates the tenuous nature of the connection between Anguissola and Teerlinc, based on their mutual acquaintance with Clovio. The connection between the two artists does not appear particularly durable in the ego network that focuses

---

[32] It has recently been argued that the miniature Clovio holds is a self-portrait of Anguissola, not an image of Teerlinc; see Leemans 2014, esp. 48.

[33] On the terminology employed here, see Prell 2012, 7–12.

upon Clovio, illustrating the tenuous nature of the triangulation outlined in the paragraph above. But an expansion of the graph based upon information regarding Teerlinc's and Anguissola's primary royal patrons suggests that the artists were likely connected in additional ways that have, until now, escaped consideration.

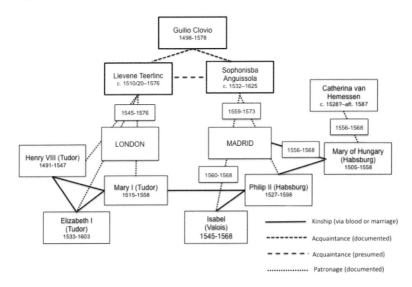

Figure 7. Network visualization: Royal Patrons (sample) of Sofonisba Anguissola and Levine Teerlinc. Credit: Author.

The expanded network graph (Figure 7) illustrates some, but by no means all, of the documented connections between the two artists and their royal patrons in England and Spain. These are indicated by dotted lines. This graph indicates, as well, some of the basic kinship ties between those patrons, based on either blood or marriage. These are indicated via solid lines, signifying the durability of the connections. Of particular interest is the range of connections between the artists and their patrons, of varying degrees and strength, suggested by consideration of this visual. Numerous potential avenues of research emerge, many rarely or not at all addressed in existing literature, a point to which we shall return.

Initiated as a partnership between faculty and the Digital Humanities Center at the University of Alabama, the multifaceted project *Global Makers: Women Artists in the Early Modern Courts* is intended to advance study in the field by addressing the scholarly needs outlined above via digital intervention.[34] Conceived as a scholarly collaborative, the goal of the project is to encourage sustained, interdisciplinary consideration of the roles that women played as hands-on producers of visual and material culture in the courts by providing a free-access space to join and upload, share, and discuss. As a digital commons, the site is designed to bring together scholars and students interested in the emerging topic of early modern women in the courts. Towards that end, the project website is designed to serve four interrelated functions. The first of these is to establish a collaborative and inclusive database cataloging women artists working between c. 1400 and 1750 in a wide variety of media, the objects they produced, and the patrons associated with them, if known. The site will also provide a bibliography of related, scholarly materials and support a forum for discussion. Finally, the *Global Makers* site will host a network mapping feature.

The first phase of the site is currently in development, and a preliminary version will be live by mid-2021. At that point, both the catalog and discussion forum functions will be available. Those who wish to contribute to the database will be able to register by submitting basic information (name, academic affiliation, etc.). After joining, users will be permitted to upload data. This function is supported by Friend of a Friend (FOAF) in tandem with Dublin Core to create a Resource Description Framework (RDF). This appears to offer advantages over a basic Dublin Core field plan, affording greater flexibility in terms of data manipulation. After users submit information, a peer-review panel will then vet the data prior to posting. A guiding principal in design of the database platform is to facilitate and support access to an open and inclusive body of information upon which future research initiatives might be based.

---

[34] The *Global Makers* title was chosen to evoke the model of the contemporary "maker" movement—one based on collaboration and an appreciation for hands-on production. The project is supported by faculty and staff of the Alabama Digital Humanities Center (ADHC) at the University of Alabama. Work is funded, in part, through a Digital Art History Grant from the Samuel H. Kress Foundation. The project also includes a pedagogical component and conference sessions. Sessions dedicated to the topic "Makers: Women Artists in the Early Modern Courts" were convened at the Renaissance Society of America Conference (Boston, 2016) and the Sixteenth Century Studies Conference (Bruges, 2017), the latter sponsored by the Society for the Study of Early Modern Women. An edited volume of essays from those sessions is currently in press.

A second phase of the website is planned in which relationships between information in the database (artist, object, patron, location) will be made available to users via network visualizations. These, much like the sample network maps discussed above, are intended to illuminate the potential connections between the artists under consideration, their patrons, and sites of work. The value of such maps to stimulating new areas of inquiry is suggested by once again referencing the network graph illustrating the kinship ties between Anguissola's and Teerlinc's patrons. This as the impact of Hapsburg patronage upon the careers of both women is a topic not previously considered.

We might profitably re-consider, for instance, the circumstances surrounding Anguissola's invitation to the court of Phillip II in light of the monarch's potential acquaintance with Teerlinc's success in London. To what degree, if any, might Phillip's decision to invite the young Anguissola to Spain, and into the household of his new bride and third wife in 1559, have been impacted by the esteem in which Mary Tudor, the king's second wife, reportedly held Teerlinc?[35] We might also consider what influence the arrival in Spain of the Flemish artist Catharina van Hemessen three years earlier (1556), in the retinue of Phillip's aging aunt, Mary of Hungary, may have served in offering a model for Anguissola's appointment to the new Spanish queen's household.

The network map also suggests avenues of future research regarding the career of Catherina van Hemessen. Like Teerlinc and Susannah Horenboult, Van Hemessen was the daughter of an artist. Her father Jan (c. 1500–aft. 1563) was a master in the Antwerp painter's guild with an elite clientele that included Margaret of Austria. Catharina apparently trained in her father's workshop and created thirteen portraits and religious paintings that bear her signature between 1548 and 1552.[36] Nevertheless, it is often suggested that she was an amateur rather than a professional artist, a designation based, in part, on Van Hemessen's absence from guild records (Van der Stighelen 1997, 68). The distinction between *amateur* and *professional* artist is, however, a difficult one to make when discussing women in the early modern period—particularly if this is based upon guild membership, documented commissions, or payments

---

[35] For the description of Teerlinc as "*molto amata dalla Regina Maria*" by Ludovico Guicciardini (1521–89) (*Descrittione di M. Lodovico Guicciardini ... de tutti i Paesi Bassi ...*, 1588), a Florentine merchant resident in Antwerp, and the artist's activities under the queen, see James 2009, 297–304.
[36] A further five paintings, three portraits and two religious images, are attributed to the artist by De Clippel 2004.

received, all of which were conditioned by custom and decorum. That Catharina was not admitted to the painter's guild is hardly surprising; the Antwerp guild was not as open to female membership as was that in nearby Bruges (Wallen 1971, 76–77).[37] In either case, Van Hemessen was appointed a lady-in-waiting at the court of Mary of Hungary, Regent of the Netherlands (r. 1533–55) (Doyle 2000). Precisely when that occurred is unclear, but an ordinance dated 1555 refers to the artist as "kleine Catheline" (Gellman 2011, 352). Van Hemessen had married Chrétien de Morien, organist at Antwerp Cathedral, in 1554, and the couple accompanied Mary to Spain following the abdication and retirement of her elder brother, Emperor Charles V, in 1556.[38] The couple returned to Antwerp in 1558, following Mary's death (Harris and Nochlin 1976, 105).

As no signed works by Catharina van Hemessen are known after 1552, it is generally assumed that the artist ceased painting following her marriage and court appointment.[39] This seems presumptive though, particularly as her skill as a painter likely led to the prestigious position in the regent's household. While the absence of archival evidence and attributed works from the period of Van Hemessen's employ in Mary's household prohibits definitive determination of her activities there, reference to the experiences of her near contemporaries, Teerlinc and Anguissola, is instructive. That suggests that women painters—married or unmarried—who attained court positions might be expected to continue their artistic practice; however, given the rules of decorum that circumscribed female behavior, this likely meant the cessation of documented commissions. Indeed, Anguissola's experiences in the household of Philip II, and signatory abstinence following her appointment, suggest that similar concerns may have attended Van Hemessen's role and potential artistic production at the court of his aunt.

---

[37] On female guild membership in the two cities in the fifteenth century, see Harris and Nochlin 1976, 19 and 27. A quarter of the Bruges' guild membership was female by 1480 while Antwerp had only one female member between 1453 and 1500; for this, see Greer 2001, 180. The 1585–86 Antwerp guild registers document twenty-two widows who paid dues as a means of continuing to market products of their husbands' production; see Honig 1998, 16–17.

[38] On the retirement, see Baker-Bates 2013.

[39] For a notable exception, and a caution that "It is surely premature to say that [Heemskeerk] did not paint after her marriage, or that her role as lady-in-waiting precluded painting for the queen and her court," see Gellman 2011, 354.

As these examples suggest, the value of network mapping to stimulating discourse and future lines of inquiry in the study of women artists in the early modern courts is substantial. As the *Global Makers* project moves forward, and the various features outlined above become fully functional, it is hoped that the project will serve a vital role in advancing research in this emerging field.

WORKS CITED

Bailey, Jefferson, and Lily Pregill. 2014. "Speak to the Eyes: The History and Practice of Information Visualization." *Art Documentation: Journal of the Art Libraries Society of North America* 33.2 (Fall): 168–91.

Baker-Bates, Piers. 2013. "The 'Cloister Life' of the Emperor Charles V: Art and Ideology at Yuste." *Hispanic Research Journal* 14.5: 427–45.

Bal, Miek, ed. 2005. *The Artemisia Files: Artemisia Gentileschi for Feminists and Other Thinking People.* Chicago: University of Chicago Press.

Baldwin, Pamela Holmes. 1995. "Sofonisba Anguissola in Spain: Portraiture as Art and Social Practice at a Renaissance Court." PhD Dissertation, Bryn Mawr College.

Bath, Michael. 2008. *Emblems for a Queen: The Needlework of Mary, Queen of Scots.* London: Archetype.

Buffa, Paolo, ed. 1994. *Sofonisba Anguissola e le sue sorelle.* Milan: Leonardo Arte.

Campbell, Lorne, and Susan Foister. 1986. "Gerard, Lucas, and Susanna Horenbout." *The Burlington Magazine* 128: 719–27.

Campbell, Stephen J. 2004. "Introduction." In *Artists at Court: Image-Making and Identity (1300–1500)*, edited by Stephen J. Campbell. 9–18. Boston: Isabella Stewart Gardner Museum.

Christiansen, Keith, and Judith W. Mann, eds. 2001. *Orazio and Artemisia Gentileschi: Father and Daughter Painters in Baroque Italy.* New York: The Metropolitan Museum of Art.

Cole, Michael. 2020. *Sofonisba's Lesson: A Renaissance Artist and Her Work.* Princeton: Princeton University Press.

De Clippel, Karolien. 2004. *Catharina van Hemessen (1528–c. 1567): een monografische studie over een "uytnemende wel geschickte vrouwe in de conste der schilderyen."* Brussels: Koninklijke Vlaamse Academie van België voor Wetenschapen en kunsten.

Doyle, Daniel R. 2000. "The Sinews of Habsburg Governance in the Sixteenth Century: Mary of Hungary and Political Patronage." *Sixteenth Century Journal* 31.2: 349–60.

Droz-Emmert, Marguerite. 2004. *Catharina van Hemessen: Malerin der Renaissance.* Basel: Scwabe.

Drucker, Johanna. 2013. "Is There a Digital Art History?" *Visual Resources* 29: 5–13.

Drucker, Johanna, Anne Helmreich, Matthew Lincoln, and Francesca Rose. 2015. "Digital Art History: The American Scene." *Perspective* 2. Online. Accessed 25 February 2017. http://perpective.revues.org/6021.

Edmond, Mary. 2003. "Teerlinc, Levina." *Grove Art Online.* Oxford University Press. Accessed 26 November 2016. http://www.oxfordartonline.com/subscriber/article/grove/art/T083626.

Fantoni, Marcello. 2012. "Introduction." In *The Court in Europe*, edited by Marcello Fantoni, 11–24. Rome: Bulzoni.

Ferino-Pagden, Silvia, ed. 1995. *Sofonisba Anguissola: Die Malerin der Renaissance.* Vienna: Kunsthistorisches Museum Vienna.

Ferino-Pagden, Silvia, and Maria Kusche, eds. 1995. *Sofonisba Anguissola: A Renaissance Woman.* Washington, DC: National Museum of Women in the Arts.

ffolliot, Sheila. 2013. "Early Modern Women Artists." In *The Ashgate Research Companion to Women*, edited by Allyson M. Poska, Jane Couchman, and Katherine A. McIver, 423–44. Burlington: Ashgate.

Fletcher, Pamela. 2015. "Reflections on Digital Art History." In "CAA Re-Views: Field Editors' Reflections," *caa.reviews* 18 June 2015. Accessed 25 February 2017. http://www.caareviews.org/reviews/2726#fnr8.

Francchia, Carmen. 2011. "Women's Artistic Production and Their Visual Representation in Early Modern Spain." In *A Companion to Spanish*

Women's Studies, edited by Xon de Rose and Geraldine Hazbun, 129–42. Rochester and Suffolk: Boydell & Brewer.

Freisen, Ilse E. 1995. "Review of the Court Artist: On the Ancestry of the Modern Artist by Martin Warnke." *Renaissance and Reformation/ Renaissance et réforme* 19: 76–78.

Frye, Susan. 1999. "Sewing Connections: Elizabeth Tudor, Mary Stuart, Elizabeth Talbot and Seventeenth-Century Anonymous Needleworkers." In *Maids and Mistresses, Cousins and Queens: Women's Alliances in Early Modern England,* edited by Susan Frye and Karen Robertson, 165–82. Oxford: Oxford University Press, 1999.

Fumagalli, Elena, and Raffaella Morselli. 2014. "Introduction." In *The Court Artist in Seventeenth-Century Italy,* edited by Elena Fumagalli and Raffaella Morselli. Rome: Bulzoni. Kindle edition. Accessed 30 November 2016.

Gamberini, Cecilia. 2016. "Sofonisba Anguissola at the Court of Philip II." In *Women Artists in Early Modern Italy: Careers, Fame, and Collectors,* edited by Sheila Barker. 29–38. Turnhout: Brepols.

Garrard, Mary. 1994. "Here's Looking at Me: Sofonisba Anguissola and the Problem of the Woman Artist." *Renaissance Quarterly* 47: 556–622.

Gellman, Lola B. 2011. "Hemessen, Catharina van." In *Concise Dictionary of Women Artists,* edited by Delia Gaze. New York and Abingdon: Routledge.

Greer, Germaine. 2001. *The Obstacle Race: The Fortunes of Women Painters and Their Work.* London: Tauris Parke.

Guerzoni, Guido, and Guido Alfani. 2007. "Court History and Career Analysis: A Prosopographic Approach to the Court of Renaissance Ferrara." *The Court Historian* 12.1: 1–12.

Hall-Van den Elsen, Catherine. 1992. "The Life and Work of the Sevillian Sculptor Luisa Roldán, with a Catalogue Raisonné." PhD dissertation, La Trobe University.

———. 1997. "Rodán, Luisa." In *Dictionary of Women Artists,* edited by Delia Gaze, 1: 1192–94. London and Chicago: Taylor & Francis.

———. 2018. *Fuerza e intimismo: Luisa Roldán, escultora, 1652-1706.* Madrid: Consejo Superior de Investigaciones Cientificas.

Harris, Ann Sutherland, and Linda Nochlin. 1976. *Women Artists: 1550-1950.* Los Angeles and New York: Alfred A. Knopf.

Honig, Elizabeth A. 1998. *Painting and the Market in Early Modern Antwerp.* New Haven and London: Yale University Press.

———. 2001/02. "The Art of Being 'Artistic': Dutch Women's Creative Practices in the 17th Century." *Woman's Art Journal* 22.2: 31–39.

Jacobs, Federika. 1994. "Woman's Capacity to Create, The Unusual Case of Sofonisba Anguissola." *Renaissance Quarterly* 47.1: 74–101.

James, Susan E. 2009. *The Feminine Dynamic in English Art, 1485-1603.* Farnham and Burlington: Ashgate.

Jaskot, Paul B., Anne Kelly Knowles, Andrew Wasserman, Stephen Whiteman, and Bejamin Zweig. 2015. "A Research-Based Model for Digital Mapping and Art History: Notes from the Field." *Artl@s Bulletin* 4.1 (Spring): 65–74.

Jones, Tanja. 2017. "Makers: Towards the Study of Women Artists in the Early Modern Courts." In *Künstlerinnen: Neue Perspektiven auf ein Forschungsfeld der Vormoderne,* edited by Birgit Ulrike Münch, Andreas Tacke, Markwart Herzog, and Sylvia Heudecker, 34–43. Vol. 4 of *Kunsthistorisches Forum Irsee.* Petersberg: Michael Imhof Verlag.

King, Catherine. 1995. "Looking a Sight: Sixteenth Century Portraits of Women Artists." *Zeitschrift für Kunstgeschichte* 58.3: 381–406.

Klein, Lisa. 1997. "Your Humble Handmade: Elizabethan Gifts of Needlework." *Renaissance Quarterly* 50.2: 459–93.

Kusche, Maria. 1989. "Sofonisba Anguissola en España: retratista en la corte de Felipe II junto a Alonso Sánchez Coello y Jorge de la Rua." *Archivo Español de Arte* 62: 391–420.

———. 1992a. "Sofonisba Anguissola, retratista de la corte Española." *Paragone* 509–511: 3–34.

———. 1992b. "Sofonisba Anguissola, vuelta a Italia, continuación de sus relaciones con la corte Española." *Paragone* 513: 10–35.

———. 1994. "Sofonisba e il ritratto di rappresentatnza ufficiale nella corte Spagnola." In *Sofonisba Anguissola e le sue sorelle,* edited by Paola Buffa, 117-52. Milan: Leonardo Arte.

Leemans, Annemie. 2014. "Tra storia e leggenda: indagini sul network artistico tra Sofonisba Anguissola, Giulio Clovio e Levina Teerlinc." *Intrecci d'arte* 3: 35–55.

Levey, S. M. 2007. *The Embroideries at Hardwick Hall: A Catalogue.* London: National Trust.

Lincoln, Matthew. 2014. "Digital Dimensions at CAA 2015." Author's blog post, 28 Nov 2014. Accessed 19 February 2017. https://matthewlincoln. net/2014/11/28/digital-dimensions-at-caa-2015.html.

———. 2016. "Social Network Centralization Dynamics in Print Production in the Low Countries, 1550–1750." *International Journal for Digital Art History* 2: 134–57.

Locker, Jesse M. 2015. *Artemisia Gentileschi: The Language of Painting.* New Haven and London: Yale University Press.

Mainz, Valerie. 1997. "Court Artists." In *Dictionary of Women Artists*, edited by Delia Gaze, 1: 37–43. London and Chicago: Taylor & Francis.

Mann, Judith. 2005. *Artemisia Gentileschi: Taking Stock.* Turnhout: Brepols.

Mason, Peter. 2015. "André Thevet, Pierre Belon, and Americana in the Embroideries of Mary Queen of Scots." *Journal of the Warburg and Courtauld Institutes* 78: 207–21.

Nochlin, Linda. 1971. "Why Have There Been No Great Women Artists?" In *Art and Sexual Politics: Why Have There Been No Great Women Artists?* edited by Thomas B. Hess and Elizabeth C. Baker, 1–39. New York: MacMillan.

Prell, Christina. 2012. *Social Network Analysis: History, Theory and Methodology.* London: Sage.

Quilligan, Maureen. 2001. "Elizabeth's Embroidery." *Shakespeare Studies* 29: 208–15.

Reiss, Sheryl E. 2013. "Beyond Isabella and Beyond: Secular Women Patrons of Art in Early Modern Europe." In *The Ashgate Research Companion to Women*, edited by Allyson M. Poska, Jane Couchman, and Katherine A. McIver, 445–67. Burlington: Ashgate.

Ruiz Gòmez, Letitia, ed. 2019. *Sofonisba Anguissola and Lavinia Fontana, A Tale of Two Women Painters.* Madrid: Museo Nacional del Prado.

Spear, Richard E. 2000. "Artemisia Gentileschi: Ten Years of Fact and Fiction." *The Art Bulletin* 82: 568–79.

Stighelen, Katlijne van der. 2011. "Amateur Artists: Amateur Art as a Social Skill and a Female Preserve." In *Concise Dictionary of Women Artists*, edited by Delia Gaze, 1: 50–67. London and London: Routledge.

Strunck, Christina. 2017. "Hofkünstlerinnen. Weibliche Karrierestrategien an den Höfen der Frühen Neuzeit." In *Künstlerinnen: Neue Perspektiven auf ein Forschungsfeld der Vormoderne*, edited by Birgit Ulrike Münch, Andreas Tacke, Markwart Herzog, and Sylvia Heudecker, 20–37. Vol. 4, *Kunsthistorisches Forum Irsee*. Petersberg: Michael Imhof Verlag.

Tittler, Robert. 2016. "The 'Feminine Dynamic' in Tudor Art: A Reassessment." *The British Art Journal* 17.1: 123–31.

Wallen, Burr. 1971. "The Portraits of Jan Sanders van Hemessen." *Oud Holland* 86.2/3: 76–77.

Warnke, Martin. (1985) 1993. *The Court Artist: On the Ancestry of the Modern Artist*, translated by David McLintock. Cambridge: Cambridge University Press. Citations refer to the 1993 edition.

Welch, Evelyn. 2004. "Painting as Performance in the Italian Renaissance Court." In *Artists at Court: Image-Making and Identity (1300–1500)*, edited by Stephen J. Campbell, 9–18. Boston: Isabella Stewart Gardner Museum.

Whiteman, Stephen H. 2014. "Digital Mapping and Art History: A Review of the Kress Summer Institute." *Ars Orientalis* 44. Accessed 26 November 2016. http://www.asia.si.edu/arsorientalis/44/44-about.asp.

Woods-Marsden, Joanna. 1998. *Renaissance Self-Portraiture: The Visual Construction of Identity and the Social Status of the Artist*. New Haven and London: Yale University Press.

Zweig, Benjamin. 2015. "Forgotten Genealogies: Brief Reflections on the History of Digital Art History." *International Journal for Digital Art History* 1: 38–49.

Contributors

Marie-Alice Belle is Associate Professor in Translation Studies at the Université de Montréal. Her research explores the intersections between translation, book studies, and cultural history in early modern Britain. She is currently PI for the international project 'Trajectories of Translation in Early Modern Britain (1473–1660): Routes, Mediations, Networks' (2018–2022). Recent publications include two volumes of essays co-edited with Brenda M. Hosington: Thresholds of Translation: Paratexts, Print, and Cultural Exchange in Early Modern Britain (1473–1660) (London: Palgrave Macmillan 2018), and Translation as 'Transformission' in Early Modern England and France, special issue of the Canadian Review of Comparative Literature, 46.2 (2019).

Peter Boot is a senior researcher at the Huygens Institute for the History of the Netherlands. He graduated in mathematics (Leiden) and Dutch literature and culture (Utrecht). In between he worked as a programmer and software consultant. He wrote his PhD thesis about annotation in digital editions and its potential implications for research in the humanities (Mesotext. Digitised Emblems, Modelled Annotations and Humanities Scholarship, 2009). His current research focuses on online response to books (on e.g. dedicated review sites or booksellers' sites) and what it can teach us about readers and reading. He also works as a consultant on digital edition projects and in other digital humanities projects.

Toby Burrows is a Senior Researcher in the Oxford e-Research Centre at the University of Oxford, and a Senior Honorary Research Fellow in the School of Humanities at the University of Western Australia. His current projects include "Mapping Manuscript Migrations" (funded by the Digging into Data Challenge of the Trans-Atlantic Platform) and "Collecting the West: how Collections Shaped Western Australia" (funded by the Australian Research Council). Recent publications include the edited book Collecting the Past: British Collectors and their Collections from the 18th to the 20th Centuries (Routledge, 2018) and "Connecting Medieval and Renaissance Manuscript Collections" in the journal Open Library of Humanities (2018). Earlier projects included HuNI: Humanities Networked Infrastructure — a virtual laboratory for building connections between data from Australian cultural collections (huni.net.au).

ISBN 978-1-64959-016-9 (paper) ISBN 978-1-64959-017-6 (pdf) ISBN 978-1-64959-037-4 (epub)
New Technologies in Medieval and Renaissance Studies 9 (2022) 305–308

Matthew Evan Davis is currently the ZKS-Lendrum Assistant Professor (Research) in the Scientific Study of Manuscripts and Inscriptions at Durham University. He previously served as a postdoctoral fellow with the Lewis and Ruth Sherman Centre for Digital Scholarship at McMaster University and as the Council for Library and Information Resources/Mellon Postdoctoral Fellow for Data Curation in Medieval Studies at North Carolina State University, serving as a technical advisor to the Piers Plowman Electronic Archive, the Siege of Jerusalem Electronic Archive, and the Medieval Electronic Scholarly Alliance. His scholarship focuses on the relationships between people, texts, and both digital and physical spaces, most recently in an ongoing virtual archive of the works of John Lydgate (minorworksoflydgate.net).

Marie-France Guénette is *Professeure assistante* of Translation at Université Laval (Canada). Her doctoral research in Translation Studies at the Université de Montréal focuses on translation and print networks around the English court of Queen Henrietta-Maria (1625–1642). Marie-France has presented her research at the conferences of the Renaissance Society of America, the Society for the History of Authorship Reading and Print, and the Canadian Society for Renaissance Studies. Her article "Channelling Catholicism through translation", forthcoming in *Status Quaestionis. Language, Text, Culture*, explores the agentic strategies employed by women as demonstrated in a corpus of translated recusant literature which was meant to circulate at the queen's court and among the English Catholic elite.

Tanja L. Jones is Associate Professor of Art History at the University of Alabama. Her research focuses on artistic identity, gender, and mobility in Early Modern Italian courts. She has published extensively on Renaissance medals, is completing a monograph dedicated to Pisanello, and directs the Makers Project (www.makers.as.ua.edu).

Travis Mullen is a digital humanist and independent scholar living in Columbia, South Carolina. His work explores the intersection between book history, media studies, network theory and renaissance studies. He has contributed code to and written about a number of large-scale digital projects at the University of South Carolina's Center for Digital Humanities including the automated collation project *Paragon* and Duke University Press' *The Carlyle Letters Online.*

Jessica Marie Otis is an Assistant Professor of History and a director at the Roy Rosenzweig Center for History and New Media at George Mason University. After receiving both her MS in Mathematics and her PhD in History from the University of Virginia, she was a CLIR-DLF Postdoctoral Fellow in

Early Modern Data Curation working on the NEH-funded *Six Degrees of Francis Bacon*. Subsequently, as the Digital Humanities Specialist in the University Libraries at Carnegie Mellon University, she co-founded the dSHARP digital scholarship center. Her research focuses on the cultural history of mathematics, cryptography, and plague in early modern England and her articles have appeared in the *Journal of British Studies*, *Digital Humanities Quarterly*, and the *International Journal of Humanities and Arts Computing*.

Claudia Resch is a senior researcher and project leader at the Austrian Centre for Digital Humanities and Cultural Heritage (ACDH-CH) of the Austrian Academy of Sciences. Current research focuses on German literature of the Early Modern period and the application of literary and linguistic computing in a corpus-based approach to textual issues. Key areas covered are historical linguistics, text stylistics, and annotation problems associated with non-standard varieties of Early Modern German. The development and the architecture of ABaC:us — Austrian Baroque Corpus, a historical thematic corpus based on German literature, derives from her initiative and research proposal. From 2012 to 2017 Claudia Resch was a lecturer at the Department for German Philology of the Ludwig-Maximilians-Universität in Munich. Since 2017, she teaches at the Department of History at the University of Vienna. Since 2020, she has also been teaching at the Department of German Studies as well as in the new master's degree programme in Digital Humanities at the University of Vienna.

Andie Silva is Assistant Professor of English (York College) and Digital Humanities (CUNY Graduate Center). Her research specialties include digital pedagogy, history of the book, and early modern British literature. Recent publications include *The Brand of Print: Marketing Paratexts in the Early English Book Trade* (2019), and articles in *Appositions: Studies in Renaissance/Early Modern Literature*, *Changing English*, and *The Journal of Interactive Technology and Pedagogy*.

Colin Wilder is assistant professor of German History and Digital History at the University of South Carolina. Since 2012, he has served as assistant and associate director of the Center for Digital Humanities at USC. Before that, he held postdoctoral fellowships at Brown University and the University of Wisconsin-Madison. He completed his PhD at the University of Chicago in 2010. He serves as technical director of the international Victorian Lives and Letters Consortium while also leading several newer projects. His historical scholarship focuses on the history of legal and political thought in Germany in the 16th through 18th centuries.

Alessandro Zammataro is a first-year D.Phil. student in Medieval and Modern Languages at the University of Oxford. He received his first doctoral degree in "Lessicografia e semantica del linguaggio letterario europeo" at the University of Catania. His research interest lies at the intersection of philology, lexicography, and the digital humanities, with a focus on both medieval culture and twentieth-century Italian literature. He is expert in the digital restoration and improvement of Medieval and Modern manuscripts. He serves as International Consultant of the Centro di Informatica Umanistica in the department of Scienze Umanistiche at the University of Catania. He is also working at the National Digital Edition of the complete works of Pirandello in collaboration with Mondadori and the National Committee of Pirandello's work. His current research focuses on Petrarch's philology and the relationship between text and figurative arts with emphasis on the material history of literature and how books and illuminations can shape the audience's perception of a literary text. His publications include "Il Canto della Vergine. Storia mistica e immagini del Medioevo nella poesia di F. Tozzi" (Aracne 2013), I libri della Memoria. La biblioteca ideale di Federigo Tozzi tra letteratura e filologia (2013).